LITERACIES, THE ARTS, AND MULTIMODALITY

Literacies, the Arts, and Multimodality

Edited by

PEGGY ALBERS
Georgia State University

JENNIFER SANDERS
Oklahoma State University

National Council of Teachers of English
1111 W. Kenyon Road, Urbana, Illinois 61801-1096

Staff Editor: Carol Roehm
Interior Design: Jenny Jensen Greenleaf
Cover Design: Pat Mayer
Cover Images: A collage of iStockphoto.com images.
iStockphoto.com/Iurii Andrieiev, iStockphoto.com/Jiri Moucka,
iStockphoto.com/David Gunn, iStockphoto.com/Marcela Barsse,
iStockphoto.com/Ekaterina Romanova

NCTE Stock Number: 32142

It is the policy of NCTE in its journals and other publications to provide a
forum for the open discussion of ideas concerning the content and the teaching of English and the language arts. Publicity accorded to any particular
point of view does not imply endorsement by the Executive Committee, the
Board of Directors, or the membership at large, except in announcements
of policy, where such endorsement is clearly specified.

Every effort has been made to provide current URLs and email addresses,
but because of the rapidly changing nature of the Web, some sites and
addresses may no longer be accessible.

Library of Congress Cataloging-in-Publication Data

Literacies, the arts, and multimodality / edited by Peggy Albers, Jennifer
Sanders.
    p. cm.
   Includes bibliographical references and index.
   ISBN 978-0-8141-3214-2 (pbk.)
    1. Computers and literacy—United States. 2. Language arts—United
States—Computer-assisted instruction. 3. Arts—Study and teaching—
United States. 4. Visual education—United States. 5. Computer literacy
—Study and teaching—United States. I. Albers, Peggy. II. Sanders,
Jennifer, 1976–
   LC149.5.L48 2010
   428.0078'5—dc22
                                          2010005426

This book is dedicated to my mother, Genevieve, who inspired my creativity and love for the arts, and my father, Francis, who encouraged independence and initiative. I also dedicate this book to my sisters and brothers who continue to support my work and interests.—Peggy Albers

To all the teachers who continue to fight the good fight.—Jenn Sanders

CONTENTS

CONTENTS

Acknowledgments

A number of people have supported this project during the
many months it was developed. First, we want to thank
NCTE's Commission on Arts and Literacies (COAL) (http://
www.ncte.org/cee/commissions/artsandliteracies), whose passion
for the arts, digital literacies, and multimodality encouraged this
project. Each year, our group meets at NCTE's Annual Convention, shares our current research and teaching, and engages in
substantive discussions about the significance of the arts, multimodality, and digital media in literacy and language arts learning.
This community of scholars encourages one anothers' thinking
and positions members to share their work with wider audiences.
We especially thank all the chapter authors who participated in
and stayed with this project, responded quickly to each of our
"rush" requests, and worked with us so graciously through every
step of the process.

We also want to thank NCTE for supporting this important
project; the editorial and production staff at NCTE have been
most helpful in completing this project. In particular, Bonny
Graham worked closely with us to prepare the proposal, and
Carol Roehm assisted us in preparing the final manuscript. We
would like to thank the many anonymous reviewers for this
project, all of whom offered substantive and very helpful feedback on all aspects of this project from the proposal and sample
chapters to the full manuscript. Thanks to Peggy's doctoral students from Georgia State University in Atlanta, Tammy Frederick, Shekema Tinch Holmes, Nicole Manry Pourchier, Alisha
White, Svetoslava Dimova, Heather Lynch, Mary Huysman,
Janelle Gardner, and Sarah Mantegna, for fine-tuning the edits
on each of the chapters. They were expeditious and thorough in
their reading of these chapters.

Jenn would like to thank the members of her writing groups for their support and brillance: Jennifer Graff, Ivy Hsieh, and Yildiz Turgut at University of Florida, and Lucy Bailey and Sandra Goetze at Oklahoma State University.

To Jenn's parents, Nam Yong and Charles Jones: thanks for being on the receiving end of many stressed and excited phone calls, and encouraging me every step of the way. To my husband, Adam: thanks for holding down the fort for days or weeks at a time when I became a writing recluse. Thanks for making me dinner when I forgot to eat and knowing when I just needed a hug.

Multimodal Literacies: An Introduction

JENNIFER SANDERS AND PEGGY ALBERS

Entangled by James Adam Sanders, woodblock print. Used with permission.

Today, more than ever before, attention is being given to the role of the arts, multimodality, and new literacies as they relate to research and practice in English language arts classrooms and operate within 21st century literacies (NCTE, http://www. ncte.org/pathways/21stcentury). This attention is significant and timely as it reflects a growing shift in how literacy is being defined and what it means to be literate in the twenty-first century. Literacy, no longer confined to communication through reading and writing of traditional printed text, has expanded and figuratively exploded, particularly within the past decade. Messages are now created, inscribed, sent, and received in multimodal ways steeped in the use of new technologies. In today's world, a literate person must be able to read and create a range of paper-based and online texts (newspapers, pamphlets, websites, books, Kindle, and so on), participate in and create virtual settings (classrooms, Second Life, Facebook, Elluminate, blogs, wikis) that use interactive and dynamic Web 2.0 tools, and critically analyze multimodal texts that integrate visual, musical, dramatic, digital, and new literacies (Albers, 2007; Doering, Beach, & O'Brien, 2007; Harste, Leland, Grant, Chung, & Enyeart, 2007; Miller, 2007). In response to these needs, 21st century literacy and language arts classroom practice and research have become more focused on multimodal literacies and ways to reconceptualize and reenvision what constitutes literacy (Albers, Vasquez, & Harste, 2008; Harste, 2003; Lewison, Leland, & Harste, 2008; Miller, 2007; O'Brien & Beach, 2009).

For educators and students, it's here—technology and the desire to create and read multimedia and multimodal texts. Children and adults alike are using visual, audio, and technology media to capture, develop, produce, and publicly publish all types of products, and these uses have certainly spilled over into the literacy and English language arts (ELA) classes. As literacy and language arts teacher educators, we continually struggle with the tension between the restrictive culture of political mandates that value traditional approaches to literacy and how we must work to develop a culture of possibilities that engage and build upon the new literacies that students bring with them to class daily. We are continually enthralled at the intensity with which young people immerse themselves in arts, multimodality, and 21st century literacies. While some see such engagement as problematic, we, like Gee (2003), see these actions as redefining the world of literacy and our most basic understanding of what it means to be literate. We argue that ELA and literacy educators, across grade levels, as well as researchers, must be knowledgeable about and be prepared to work with the tools through which such multimodal and multimedia projects are created. These stakeholders must also become familiar with how today's messages are sent, received, and interpreted; how media and technology position us both as viewers and users of multimedia texts in the world; and how such texts endow us with an identity we may or may not wish to take on (Albers & Harste, 2007; Vasquez, 2004). Yet we welcome this struggle, because we see it as an essential part of the forward trajectory of literacy, one that has already catapulted us toward reading and creating multimodal, multidimensional, and hyperlinked texts.

In light of this changing world of texts and the diverse student populations we serve, we must not only consider what we think students ought to know to be literate in the twenty-first century, but we must also ask, *What are the everyday literacies that learners bring into the classroom?* and *How can I value and integrate these literacies into my own practice?* By keeping these questions in mind, we make literacy more relevant to students while creating space in the English language arts classroom both for teachers and students alike to explore, compose, and share a range of texts with larger audiences. Further, when we keep such questions in mind, we can create multidimensional curricula that reach more populations in ways that we could not otherwise.

We begin this introduction with a woodcut print created by James Adam Sanders, simply entitled *Entangled*. Each of the sixteen layers was intentionally carved from one 12" × 16" woodblock. As each new layer was carved and printed atop previous layers, the colors, shapes, and textures combined to ultimately form a whole that would not be complete without each of the layers working in synergy. We see Sanders's artwork as a visual metaphor for the way in which we understand the nature of literacy in today's world: complex, multimodal, multimedia, digital, and transformative. We also understand that as teachers, we have the responsibility to provide students with a range of opportunities that enables them to expand their repertoire of ways in which they can communicate what and how they know. We know that when people are actively engaged with inquiry, have a desire to learn new things, and try out different digital, visual, musical, spatial, dramatic (and so on) tools and techniques, they have the potential to say and do things that we have never before imagined. Consider, for example, the work of Glynda Hull (2009), who brings together children from different continents through digital technologies to study images of boys and girls and engage in critical written and video conversations about how children are represented in images. Or consider how your own lives have been changed by the arts, multimodality, and 21st century literacies. There is more accessibility to software that allows you to alter digital photos and to send these photos to family and friends immediately through cell phone connectivity with the Internet. Think of the explosion of the hundreds of thousands of YouTube videos, created by students, teachers, and ordinary people and uploaded for educational, personal, political, and other reasons. If you missed a performance on *American Idol*, YouTube, no doubt, will have a video posted by the start of the next day. Cell phones with video capability capture a range of events and emotions. Consider the video of a Chicago student beaten by others, captured on video, and replayed by news stations across the country. These examples demonstrate how no one particular mode (written language, visual, gestural, music, digital, and so on) carries the entire message. They also serve to demonstrate how "entangled" literacy really is. That is, modes, media, and language systems are in symbiotic relationship and offer humans the potential to express what they want to say in innumerable ways, forms, and combinations. Literacy is not simply a separation of language systems that can be tested or skilled to death. It is not, nor can it be, enacted by simply adding on another communicative mode to traditional print literacy and calling it "multimodal." Literacy is entangled, unable and unwilling to be separated from the other modes, media, and language systems that constitute the very messages that are sent, read, and/or interpreted.

For us, this collection of work in *Literacies, the Arts, and Multimodality* enables us to speak about and to the trajectory of 21st century literacy research and practice. Multimodal literacies research considers the multifaceted ways in which languages (art, drama, music, movement, written/oral, math) can be studied in school contexts, and multimodal literacies instruction is pedagogy with a fundamental philosophical orientation that holds that children (and adults) learn best when *engaged* in complex, socially constructed, personally relevant, creative composition and interpretation of texts that incorporate a variety of meaningful communicative modes or symbol systems. Composing and interpreting through multimodal literacies are much like Sanders's print; the message incorporates multiple modes that work together in interactive, dynamic, and integrative ways to communicate the maker's intentions. Working with multimodal literacies is an essentially interactive and flexible, dynamic and integrative, social and cultural practice that cannot be reduced to anything less.

In this introduction, we want to offer our readers a way to define and think about the arts, multimodality, and 21st century literacies, as well as highlight the significance of each field for literacy and English language arts classrooms. After providing this conceptual framework, we will briefly introduce the chapters of research and teacher practice that are included in this compilation. We conclude with a discussion of the complex issues that arise with multimodal literacies instruction. When referring to the work of the arts, multimodality, and 21st century literacies as a whole, we will use the term *multimodal literacies*, as we believe it is inclusive of the arts, literacies, and new media.

Framing the Arts, Multimodality, and 21st Century Literacies in the English Language Arts

Concepts of *the arts*, *multimodality*, and *21st century literacies* are often used interchangeably although each has its own unique characteristics. In the following discussion, we theoretically situate each of these key concepts and make connections to relevant scholarship while considering each area's significance in the English language arts.

The Arts

As Albers and Harste (2007) have written, the arts often refer to the visual, musical, and performance arts, which include paintings, ceramics, photographs, films, plays, storytelling, concerts, and others, and are often associated with the term *aesthetics*. Engagements with the arts offer us aesthetic experiences that are pleasing and transform the very way we encounter our world. Maxine Greene (1995; 2001), a philosopher, has long argued that the arts in education enable a person to become different and look through the lenses of various ways of knowing, seeing, and feeling in a conscious endeavor to change one's perspective on the world. Learning through the arts, she argued, must not be positioned as a frill but as an intentional undertaking that enables learners to notice the noticeable, become appreciative and reflective, and understand the role of the arts in making life meaningful. Elliot Eisner (2003) has also championed the arts as developing different forms of thinking, including an ability to see qualitative relationships within and among texts, an understanding that form and content are inextricably linked, an understanding that how something is expressed is only a part of what is meant, and the awareness that not everything knowable can be expressed through written language. The arts, argued Greene, leads to informed or critical talk by positioning learners as active viewers and perceivers while providing more precise and imaginative language to elucidate a deeper perception of the everyday world.

A number of scholars have reported on the effects of the arts on literacy (i.e., Blecher & Jaffee, 1998; Deasy, 2002; Ehrenworth, 2003; Olshansky, 1994; Rose, Parks, Androes, & McMahon, 2000; Smagorinsky & Coppock, 1993; Wolf, 1998), and several important works are highlighted here to help to contextualize the significance of the arts in language arts instruction.

In 2007, Burnaford, Brown, Doherty, and McLaughlin wrote *Arts Integration Frameworks, Research and Practice: A Literature Review*, an extensive and comprehensive review of arts-based practice and research primarily conducted in the United States that was written between 1995 and 2007. They presented the historical context around which arts-based instruction and research emerged, current theories that inform practice and research, and a range of studies that described methods and practices in the field. In presenting this collection of work, Burnaford et al.'s work situates the significance that the arts play in teaching, learning, and research.

Beth Olshansky's important work (1994, 2006, 2008) in the arts and writing has demonstrated time and again that both language systems must be treated equally in literacy learning and that when viewed from this perspective, both children's writing and art-making grow. After observing more than 400 students at all elementary grades during a two-year study of their art and story-making, Olshansky (1994) concluded that integrated art and writing instruction supports diverse learners and enriches the composing processes: "without the burden of needing to create representational images, their minds are free to discover images and make meaning out of their own abstract creations. Their ideas are imaginative and their language in discussing them is unusually descriptive" (p. 352). Olshansky's (2006) conclusion is supported by the children's own words: "pictures paint the words on paper for you so your words are much better. The words are more descriptive. Sometimes you can't describe the pictures because they are so beautiful" (p. 531). For these children, literacy, as experienced with and through the arts, was engaging, supportive, and allowed more informed, precise, and descriptive talk.

Another landmark synthesis of research in the arts, including connections to literacy learning, was conducted by James Catterall, Lois Hetland, and Ellen Winner and edited by Richard Deasy (2002) under the auspices of the National Endowment for the Arts and the U.S. Department of Education. This compendium of research, titled *Critical Links: Learning in the Arts and Student Academic and Social Development* and available online at http://www.aep-arts.org, presents summaries and critiques of sixty-two studies, both qualitative and quantitative, in the arts and arts integration. In sum, Deasy states that the studies in the compendium "suggest that well-crafted arts experiences produce positive academic and social effects" (p. iii). Two studies, in particular, demonstrated how the inclusion of drama in the reading curriculum improved students' comprehension and the teacher's use of effective instructional practices to support reading (Rose et al., 2000; Wolf, 1998). Only three studies of visual arts processes or instruction were included in the compendium, and all of these studies addressed the positive role of the visual arts, particularly drawing, in enhancing literacy instruction (Burger & Winner, 2000; DeJarnette, 1997; Wilhelm, 1995). Larry Scripp synthesized the research on music for this compendium and found "positive significant associations between music and achievement in reading" (Deasy, 2002, p. 133). However, Scripp also concluded that "further practitioner research is needed to specify how these links can be best and most consistently achieved" (p. 133). Throughout *Critical Links*, authors called for further research that conveys the intricate details and the teaching and learning results of arts-integrated instruction; *Literacies, the Arts, and Multimodality* answers this call for research with thirteen chapters that systematically describe the instructional practices and learning outcomes of research in multimodal literacies.Collectively, these studies demonstrate the power of arts-integrated instruction. The research also represents how the arts encourage a different type of language learning, one that enables children to authentically tell their cultured stories, to speak through art, and to understand stories more deeply through informed viewing of art.

Multimodality

As articulated by the work of Halliday (1985), Hodge and Kress (1988), and Kress and van Leeuwen (2006), multimodal communication is comprised of multiple "modes" or communicative forms (i.e., digital, visual, spatial, musical, etc.) within various sign systems that carry meanings recognized and understood by a social collective. In multimodal theory, Kress and Jewitt (2003) identify four aspects that comprise one's representation of meaning: materiality, framing, design, and production, all of which come into play when texts are constructed.

Materiality refers to the materials and resources used to represent meaning (still images, music, transitions, fabric, as well as ideas, concepts, etc.), and their affordances, or the qualities of that material/resource and its potential to communicate messages in various ways. *Framing* defines the way in which elements of a visual composition operate together, are spaced, show dis/continuities in color, connect (or not) with each other, or "move" on the canvas (Kress & van Leeuwen, 2001). Within digital texts such as PowerPoint presentations, webpages, and digital films, framing involves placement of a visual image, selection of the best image for the intention of the message, and choices concerning text or image size and font types. In creating such texts, the textmaker considers how each of these elements interrelates and how this relationship will inform a viewer's interpretation.

Design, the conceptual side of expression (Kress & van Leeuwen, 2001) and separate from the actual product, refers to how people make use of the materials and resources that are available to them at a particular moment to create their representation.

Lastly, *production* refers to the creation of and organization of the representation; production includes the actual product or text (website, movie, podcast, visual text, dance, play, etc.), as well as the technical skills (skills of the hand, eye, ear, body) used when working with media to create the text. Additionally, within multimodality inherently lies a critical perspective enacted when examining the textmaker's choices regarding the materials used, how those materials are framed and designed, and how such decisions are realized and situated within the creator's beliefs.

Scholarship in multimodality has grown significantly within the past decade, and to contextualize multimodality within literacy practice, we present two studies. In a two-year study called the Games-Play Project that involved an artist, an architect, and teachers of 4- and 5-year-olds, Kate Pahl (2007) examined children's multimodal drawings, created as part of the architectural planning for their new playground, of games they liked to play. Pahl considered how teachers might view and extend their students' texts by considering the variety of multimodal literacy practices demonstrated and associated with the texts. The children's multimodal drawing artifacts revealed details of what Rowsell and Pahl (2007) called "sedimented" identities, or traces of past experiences visually shown in the drawings. If educators read such multimodal texts to uncover the child's sedimented experiences, they may find connections between home, school, and other spaces and facilitate conversations that bridge home and school literacy practices. The work of Rowsell and Pahl demonstrated the multimodal nature of learning in that children designed and produced, through the modes of art and writing, the space they thought they needed to play their games. Further, in framing their ideas and the drawings, they revealed themselves as individuals, as members of families, and as members of their school through art and writing.

Albers and Frederick (2009) studied seven teachers' visual texts created over a semester. Like Rowsell and Pahl (2007), they found teachers included elements or traces of practice, interests, and ideologies that appeared across texts. They concluded that these "(re)marks" enabled researchers and educators to see learners' ongoing discourses through these elements. Norris's (2004) work in multimodal analysis has located how modes operate in human interaction. In her comprehensive methodological approach to understand this interaction, she described the complex nuances within and across modes that are made visible within such analysis. According to Kress (2003), "the world told" is vastly different from "the world shown" (p. 1), and all texts are "entirely in the realm of ideology" (Kress & van Leeuwen, 2006, p. 12). As such, a number of critical literacy scholars have argued that reading and analyzing modes must be critical (Albers et al., 2008; Callow, 2005; Harste, Leland, Grant, Chung, & Enyeart, 2007; Lewison, Leland, & Harste, 2008; Lewison & Heffernan, 2008) because they position not only the viewers to read in a particular way, but position the subject of the image in particular ways.

These teachers and researchers interested in multimodality help us see how students' and teachers' lives are revealed in the design, framing, and production of their texts and reveal the critical nature, or ideologies, of such creations. Across this work, researchers collectively have shown the significance of studying the dynamic and interactive nature of students' image production within classroom contexts as a crucial part of literacy practice and research.

21st Century Literacies

In concert with the arts and multimodality is 21st century literacies studies (Albers & Harste, 2007; Alvermann, 2008; O'Brien & Beach, 2009; NCTE Pathways–21st Century Literacies), also known as new literacies, or literacy in a digital and high-tech world, which gestures toward a shift in perspective or mindset, (Kist, 2005; Lankshear & Knobel, 2003; 2007). Lankshear and Knobel (2007) identified two interrelated elements in 21st century literacies: (1) new technical stuff, and (2) new ethos. Both of these elements are necessary components when engaging in 21st century literacies work. When thinking about "new technical stuff," Lankshear and Knobel argued that it not only involves new uses of technology but also necessitates new ways of being and interacting in the world (p. 7). That is, new technologies can be used in new ways (Facebook, blogs) to do the same kinds of things we already know (phones, letters). Further, when integrated into literacy practices, this "new technological stuff" allows educators and students to create something significantly novel (self-running PowerPoints, Podcasts, YouTube videos, for example). In essence, this new technical stuff allows us to technologize our existing practices *and* creates space for us to move beyond mere technologizing; that is, we do not include technology because we should, but because it allows for greater participation, collaboration, and distribution of knowledge that has not been possible with our previous uses of technology (Albers, Vasquez, & Harste, 2008). For example, students across the world create podcasts, or digitized audio recordings, accessible by all who know the URL link. Once confined to classrooms, student learning can now be shared worldwide (Hull, 2009). The "new ethos stuff" develops from the new technology. Central to "new ethos stuff" is not that we use technology to reorganize old practices (look up information online, use PowerPoint as colorful overhead transparencies, or write documents using word processing), but that we develop new ways of being when working with new technologies: sharing, experimenting, innovating, and creative rule-breaking (video podcasts, photo editing, and morphing of images, for example).

To conceptualize 21st century literacies in this way is to understand that communication is socially motivated and engaging, should work toward social action, and should be informed by global perspectives (NCTE Pathways). Consider how two social networking sites, Facebook and Twitter, have changed the face of social and global communication. Young children through adults access these sites multiple times a day, writing, talking in real time, and sharing a range of texts from photos to videos, drawings to audiocasts, and so on. Lenhart, Madden, Macgill, and Smith (2007) reported that 93 percent of teens use the Internet much more than they had in the past, and more than half of them had created profiles on social networking sites. Consider how social networking sites, the Internet, and television contributed, in synchronicity, to the nearly unprecedented worldwide fame of Susan Boyle, a middle-aged woman from Scotland who sang a show tune from *Les Miserables* on *Britain's Got Talent*. Photos, written text, interviews, history, and past singing engagements of Ms. Boyle, a woman previously unknown to the public, emerged onto the global scene literally overnight. In a short matter of two weeks, Ms. Boyle's video from *Britain's Got Talent 2009* had been viewed 47,309,919 times, and as of this writing several months later, more than 78 million.

Or consider how the cell phone has become a tool of communication that allows the user to send, receive, and forward a range of messages that are multimodal, messages that are visual, aural, spatial, and/or dramatic. Users scroll through text messages, create simple but interesting drawings, locate themselves via its built-in Global Positioning System, or "tweet" friends using Twitter to let them know they have arrived, all with just the touch of a finger. Just as literacy is not simply about reading and writing anymore, the cell phone is no longer merely for making and receiving phone calls; its name has become a misnomer. The capability of this one device has led people to reimagine and reinvent communication. In sum, social networking sites and modern tools of communication offer us a range of ways in which we can create simple messages or complex texts and have brought about cultural shifts in communication. In today's world, much of our communication is multimodal and requires facility with new forms of composition and interpretation.

To contextualize 21st century literacies into classrooms, Vivian Vasquez's work with teachers and children in the Washington, D.C. area is of particular note. Vasquez has initiated a number of 21st century literacies projects that invite learners to understand the role of critical literacy in different spaces and places. In one project called the "DC Area Literary Map Podcast" (Albers, Vasquez, & Harste, 2008), Vasquez aimed to create a project that would (1) help teachers become more resourceful when choosing books for students; (2) move beyond the immediate needs of students; (3) be generative, ongoing, and sustainable beyond the life of the course; and (4) be accessible to a larger audience outside of the class. Teachers generated questions around a book that reflected a social issue, found other texts (music, visual, photos of statues, poems, among others) that might accompany this book, and then created a four-minute podcast that addressed their learning about the social issue. These podcasts were then posted on Vasquez's blog and those interested in critical literacy with picture books could listen. This important work with teachers in the "new technology stuff" enabled them to move into the "new ethos stuff," or a shift in mindset about both the content that they wanted to teach and the possible ways in which to communicate this critical perspective across multiple spaces. Through such projects, teachers create something significantly new, experiment with new technologies, and share innovative learning that moves well beyond the four walls of the classroom.

The Scope of This Book

NCTE's Pathways Program—21st Century Literacies—has initiated a national effort to bring to the foreground the significance of the arts, multimodality, and 21st century literacies, and has challenged educators and researchers to consider how these three areas are significant in teaching and research in today's English language arts classrooms. As an active commission of NCTE, the Commission on Arts and Literacies (COAL) took on this challenge and developed this edited book in which connections among literacy and the arts, multimodality, and new literacies are addressed and positioned as significant to the English language learning of all students.

The chapters within this book arise from the work of teachers, teacher educators, and researchers from across the country who have substantively integrated the arts, digital media, drama, film, sound, and Web 2.0 tools into literacy and language arts instruction. Written by members of COAL, teachers and researchers whose interests span K–12 and university settings, *Literacies, the Arts, and Multimodality* is aimed at two specific English language arts and literacy audiences: (1) K–12 teachers and (2) teacher educators and researchers in college/university settings. With these two audiences in mind, we share theoretically grounded and well-documented teaching and research, writing that enables teachers, teacher educators, and researchers to adapt and implement the ideas and methodologies presented in the chapters into their work. The chapters serve as concrete demonstrations of how to integrate the arts, multimodality, and 21st century literacies into classroom practice and research, and highlight the significance of these three areas in the teaching and learning of the English language arts. Authors within these chapters worked with students across ages, including preservice and inservice teachers; across urban, suburban, and/or rural communities with diverse cultural demographics; and within an array of geographical regions. This book represents a breadth of multimodal literacies work across a range of contexts, wherein lies both its merit and its limitations. First, we provide a brief overview of the chapters, and then we take some space to problematize and complicate the issues involved in implementing multimodal literacies research and practice.

Jerome Harste, a key thinker in areas of literacy and literacy and arts integration, defines and describes multimodality in Chapter 1. In this invited chapter, Harste urges readers to consider multimodal events and texts as a whole instead of breaking them into the various types of literacies within. He also addresses why multimodality is a central construct for literacy in the twenty-first century and challenges educators to rethink curriculum in multimodal ways that promote social consciousness.

In Chapter 2, "Saying 'Yes' to Music: Integrating Opera into a Literature Study," Sharon Blecher and Gail Burton describe the integral role music plays in their first- and second-grade curricula. They demonstrate how music frames their school day, enhances children's understanding of story, specifically fairy tales, and enables children to engage in authentic musical and literary inquiry. In this chapter, readers see how drama, visual arts, music, and the genre of fairy tales were integrated to help children broaden their thinking and extend the possibilities for learning in unique and phenomenal ways. Our third chapter addresses the integration of audio modes and literacy. "Opening Doors, Unlocking Writers: A Classroom Exploration of Picture Books with Sound" by Joanna Robertson, is a skillful interweaving of theory and practice that examines teacher and student transactions with multimodal picture books that incorporate elements of sound. This case study research was conducted with a fourth- and fifth-grade teacher and her students and shares both teacher practice and student responses to these multimodal picture books. The chapter concludes with a discussion of the hybridity of texts—the mixture of different discourses or ways of speaking within a social community like a classroom, of students' literacy practices, and of teacher's pedagogical design, along with a bibliography of fifteen picture books that integrate sound elements.

Three chapters in this collection focus on the integration of the arts and writing: Chapter 4, "Inventing a Drama World as a Place to Learn;" Chapter 5, "Relationships between Artistic and Written Composing;" and Chapter 6, "Seeing, Writing, and Drawing the Intangible: Teaching with Multiple Literacies." In Chapter 4, Esther Gray and Susan Thetard present their research investigating how Susan's high school students express the complexities of the Holocaust through process drama and writing in role. Gray and Thetard describe how they carefully designed the dramatic contexts to discourage students from oversimplifying the events or from resorting to mere tragedy narratives. Findings from the data illuminate the ethics and insights students gained about the Holocaust-era and about themselves as actors. This chapter raises important points related to critical literacy and identifies key considerations for teachers who plan to implement drama in their own literacy classrooms.

In Jennifer Sanders's phenomenological study presented in Chapter 5, she examines the similarities, differences, and relationships between the composing processes of art and writing for six fourth-grade students who engaged in an art-infused writing workshop throughout the school year. The unique findings of this research are the inductive identification of seven relationships that emerged from the students' written and artistic composing processes and the description of how students learn to transfer what they understand about composing in art to writing and writing to art. In Chapter 6, Michelle Zoss, Richard Siegesmund, and Sherelle Jones Patisaul describe the origin and adaptation of a "backpack lesson" in which middle school students draw their backpacks, listen to a piece of literature that describes the things soldiers "carry" with them, and engage in a metaphorical writing activity about what they literally and figuratively carry in their backpacks. Through multimodal instruction that is engaging, challenging, and personally relevant for the students, rich learning and writing result. This lesson is conveyed so clearly and explicitly that teachers of all levels will find it easy to follow and adapt in their own classrooms.

The next two chapters examine ways to read images. In Chapter 7, "Reading Art, Reading Lives," Peggy Albers analyzes the visual texts created by urban students in English language arts classrooms across grade levels and identifies three distinct genres that emerged. Teachers and researchers alike can benefit from Albers's careful and descriptive structural analysis of students' visual texts and will come to understand how such analysis allows viewers insight into students' understanding. In Chapter 8, "Reading Illustrations," Ray Martens, Prisca Martens, Keri Croce, and Catherine Maderazo present a study of how a group of third graders in a diverse, urban classroom learned to read picture books with more depth and understanding through explicit instruction in reading both the written and visual texts. These art and literacy teachers and teacher educators provide evidence of how students translated their understanding of art and written text in their own illustrated texts and share practical implications for both teachers and researchers.

In Chapter 9, "An Arts-Integrated Unit: Learning 21st Century Literacies While the Teachers Are on Break," Beth Berghoff, Cindy Borgmann, Melissa Helmerick, and Carol Thorne describe how four fifth-grade classroom teachers, the art teacher, music teacher, and media specialist worked together to teach an integrated unit on Native Americans to students in a low-income, diverse elementary school. Three of the teachers, however, became the main initiators and actors in this effort at arts integration, and the authors of this chapter discuss their struggles, decisions, and successes that resulted. Research such as this that explicitly focuses on connections of teachers' content and pedagogical knowledge to their practice is scarce, and this chapter allows readers to follow the art and music teachers through their own learning processes to their subsequent instructional practices.

The final four chapters in this collection consider the various applications for digital video composing in English language arts classrooms. In Chapter 10, "Silencing Stories" Adrienne Costello describes, through ethnographic case study, one teacher's implementation of digital video composing and informal classroom drama in an urban middle school. In a strong and engaging voice, Costello recounts how multimodal teaching and learning can be fraught with "daunting challenges" and discusses the complexities involved in a teacher's struggle to incorporate progressive, multimodal literacies practices. In the theoretically substantive Chapter 11 entitled "Toward a Multimodal Literacy Pedagogy:

Digital Video Composing as 21st Century Literacy," Suzanne Miller argues that multimodality is not "local and adolescent, but global and multigenerational," and that educators must understand 21st century literacy curriculum and pedagogy as integrating engagements that are multimodal in design and practice. Miller's four guiding principles for implementing digital video in English Language Arts classrooms are explained in clear detail, using real classroom instruction as examples, so that readers can understand how they can purposefully and meaningfully create socially oriented, multimodal literacies instruction.

In Chapter 12, "Bringing Filmmaking into the English Language Arts Classroom," Bruce Robbins describes how he and a ninth-grade English teacher collaborated on an instructional unit that integrated classic literature analysis with digital filmmaking by highlighting connections between elements of literary and cinematic storytelling. This chapter details their instructional process and provides evidence of students' progress, learning, and engagement. Robbins offers educators insights into essential components of filmmaking, describes challenges one might face, and provides a thorough picture—from conception to completion—of what successful English literature and digital filmmaking integration might look like. And finally, Chapter 13, "Digital Literacies, Aesthetics, and Pedagogies Involved in Digital Video Production" takes an aesthetic perspective on the production of and response to digital video composing. Richard Beach and Thom Swiss assert that the aesthetic appeal of digital video lies in its social impact and reception. They identify six digital literacy components of multimodality (interactivity, modularity, automation, collection or appropriation, and embodiment), demonstrate how these components were employed by students to do aesthetic work, and show how the teacher guided students in reflecting on their aesthetic decisions.

The Issues Complicating Multimodal Literacies

In most of the chapters in this book, working with multiple literacies looks easy. Many of the classrooms into which we get a glimpse are led by talented weavers of multimodal curricula or by teachers who collaborated with researchers or colleagues. But as anyone who has attempted a multimodal literacies curriculum knows, it's hard work, and it doesn't always go as smoothly as you hoped. There are several issues that may arise to complicate successful and effective arts or technology integration including securing resources or an instructor's comfort level and buy-in in using new technologies, as well as the potential for multimodal work to become chaotic. Resourcing units of instruction in which new technologies are required can be challenging, particularly if the school already struggles with its budget for textbooks, paper, and pencils. Although arts materials and technology equipment continually become more affordable, the costs quickly add up when teachers work with twenty-five to forty students in each classroom. Authors in these chapters do address issues of costs and offer some insight into resourcing such curricula.

Perhaps more significant is that as educators, we know teachers teach what they know best, what they are most comfortable with, and what they enjoy. How do we convince a teacher who thinks her voice sounds like a diesel grinding through gears to sing with her or his students? How do we convince a teacher who dislikes writing to implement an arts-infused writing workshop? A teacher's comfort level with his or her own artistic abilities or technological skills can be one of the biggest deterrents to implementing multimodal literacies instruction. When we read chapters like Sharon Blecher and Gail Burton's, we notice that at least one of the teachers has a wealth of musical knowledge to support their collaborative instruction. Would teachers with limited music (or other arts) knowledge be willing to attempt multimodal literacies instruction? It certainly takes risk and courage to move outside of our comfort zone and attempt novel practices.

In fact, Bruce Robbins, author of Chapter 12, approached six teachers about working with him to infuse digital filmmaking into their language arts instruction, and he was consistently met with resistance because the teachers didn't feel comfortable with "all that technical stuff." Teachers who lack skills or experience with the arts or new literacies are a lot like struggling readers—they avoid what they are not good at. Robbins and the other three authors of chapters on digital video composing help teachers new to technology become familiar with the essential components of effective instruction and learn successful practices that will assist them in their first attempts at multimodality. Blecher and Burton help teachers leery of integrating the musical arts into practice through their thorough description of their approaches, examples, and sets of related texts. Having a classroom music library makes the music and music players readily available so that cross-curricular connections can be made more frequently and even spontaneously. Blecher and Burton also remind readers of free resources for music such as YouTube and the allies teachers can find in their students' parents. Linda Labbo, 2003, notes an exemplary website for gallery art as well: ArtsConnectEd at http://www.artsconnected.org. For teachers who do not feel comfortable singing or playing music, using professional recordings is a much more probable entry point into multimodal literacies instruction. Educators and researchers invested in multimodal literacies will need to find more of these non-threatening paths into multimodal literacies curricula for teachers who have limited experience or expertise with the arts or technology. This book serves as one such entry point for teachers new to multimodal literacies instruction, as it will help readers envision the possibilities and see successful multimodal literacies instruction at work.

A third factor complicating multimodal curricula is the fact that teacher collaboration is often necessary to implement some types of multimodal literacies instruction, and if teacher "buy-in" is weak, collaboration can quickly turn into one or two people carrying the burden of the planning and implementation. Acquiring teacher buy-in can be a challenge if some of the collaborating teachers are not personally invested in multimodal literacies, as in cases where a special area teacher proposes the curriculum to the regular classroom teachers or when researchers bring multimodal literacies curricula to classroom teachers. In Chapter 9, *An Arts-Integrated Unit*, Beth Berghoff and her colleagues describe a project that included a librarian, music and art teachers, and classroom teachers that results in less than equal collaboration. The music and art teachers ultimately assumed responsibility for the planning of the integrated unit because they knew firsthand the educational benefits students could experience from arts integration. Individuals may be disappointed in the degree of collaboration and buy-in that occurs with some participating teachers, but even though there may be initial resistance to curriculum integration, teachers may buy-in to integration the following year, or the year after. In a study on integrating reading strategy instruction in the middle school science curriculum that Jenn Sanders worked on with a research team at the University of Florida, the teacher buy-in was noticed most strongly in the two years following the initial implementation (Fang et al., 2008). It may take time for teachers to make the curriculum their own and experiment with integration on their own terms, in their own time. So while initial teacher buy-in may appear negligible, collaborators may see greater investment and ownership of the curriculum in the following years. To advocate the benefits of multimodal literacies, some educators may be willing to take the lead during the first round of arts or new literacies integration in order to apprentice teachers less familiar with multimodal literacies instruction. True collaboration and/or a higher buy-in may follow soon after.

A common observation and finding from the work presented in this book is that multimodal literacies instruction enables more children to enter into academic thinking and literacy than uni-dimensional forms of literacy instruction. We feel confident in saying that the researchers and educators in this book all believe that multimodal literacies instruction has the power to reach students marginalized because of a mismatch in school and home cultures or because they do not conform to the traditional institutionalized academic learning styles. No matter how hard we wish it could be, however, multimodal literacies instruction is not a cure-all. Adrienne M. Costello so eloquently states in Chapter 10, "Amid the promise that 21st century literacies hold for students and teachers, we cannot overlook the challenges that are still faced by teachers in complicated contexts as they attempt to adopt transformational teaching practices, and the personal and pedagogical choices they make in the face of such challenges." The students in Mr. Bradley's class in Costello's chapter did not end up benefitting from the multimodal digital literacies instruction to which they were exposed, and they may have even been hurt by their teacher's withdrawal of this instruction. This teacher sent a pretty explicit message that these students were not good enough to participate in this special project. Similarly, Jenn would have loved to report that an arts-integrated writing curriculum kept Louis, the boy in the vignette in Chapter 5, in school, but it didn't. It kept him engaged while he was in school, but arts-integrated writing did not "save" Louis. He was still expelled from the public arts magnet school he was attending for not doing his other school work.

Whatever the challenges, we suggest that the arts, multimodality, and 21st century literacies are here, are important to literacy and language arts learning, and must be a part of curriculum. Not only must we embrace these aspects of language learning, but we must begin to play with them as students do daily. As James Gee (2003) argued, if students were invested in their school work as much as they are in their video game playing, we would have energized and enthusiastic learners excited to come to school. If multimodal literacies instruction is only reserved for special times during the week, for the "good" kids, or the privileged students, the ones who conform, then the effects contradict the social justice goals for multimodal literacies pedagogy of access for and engagement of all learners. A teacher's expectations, cultural incongruencies between a teacher's background and the students', a teacher's inexperience with managing a multimodal literacies curriculum, and his or her pedagogical beliefs-in-practice can be determining factors in the success or failure of the instruction. The question remains, how do we best advocate for effective multimodal literacies instruction amidst these complexities? This is not a question to which there is an easy answer, but we think that you will find many practical suggestions that contribute to a fuller understanding of the possibilities throughout this book. As Sanders's woodprint helps us remember, multimodal literacies research and practice is entangled; one informs the other and generates continual layers as new ideas emerge and are integrated. We believe such work will make an impact in the social, emotional, and academic lives of many children, and we argue that it is well worth traversing the challenges.

Works Cited

Albers, P. (2007). Visual discourse analysis: An introduction to the analysis of school-generated visual texts. In D. W. Rowe, R. T. Jiménez, D. L. Compton, D. K. Dickinson, Y. Kim, K. M. Leander, & V. J. Risko (Eds.), *56th yearbook of the National Reading Conference* (pp. 81–95). Oak Creek, WI: National Reading Conference.

Albers, P., & Harste, J. C. (2007). The arts, new literacies, and multimodality. *English Education, 40*(1), 6–20.

Albers, P., Harste, J. C., Vander Zanden, S., & Felderman, C. (2008). Using popular culture to promote critical literacy practices. In Y. Kim, V. J. Risko, D. L. Compton, D. K. Dickinson, M. Hundley, R. T. Jiménez, K. M. Leander, D. W. Rowe (Eds.), *57th yearbook of the National Reading Conference,* (pp. 70–83). Oak Creek, WI: National Reading Conference.

Albers, P., Vasquez V. M., & Harste, J. C. (2008). A classroom with a view: Teachers, multimodality, and new literacies. *Talking Points, 19*(2), 3–13.

Alvermann, D. E. (2008). Why bother theorizing adolescents' online literacies for classroom practice and research? *Journal of Adolescent and Adult Literacy, 52*(1), 8–19.

Blecher, S., & Jaffee, K. (1998). *Weaving in the arts: Widening the literacy circle.* Portsmouth, NH: Heinemann.

Burger, K., & Winner, E. (2000). Instruction in visual art: Can it help children learn to read? *Journal of Aesthetic Education, 34*(3–4), 277–293.

Burnaford, G. (with Brown, S., Doherty, J., & McLaughlin, H. J.). (2007). *Arts integration frameworks, research & practice: A literature review.* Washington, DC: Arts Education Partnership.

Callow, J. (2005). Literacy and the visual: Broadening our vision. *English teaching: Practice and critique, 4*(1), 6–19.

Deasy, R. J. (Ed.). (2002). *Critical links: Learning in the arts and student academic and social development.* Washington, DC: Arts Education Partnership. Retrieved from http://www.aep-arts.org/files/publications/CriticalLinks.pdf

DeJarnette, K. G. (1997). *The arts, language, and knowing: An experimental study of the potential of the visual arts for assessing academic learning by language minority students* (Unpublished doctoral dissertation). University of California, Los Angeles.

Doering, A., Beach, R., & O'Brien, D. (2007). Infusing multimodal tools and digital literacies into an English education program. *English Education, 40*(1), 41–60.

Ehrenworth, M. (2003). Literacy and the aesthetic experience: Engaging children with the visual arts in the teaching of writing. *Language Arts, 81*(1), 43–51.

Eisner, E. W. (2003). Artistry in education. *Scandinavian Journal of Educational Research, 47*(3), 373–384.

Fang, Z., Lamme, L., Pringle, R., Patrick, J., Sanders, J., Zmach, C., Charbonnet, S., & Henkel, M. (2008). Integrating reading into middle school science: What we did, found, and learned. *International Journal of Science Education, 30*(15), 2067–2089.

Gee, J. P. (2003). *What video games have to teach us about learning and literacy*. New York: Palgrave Macmillan.

Greene, M. (1995). *Releasing the imagination: Essays on education, the arts, and social change*. San Francisco: Jossey-Bass.

———. (2001). *Variations on a blue guitar: The Lincoln Center Institute lectures on aesthetic education*. New York: Teachers College Press.

Halliday, M. A. K. (1985). *An introduction to functional grammar*. London, UK: Edward Arnold.

Harste, J. C. (2003). What do we mean by literacy now? *Voices from the Middle, 10*(3), 8–12.

Harste, J. C., Leland, C. H., Grant, S., Chung, M.-H., & Enyeart, J. A. (2007). Analyzing art in language arts research. In D. W. Rowe, R. T. Jiménez, D. L. Compton, D. K. Dickinson, Y. Kim, K. M. Leander, & V. J. Risko (Eds.), *56th yearbook of the National Reading Conference* (pp. 254–265). Oak Creek, WI: National Reading Conference.

Hodge, R., & Kress, G. (1988). *Social semiotics*. Cambridge, UK: Polity Press.

Hull, G. A. (2009, February). *Social networking on the Internet: Global youth, digital media, and 21st century literacies*. Paper presented at the meeting of the International Reading Association Research Conference, Phoenix, AZ.

Kist, W. (2005). *New literacies in action: Teaching and learning in multiple media*. New York: Teachers College Press.

Kress, G. (2003). *Literacy in the new media age*. New York: Routledge.

Kress, G., & Jewitt, C. (2003). Introduction. In C. Jewitt & G. Kress (Eds.), *Multimodal literacy* (pp. 1–18). New York: Peter Lang.

Kress, G., & van Leeuwen, T. (2001). *Multimodal discourse: The modes and media of contemporary communication*. London, UK: Edward Arnold.

———. (2006). *Reading images: The grammar of visual design* (2nd ed.). New York: Routledge.

Labbo, L. D. (2003). An exemplary museum website: ArtsConnectEd http://www.artsconnected.org/ [sidebar]. *Language Arts, 81*(1), 48.

Lankshear, C., & Knobel, M. (2003). *New literacies: Changing knowledge and classroom learning*. Philadelphia: Open University Press.

———. (2007). Sampling "the new" in new literacies. In M. Knobel & C. Lankshear (Eds.), *A new literacies sampler* (pp. 1–24). New York: Peter Lang.

Lenhart, A., Madden, M., Macgill, A. R., & Smith, A. (2007). *Teens and social media: The use of social media gains a greater foothold in teen life as they embrace the conversational nature of interactive online media*. Washington, DC: Pew Internet and American Life Project. Retrieved from http://www.pewinternet.org/~/media//Files/Reports/2007/PIP_Teens_Social_Media_Final.pdf.pdf

Lewison, M., & Heffernan, L. (2008, December). *Politicizing reader response through editorial cartooning*. Paper presented at the annual meeting of the National Reading Conference, Orlando, FL.

Lewison, M., Leland, C., & Harste, J. C. (2008). *Creating critical classrooms: K–8 reading and writing with an edge*. New York: Erlbaum.

Miller, S. M. (2007). English teacher learning for new times: Digital video composing as multimodal literacy practice. *English Education, 40*(1), 61–83.

National Council of Teachers of English. Pathways for 21st century literacies. Retrieved from http://www.ncte.org/pathways/21stcentury

O'Brien, D., & Beach, R. (2009, February). *Students' engagement with digital literacy/writing tools*. Paper presented at the meeting of the

International Reading Association Research Conference, Phoenix, AZ.

Olshansky, B. (1994). Making writing a work of art: Image-making within the writing process. *Language Arts, 71*(5), 350–356.

———. (2006). Artists/writers workshop: Focusing in on the ART of writing. *Language Arts, 83*(6), 530–533.

———. (2008). *The power of pictures: Creating pathways to literacy through art, grades K–6.* San Francisco: Jossey-Bass.

Pahl, K. (2007). Creativity in events and practices: A lens for understanding children's multimodal texts. *Literacy, 41*(2), 86–92.

Rose, D. S., Parks, M., Androes, K., & McMahon, S. D. (2000). Imagery-based learning: Improving elementary students' reading comprehension with drama techniques. *Journal of Educational Research, 94*(1), 55–63.

Rowsell, J., & Pahl, K. (2007). Sedimented identities in texts: Instances of practice. *Reading Research Quarterly, 42*(3), 388–404.

Sanders, James Adam. (2009). *Entangled* [Woodblock print].

Smagorinsky, P., & Coppock, J. (1993, April). *Broadening the notion of text: An exploration of an artistic composing process.* Paper presented at the annual meeting of the American Educational Research Association, Atlanta, GA.

Vasquez, V. M. (2004). *Negotiating critical literacies with young children.* Mahwah, NJ: Erlbaum.

Wilhelm, J. D. (1995). Reading is seeing: Using visual response to improve the literary reading of reluctant readers. *Journal of Reading Behavior, 27*(4), 467–503.

Wolf, S. A. (1998). The flight of reading: Shifts in instruction, orchestration, and attitudes through classroom theatre. *Reading Research Quarterly, 33*(4), 382–415.

Multimodality

JEROME C. HARSTE
Professor Emeritus, Indiana University

One problem in talking about literacy as multimodal is that there is a proliferation of literacies: oral literacy, visual literacy, computer literacy, mathematical literacy, geographical literacy, etc. A second problem in talking about literacy as multimodal is that *any* literacy is multimodal, meaning that it typically involves more than one literacy. For example, written language literacy involves visual literacy (if pictures or graphs are used), oral and gestural literacy (if the text is read), and other variations. For all of these reasons, I like to think about multimodality in terms of particular events (such as reading an advertisement) and try to understand those events in terms of the social practices that sustain it. In the case of an advertisement, I like to understand how the messages perpetuate certain lifestyles and shopping habits. From this perspective, my research questions become the following: How are multiple sign systems used? To what end? What social practices are maintaining their use? Said differently, I think of the use of multiple sign systems as a semiotic resource involving "language" (broadly defined as any sign system or combination of sign systems recognized by a culture), vision, and action. An advertisement often contains written language, a provocative picture, and a social intent or function. An ad, then, is an example of a set of semiotic resources that have been taken up and enacted. This enactment, I assume, is a culturally valued social practice that has as its intent to communicate meaning. Seeing multimodality in this way focuses attention on the definition of literacy that is in operation, the social practices that sustain that definition, and the pragmatic effects of that definition as "read" by others.

Although there is a good deal of hyperbole about the "new literacies" these days, new literacy researchers are doing what we early literacy researchers (Goodman, 1978; Harste, Woodward, & Burke, 1984; Teale & Sulzby, 1986) were doing in the late '70s and early '80s, namely, watching children as they engaged in literacy. We watched children handle books and write messages, whereas today's researchers are watching children play computer games, text message each other, and expose themselves and their world on YouTube (Lewis, 2007). Between then and now it is clear that our definitions of literacy have expanded (Myers, 1996) as have the social practices that sustain these new literate forms (Street, 2003; Knobel & Lankshear, 2007). The school no longer has a stronghold on what literate forms dominate. Instead, other forms are informing literacy in much more expansive ways. Gunter Kress (2003) said, "In this 'New Media Age' the screen has replaced the book as the dominant medium of communication. This dramatic change has made the image, rather than writing, the center of communication" (p. 1). James Gee (1996) argued that children are learning more about what it means to be literate outside of school than they are learning inside of school. School officials might "read" some websites as immoral, iPhones as disruptive, and teenagers as "impossible," but pragmatically there are new ways to be literate in today's world. I, along with the authors in this volume, see multimodality and these new literacies as potentially deepening our understanding of literacy, and as helping us create a more viable twenty-first-century English language arts curriculum.

Multimodality as a Vehicle for Understanding Literacy

Each sign system (language, art, music, mathematics, dance, and drama) has a technical component as well as a relational component. Although there are technical aspects to using art effectively as a sign system (Albers, 2007a), art provides new ways of relating, being, and belonging in the world. This is true for all literacies; each has a technical component as well as a relational component. Knobel and Lankshear (2007) argue that educators typically worry about the technical aspects of the new literacies when introducing them into classrooms and ignore the "ethos" or the new ways of belonging that these new technologies offer. Both dimensions—the technical and the relational—are important. Nonetheless, as Knobel and Lankshear argue, it is the affordance of these new ways of being that marks a new literacy's lasting value.

In similar fashion, it might be more valuable to talk about multimodality in terms of affordances rather than in terms of popularity. Rather than argue why art and music are important even during tight economic times, it might be more productive to explore what art and music allow us to do—its technical and relational affordances—that language and mathematics don't.

I remember evaluating the Wingate reading and language arts program on the Navajo reservation (Harste, 1978). While the officials at the Bureau of Indian Affairs were concerned about the children's lack of growth in reading and writing English, I was blown away by the artwork that graced the walls of these classrooms. Like Karen Grady's (2002) and Peter Cowan's (2004) work in documenting how Hispanic adolescents use low-rider art to maintain a sense of cultural identity, the children at Wingate were using their artistic ability to maintain their cultural identity and way of knowing even in a setting where this way of knowing wasn't officially valued. As a result of this experience, I joined a host of sociolinguists in hypothesizing that different cultural groups have different ways of knowing and being in this world. Although linguistics may be the dominant way of knowing for children of a European heritage, art or music or dance may be a dominant way of knowing for children raised in other cultural traditions.

Stating it this way is problematic, however. Like Elliot Eisner (1982) and Maxine Greene (1988), I am not interested in suggesting that sign systems are in competition with one another. Each affords a particular type of meaning. I think about literacy broadly as all of the ways that humankind has for mediating their world. A language arts program, by this way of thinking, ought to expand our communication potential not just in language but in all the ways there are to know and mean. Like Halliday (1975), I assume that each of the sign systems has something unique to contribute to meaning making or it would cease to exist. This stance positions me as a social semiotician, or someone interested in signs and how humankind uses sign systems—art, music, language, mathematics, dance, and drama—to mediate and transmediate themselves and their world. Although there are some who see sign systems in terms of learning styles and advocate different kinds of instruction for different kinds of learners (Carbo, Dunn, & Dunn, 1986; Gardner, 1993), I assume that the use of multiple sign systems enhances everyone's learning as well as meaning making.

Fortunately, there is more and more research to support this view. Carger (2004) reported on the positive influence that the visual arts have on learning for bilingual children. The Arts Education Partnership (Stevenson & Deasy, 2005) released its study of an arts-integrated approach to learning in ten urban schools and found significant gains in achievement, especially among struggling learners. The Center for Inquiry in Indianapolis, a public school, with which I am closely associated, advocates inquiry-based instruction, multiple ways of knowing, and critical literacy. Although it is difficult to know how much of its success with African American children is attributable to multiple ways of knowing per se, the fact remains that the school has consistently outscored other schools serving a similar inner-city population. Scores on the Indiana State Test of Education Progress (ISTEP), in fact, suggest that students at the center do as well as students attending suburban schools around Indianapolis (Harste, Leland, Schmidt, Vasquez, & Ociepka, 2004).

Even multimodal discourse styles make a difference. Kathryn Au (1979) showed that Hawaiian children learned better through a "talk story" form of instruction than through instructional approaches that ignored their cultural ways of knowing. Lewis, Thompson, Celious, & Brown (2002) have used hip-hop to help African American students find relevance in life as well as their school subjects, including philosophy. Scollon and Scollon (1981) have pointed out that school-based discourses that incorporate essayist practices conflict with the values, attitudes, and ways with words embedded in some Athabascan home- and community-based discourses. Their work, to some degree, spawned a culturally responsive school movement, the effects of which can be seen in the work of a host of scholars. McCarty and Watahomigie

(1999) have shown, for example, that when indigenous students and teachers share the same cultural values, learning is enhanced.

These research studies suggest that sign systems position people in particular ways that affect learning. When we took this thinking to our curricular work with children at the Center for Inquiry, for example, we found that children who were invited to think about what Indianapolis looked like in art and what it looked like in music explored aspects of the city that enriched our study of Indianapolis in new ways. We had no idea, for example, that Indianapolis was once the heart of an important movement in literature or that Whitcomb Riley and Mark Twain worked hand-in-hand in legitimizing the use of dialect in literary texts. Although we knew Indianapolis had been associated with the jazz movement, hearing what Indianapolis sounds like in music brought new appreciation of the city's heritage as well as its influence on blue grass and country music.

Multimodality as a Social Practice for Rethinking Curriculum

From the perspective of identity, sign systems have a critical edge. Although critical theorists are interested in what counts as literacy in a society, they are even more interested in what social practices are in place (Luke & Freebody, 1997). They argue that in order to change what counts as literacy, the social practices— the practices that give certain sign systems more clout than other sign systems—need to change. It is important that teachers think about what social practices they have in place in their classroom. Which literacies are supported or not supported? Who do these practices benefit and who do they hurt? Literacy, after all, cuts both ways. Regardless of the modalities we value, literacy cuts some people in while it cuts other people out.

It is important to evaluate the kinds of literate practices that are valued in schools. The Internet, for example, is a good illustration of how literacy in multimodal form has transformed our ways of being in the world. Children daily invent new ways of being in the world using today's technology. While I can't imagine how I ever got any work done before computers, email, and the

Internet, children can't imagine life without iPods, iPhones, and Facebook. Although many social networking sites are off-limits to children at school, children still access them outside of school—at home, at friends' homes, and in public libraries. Social networking as a social practice invites educators to think about what they might do curricularly. Students can analyze these sites for what they say (visually, musically, and linguistically), generate discussions about these sites, and think through the moral and ethical use of these sites.

Like other educators, I want children to experience both the world of print and the world of technology. I want children, even children in the twenty-first century, to use literature to explore who they are as well as how moral and ethical they might be. That said, I worry about how we, including children, are being manipulated by media. As an educator, I want to have students who become agents of text rather than victims of text, regardless of the sign systems involved. That is, I want students to be able to actively read, interpret, talk back to texts, as well as identify the many visible and invisible messages that comprise these texts.

Although a lot of this work still needs to be done, there are educators who wish to move the study of art from drawing, painting, and the fine arts to be the study of our visual culture more generally (Duncum, 2001; Freedman, 2003). In this spirit and to these ends, some of us (Albers, Harste, Vander Zanden, & Felderman, 2008; Harste, Leland, Grant, Chung, & Enyeart, 2007; Lewison, Leland, & Harste, 2008a) have begun by looking closely at the systems of communication in multimodal texts in an effort to help students read, interpret, and create multimodal texts that "talk back" (Giroux, Lankshear, McLaren, & Peters, 1996) to the dominant visual messages being presented in our culture. To illustrate the curricular potential of seeing multimodality as a semiotic resource for rethinking curriculum, I want to walk you through an analysis of two multimodal texts, an ad and a counter-narrative, created in a workshop exploring the teaching of reading and writing through the arts. I see these two examples as highlighting the changing nature of literacy as well as demonstrating how our curricular practices can become more critical.

Ads as Curricular Resources

One of the assumptions social semioticians make about a multi-modal text is that all signs are motivated. By this we mean that there is nothing random in a multimodal text; what is there was done for a purpose.

Kress and van Leeuwen (2006) said that we often think of art as abstract and language as concrete. Using a very young child's rendering of an elephant, they demonstrated that the child's drawing of an elephant provided much more information about what the child knew about elephants than the child did by saying, "This is an elephant." The contour drawing showed the elephant with a trunk, four legs, large head, eyes (and other elements), whereas the oral statement was abstract and didn't offer the details of the visual rendering.

Visual discourse analysis (Albers, 2007b) builds on Kress and van Leeuwen's (2006) framework for unpacking visual images by inviting the user to analyze texts systematically, drawing upon structural analysis as well as the discourses (Gee, 2005) that underpin the message of the text. In this first image, I use the framework of language, vision, and action for unpacking the definition of literacy that is in operation, the social practices that sustain this definition, and the pragmatic effects of this definition as read by others.

Language. Figure 1.1 is my close rendition of an ad I saw in a magazine some time ago. The first thing I noticed was that there wasn't much language. "Ralph Lauren Children" is on the bottom of the ad while "Ralph Lauren," the adult clothing label, is on the top, behind the head of the child model. The placement of the written texts suggests that Ralph Lauren serves one not only from head to toe but through life, from childhood to adulthood. It is not accidental that "r-e-n" shows up behind the head of the little girl, thus inviting the reader to make a link between the "r-e-n" at the end of "Children" and the "r-e-n" at the end of "Lauren." The print for the adult "Ralph Lauren" is red and larger than the print for "Ralph Lauren Children," thereby suggesting that the name, Ralph Lauren, unifies one's world.

FIGURE **1.1.** *An artist rendering of a Ralph Lauren ad.*

Vision. The focal point in this ad is a blond-haired little girl wearing a flowered, summer, short-sleeved dress with a sweater thrown over her shoulder. The background appears to be a beach with a blue sky. The girl is making eye contact with the viewer, suggesting poise as well as self-assurance. She is the epitome of sophisticated grace. The message being sent is to connect the clothing label Ralph Lauren with sophistication. Thus, in this ad, the viewer understands that it's never too early to make this association. With the sweater thrown over the young girl's shoulder, we rightfully think a cool beach, not Hawaii, but probably New England prep, and the Hamptons.

Action. The designer and creator of the original ad has the child model looking down upon the viewer, a move that forces the viewer to look up. By positioning the model in this way, the creator of the original ad has suggested that this is the lifestyle to be achieved. Using a little blond-haired girl as the model further suggests that this lifestyle is a given, the dominant and mainstream goal of members of this culture.

Discussion. Although the creator of the original ad seemed to know what she or he was doing and what messages she or he wanted to send, it is not always clear that readers of this ad are as critical as one might hope. In a study, we (Albers, Harste, Vander Zanden, & Felderman, 2008) asked preservice teachers and fifth graders to read this ad and seven other ads. Typical responses for this ad included the following: "I like their clothes and style and I think this is a cute outfit." "It made me want those clothes for myself." ". . . it is subtle and reminds me of a photograph I could take." "I like this ad because of its simplicity and clean image. The ad was not too cluttered or flashy and it was clear what was being sold." In terms of social practices, consumerism motivates ads of this sort. An uncritical reader perpetuates these social practices. Pragmatically the assumption is made that readers will not read against the grain but rather buy into the message and lifestyle being sold—the goal of all messages of consumerism. Creators of ads want us to participate vicariously in the ad, to see ourselves in the role played by the models in the ad, and to buy the product or the lifestyle. Our data not only suggested that the creators of this ad were successful, but that we as educators need to create curriculum that supports the critical reading of multimodal texts (for other frameworks that might be used, see Albers, 2007b; Harste, 2008; Harste, Leland, Grant, Chung, & Enyeart, 2007).

Counter-Narrative as a Curricular Resource

There is some evidence that having students create counter-narrative texts supports the development of a critical stance (Burn & Durran, 2007). In creating a counter-narrative text, students first have to uncover the dominant system of meaning that is operating and then think of what alternative systems of meaning might be highlighted given a different set of values. Figure 1.2 is a poster developed by one of the students I taught in a workshop on the teaching of reading and writing using the arts.

Language. There are only two pieces of language on this poster. "Art War" on the top of the page and "Nobody Wins" on the bottom of the page. The alignment of "Art" and "War" on the top of the page, done to ensure the viewer takes notice of the number of letters each word shares, suggests that a parallelism exists between the two concepts. The letters making up "Art" and "War" are large and open suggesting a larger-than-life status.

Vision. The focal point of the poster is the visual of two boxers slugging it out. Neither boxer is particularly attractive. As readers we have to assume this was intentional. The crossed paintbrushes at the top of the page conjure up images of crossed swords, the traditional symbol of might.

Action. Pragmatically, the message is clear. If art is pitted against other sign systems, nobody wins. This message is a counter-narrative to the typical response of cutting art and music programs in an effort to get back to basics. Importantly, because cutting art and music programs is typically a political response, this fact, in itself, is evidence that art is a tacit, if not explicit, system of meaning operating in our society. This poster, then, not only works to make viewers conscious of the dominant system of meaning operating in society but talks back to it as well. The social action in this instance is a demonstration of an alternate stance that might be taken.

Discussion. While work in studying the grammar of visual design is just beginning, I have found the frameworks presented by Kress and van Leeuwen (2006) and Albers (2007b) to work surprisingly well for studying cereal boxes, advertisements, public sculptures, scenes in movies as well as some forms of graffiti. Art,

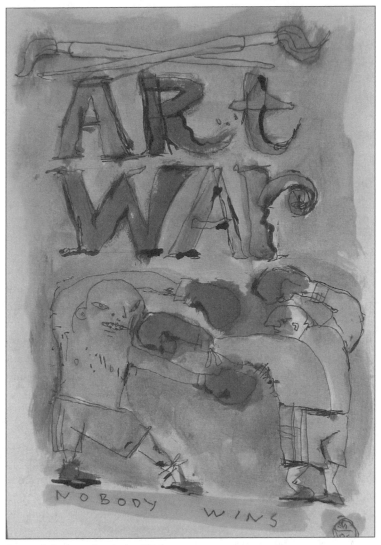

FIGURE **1.2.** *A student's* Art War *poster.*

like language, is a semiotic (or meaning-centered) system. According to Halliday (1975), and regardless of the complexity of the form, in order to interpret that message, one simultaneously has to attend to the field (the setting, the content of the message, as well as what is happening), the mode (the various sign systems involved and what messages each carry), and the tenor (the relationship depicted between and among people including how you as the reader of this text are positioned and what identity you are asked to take on). In my mind, curriculum for the twenty-first century needs to explicitly include the critical reading and making of multimodal texts.

Classroom Practices as a Curricular Resource

The Center for Inquiry in Indianapolis began implementing multiple ways of knowing curriculum using picture books that raised important social issues (for an annotated list of picture books we used, see Harste, Breau, Leland, Lewison, Ociepka, & Vasquez, 2000; Leland, Harste, Berghoff, Bomer, Flint, Lewison, & Möller, 2002; Lewison, Leland, & Harste, 2008b). Semiotically, picture books were defined as those in which the message of the book was conveyed by both the print and the picture. Because the social issues that the books addressed coincided with social issues that the students themselves were facing, we simply read these books aloud to open up the conversation. Once students began to make personal connections, they began to unpack issues and offer suggestions for how things should be. Many of the books we read then led to social action projects that students took into the community. Importantly, the reading of picture books that presented social issues put a new set of social practices in place. These social practices redefined what it meant to be literate in this classroom. When students had learned about the grammar of visual design (Kress & van Leeuwen, 1996), they then read pictures with a new set of eyes, and these books were often deconstructed in important and telling ways.

Vivian Vasquez (2004) turned the walls of her prekindergarten classroom into a "learning wall" (what researchers would call "an audit trail") of the social issues and social action that her students took over the course of a year as a result of the books they read and the classroom conversations that ensued. Her study demonstrated that critical literacy was enhanced when children read, interpreted, and responded to texts from a multimodal perspective. Further, she found that even very young children were able to take on both a critical and multimodal stance to make sense of their everyday world and world of school.

Dorothy Heathcote has been a longtime advocate of process drama. Although process drama (Wagner, 1999) is not a new literacy, one of its strengths is that it allows students to try on a new way of being in the world. There is, after all, nothing sacrosanct about how multimodality and the new literacies position people. There are, as Carole Edelsky (2006) has pointed out, lots of people using the new literacies to position themselves and us in very unsavory ways. Because so many schools block their students' use of various Internet sites (rather than talk about the moral and ethical issues these sites raise), it is important that educators use the old literacies in new ways, to serve new purposes. What students learn from process drama they can apply to how they position themselves in a world with or without iPods, iPhones, and YouTube. What is key, I think, is making this agenda—to think curriculum—explicit.

I see the key to instruction in this multimedia era, like it has been all along, as using the child as a curricular informant. By "kidwatching" (Goodman, 1978), we teacher-researchers can attend to the new literacies that children bring with them to school as well as with their ways of knowing. Instructionally, we need to start from that base as we learn to be critically literate ourselves in this multimedia era. Like everything else, we as teachers cannot do for children what we cannot first do ourselves. But this is not bad news. Like all good instruction, critical multimodal literacy is an ongoing inquiry, one in which you, the students in your classroom, and I can simultaneously engage.

Works Cited

Albers, P. (2007a). *Finding the artist within: Creating and reading visual texts in the English language arts classroom.* Newark, DE: International Reading Association.

———. (2007b). Visual discourse analysis: An introduction to the analysis of school-generated visual texts. In D. W. Rowe, R. T. Jiménez, D. L. Compton, D. K. Dickinson, Y. Kim, K. M. Leander, & V. J. Risko (Eds.), *56th yearbook of the National Reading Conference* (pp. 81–95). Oak Creek, WI: National Reading Conference.

Albers, P., Harste, J. C., Vander Zanden, S., & Felderman, C. (2008). Using popular culture to promote critical literacy practices. In Y. Kim, V. J. Risko, D. L. Compton, D. K. Dickinson, M. Hundley, R. T. Jiménez, K. M. Leander, D. W. Rowe (Eds.), *57th yearbook of the National Reading Conference* (pp. 70–83). Oak Creek, WI: National Reading Conference.

Au, K. H.-P. (1979). Using the experience-text relationship method with minority children. *The Reading Teacher, 32*(6), 677–679.

Burn, A., & Durran, J. (2007). *Media literacy in schools: Practice, production, and progression.* London, UK: Paul Chapman.

Carbo, M., Dunn, R., & Dunn, K. (1986). *Teaching students to read through their individual learning styles.* Boston: Allyn and Bacon.

Carger, C. L. (2004). Art and literacy with bilingual children. *Language Arts, 81*(4), 283–292.

Cowan, P. (2004). Devils or angels: Literacy and discourse in lowrider culture. In J. Mahiri (Ed.), *What they don't learn in school: Literacy in the lives of urban youth* (pp. 47–74). New York: Peter Lang.

Duncum, P. (2001). Visual culture: Developments, definitions, and directions for art education. *Studies in Art Education, 42*(2), 101–112.

Edelsky, C. (2006, February). *What's resisted, who's resisting, and other questions.* Paper presented at the Ethnography in Education Research Forum, University of Pennsylvania, Philadelphia, PA.

Eisner, E. W. (1982). *Cognition and curriculum: A basis for deciding what to teach.* New York: Longman.

Freedman, K. (2003). *Teaching visual culture: Curriculum, aesthetics, and the social life of art.* New York: Teachers College Press.

Gardner, H. (1993). *Frames of mind: The theory of multiple intelligences.* New York: Basic Books.

Gee, J. P. (1996). *Social linguistics and literacies: Ideology in discourses* (2nd ed.). London, UK: Taylor and Francis.

———. (2005). *An introduction to discourse analysis: Theory and method.* New York: Routledge.

Giroux, H. A., Lankshear, C., McLaren, P., & Peters, M. (1996). *Counternarratives: Cultural studies and critical pedagogies in postmodern spaces.* New York: Routledge.

Goodman, Y. M. (1978). Kidwatching: An alternative to testing. *National Elementary Principal, 57*(4), 41–45.

Grady, K. (2002). Lowrider art and Latino students in the rural Midwest. In S. Wortham, E. G. Murillo, Jr., & E. T. Hamann (Eds.), *Education in the new Latino diaspora: Policy and the politics of identity* (pp. 169–192). Westport, CT: Ablex.

Greene, M. (1988). *The dialectic of freedom.* New York: Teachers College Press.

Halliday, M. A. K. (1975). *Learning how to mean: Explorations in the development of language.* London, UK: Edward Arnold.

Harste, J. C. (1978). *Navajo school evaluation report: Wingate language arts program—grades 5–8* (mimeographed). Bloomington, IN: Division of Teacher Education, Indiana University.

———. (2008). Visual literacy. In M. Lewison, C. Leland, & J. C. Harste, *Creating critical classrooms: K–8 reading and writing with an edge* (pp. 52–59). New York: Erlbaum.

Harste, J. C., Breau, A., Leland, C., Lewison, M., Ociepka, A., & Vasquez, V. (2000). Supporting critical conversations in classrooms. In K. M. Pierce (Ed.), *Adventuring with books: A booklist for pre-K–grade 6* (12th ed., pp. 507–554). Urbana, IL: National Council of Teachers of English.

Harste, J. C., Leland, C. H., Grant, S., Chung, M.-H., & Enyeart, J. A. (2007). Analyzing art in language arts research. In D. W. Rowe, R. T. Jiménez, D. L. Compton, D. K. Dickinson, Y. Kim, K. M. Leander, & V. J. Risko (Eds.), *56th yearbook of the National Reading Conference* (pp. 254–265). Oak Creek, WI: National Reading Conference.

Harste, J. C., Leland, C., Schmidt, K., Vasquez, V., & Ociepka (2004). Practice makes practice, or does it? The relationship between theory and practice in teacher education. *Reading Online, 7*(4). Retrieved from http://www.readingonline.org/articles/art_index.asp?HREF=harste/index.html

Harste, J. C., Woodward, V. A., & Burke, C. L. (1984). *Language stories and literacy lessons.* Portsmouth, NH: Heinemann.

Knobel, M., & Lankshear, C. (Eds.). (2007). *A new literacies sampler.* New York: Peter Lang.

Kress, G. (2003). *Literacy in the new media age.* New York: Routledge.

Kress, G., & van Leeuwen, T. (1996). *Reading images: The grammar of visual design*. New York: Routledge.

————. (2006). *Reading images: The grammar of visual design* (2nd ed.). New York: Routledge.

Leland, C. H., Harste, J. C., Berghoff, B., Bomer, R., Flint, A. S., Lewison, M., & Möller, K. (2002). Critical literacy. In A. A. McClure & J. V. Kristo (Eds.), *Adventuring with books: A Booklist for pre-K–grade 6* (13th ed., pp. 465–487). Urbana, IL: National Council of Teachers of English.

Lewis, C. (2007). New literacies. In M. Knobel & C. Lankshear (Eds.), *A new literacies sampler* (pp. 229–238). New York: Peter Lang.

Lewis, R. L., Thompson, M. E., Celious, A. K., & Brown, R. K. (2002). Rap music, is it really all bad? Why hip-hop scholarship is important. *Perspectives*, 8(2), 67–69.

Lewison, M., Leland, C., & Harste, J. C. (2008a). *Creating critical classrooms: K–8 reading and writing with an edge*. New York: Erlbaum.

————. (2008b). An annotated list of picture books, chapter books, videos, songs, and websites. In M. Lewison, C. Leland, & J. C. Harste, *Creating critical classrooms: K–8 reading and writing with an edge* (pp. 315–345). New York: Erlbaum.

Luke, A., & Freebody, P. (1997). The social practices of reading. In S. Muspratt, A. Luke, & P. Freebody (Eds.), *Constructing critical literacies: Teaching and learning textual practice* (pp. 185–223). Creskill, NH: Hampton Press.

McCarty, T. L., & Watahomigie, L. J. (1999). Indigenous community-based language education in the USA. In S. May (Ed.), *Indigenous community-based education* (pp. 79–94). Philadelphia: Multilingual Matters.

Myers, M. (1996). *Changing our minds: Negotiating English and literacy*. Urbana, IL: National Council of Teachers of English.

Scollon, R., & Scollon, S. B. K. (1981). *Narrative, literacy and face in interethnic communication*. Norwood, NJ: Ablex.

Stevenson, L. M., & Deasy, R. J. (2005). *Third space: When learning matters*. Washington, DC: Arts Education Partnership.

Street, B. (2003). What's "new" in new literacy studies? Critical approaches to literacy in theory and practice. *Current Issues in*

Comparative Education, 5(2), 77–79. Retrieved from http://www.
tc.columbia.edu/cice/Archives/5.2/52street.pdf

Teale, W. H., & Sulzby, E. (1986). Introduction: Emergent literacy as
a perspective for examining how young children become readers
and writers. In W. H. Teale & E. Sulzby (Eds.), *Emergent literacy:
Writing and reading* (pp.vii–xxv). Norwood, NJ: Ablex.

Vasquez, V. M. (2004). *Negotiating critical literacies with young children*. Mahwah, NJ: Erlbaum.

Wagner, B. J. (1999). *Dorothy Heathcote: Drama as a learning medium*
(Rev. ed.). Portsmouth, NH: Heinemann.

Saying Yes to Music: Integrating Opera into a Literature Study

SHARON BLECHER AND GAIL FURLINE BURTON
Oberlin City Schools, Oberlin, Ohio

I don't want to go to Mexico, no more, no more . . .

Miss Mary Mack, Mack, Mack all dressed in black,
    black, black.
With silver buttons, buttons, buttons all down her
    back, back, back.

Children sing hand-clapping games while waiting for their buses at the end of a long day (Figure 2.1); they are re-energized by the songs and the laughter of friends.

Gonna jump so high, I'll touch the sky . . .

Teddy bear, Teddy bear touch the ground . . .

Cinderella dressed in yellow went upstairs to find
    her fellow . . .

Jumping and singing to the rhythm of the twirling rope, inviting others to jump in and feel the music pulsing up from the ground through their feet and into their hearts, children dance their happiness.

Valuing the music that children bring into the classroom and incorporating it into their work gives students voice in unexpected ways. We share a class of first and second graders in a multi-age setting where the visual arts, music, and movement are valued

FIGURE 2.1. *These girls participate in a hand-clapping game.*

modes that help us integrate and enhance the instruction of reading, writing, science, social studies, and math. In this chapter, we want to share how we created a transdisciplinary, inquiry-based examination of fairy tales and opera and how this work led to students' interest in both story and music while at the same time built literacy skills in reading, writing, art, and drama. This work resulted in an in-depth study of Mozart's (2000) *The Magic Flute* that incorporated wonderful parent and community involvement. We end this chapter with suggestions for teachers so that they can create such inquiry in their own classrooms. Although this work is located in an elementary classroom in the Midwest, we believe that these ideas will work in a range of settings and across all ages.

We bring a mix of backgrounds and appreciation for music to our students in Eastwood School's Open Room in Oberlin, Ohio. Sharon, who grew up in museums and concert halls, developed an appreciation for a variety of musical forms, knowledge of musicians, and a keen ear for their unique sounds. Sharon enjoys season tickets to the Oberlin College Recital Series, plays piano, and can name a classical piece and its composer "in three notes." In contrast, Gail grew up with little music, art, or books in her home, unless you count *American Bandstand* and the set of encyclopedias on the family bookshelf. Gail cannot tell Rachmaninoff from Tchaikovsky and never dreamed she would be studying opera with 6- and 7-year-olds. Yet she has come to appreciate what music can bring to her work with children. Both of us have open minds, risk-taking attitudes, and a willingness to learn along with our students. Both of us agree that making music part of the day has made our open classroom a more joyful place and the teaching of all content areas more textured. Music allows us to get deep inside the fabric of the subject in which we are immersed, rest in soft nooks, wiggle through interesting strands, and problem-solve our way through bumpy places.

Why Music in the Elementary Classroom?

Music of all kinds can enhance almost everything students find themselves doing throughout the day. Music compels us to listen, to engage with the shifts in sound, and to imagine its stories. Our classroom is filled with music from the moment students enter to the time they leave. Vivaldi, Mozart, Bach, Rachmaninoff, Branford Marsalis, Ella Fitzgerald, Duke Ellington, The Beatles, Johnny Cash, and other musicians greet our students daily. Music plays while children sign in, do room jobs, select books to read, share news, and write in their journals. Just as we share our music with them, our students bring in their own CDs. We respect what our students bring to the mix and find ourselves being introduced to new artists and musical forms. Children love to teach their friends about rap, sing songs from their favorite movies, and share music they hear at home, all of which builds bridges with school. As Elliot Eisner (2003) argued, we are transforming children's "brains into minds" by giving our students many opportunities to actively experience music (p. 341).

Music is part of everything we do with our students. Celebrating Black History month, watching a flower grow, researching and writing biographies, starting a new month, studying another country, and beginning a new reading theme are all invitations to musical adventure. The snow falling or the sun breaking through the winter clouds are reasons to stop the chatter and celebrate these special moments with music. Our students have come to expect music throughout the day and are not surprised when we say, "Here's our new work. What music shall we listen to?"

Genre Studies: A Focus on Fairy Tales

How do we use music in the classroom when we start a new literature study? How does music enhance our reading and writing? How does it allow our students to uncover layers of understanding and get inside the stories we are studying? How does music help our students visualize setting and understand nuances of character and emotion in stories? In the next several sections of this chapter we will begin to answer these questions through a discussion of one particular kind of literature study—fairy tales. In the process, we will help the reader discover that opera ties music and story together in powerful ways.

Our initial study begins with our students reading many versions of *Cinderella*, *The Frog Prince*, and other fairy tale text sets, or collections of different versions of the same story. We pose questions that encourage our students to compare and contrast these stories: "*What story elements must be present in a fairy tale? What kinds of characters are found in fairy tales? Do fairy tales all have happy endings? Is magic important? How does the number three have significance?*" To develop an understanding of story and to invite inquiry, we create charts and note beginnings, endings, and problems created and solved. Students research different versions of each fairy tale, generate questions, and read to find the answers. For example, they ask, "Are there balls in every *Cinderella* story? Are there always glass slippers and fairy godmothers? Does the frog turn back into a prince in every version of *Frog Prince*?" Reading to answer questions stretches students' thinking and builds comprehension.

Why Opera Study?

Because so many fairy tales have been turned into operas, opera has become a natural extension of the literature we read, the storytelling we do, and the music we enjoy. Charles Fowler (cited in Purrington, Rinehart, & Wilcox, 1990) in *Music! Words! Opera!* says:

> Opera is just another way—a dramatic and musical way—to tell a story. Music adds an important dimension of feeling. It expresses the atmosphere of the scene, the moods of the characters, and the emotional impact of the events (p. ix).

Opera integrates several art forms—music, art, drama, dance, and poetry. It requires students to employ all of their senses as they interpret the worlds created by composers and librettists. Fowler argued that "As a form of human expression, opera challenges students to reach beyond speaking and writing and to think more comprehensively about their own ability to express and to communicate" (p. ix). Furthermore, opera surprisingly parallels fairy tales in that princes, queens, magic, and the number three often characterize this genre.

Can opera make space for different kinds of learners? Can it offer children whose school day is filled with music and the rhythm of clapping games like "I don't want to go to Mexico, no more, no more" the opportunity to build on their strengths and to tap into their interests? And, can it help emergent readers find another way *in* to acquire the literacy skills they need? Our work with music and genre study through inquiry over many years has enabled us to research these questions, and we suggest that such inquiry does indeed develop young children's literacy.

Fairy Tale Operas

Many fairy tales have been turned into operas and have familiar melodies or songs that lend themselves to this genre study. Gioachino Rossini's (1993) *La Cenerentola* is an opera version of *Cinderella*. The opera differs from other versions because it is missing the magical elements and the traditional fairy godmother. Matching bracelets take the place of the glass slippers. Yet its many areas of commonality with other Cinderella tales allow it to contribute to a discussion of what makes a Cinderella story a Cinderella story. Filled with glorious music, some of it sounding traditionally Chinese, Giacomo Puccini's (1990b) *Turandot,* set in ancient times in Peking, China, is also an opera that we have used with fairy tales. It includes the important number three, riddles, princes, and beheadings, and encourages listeners to predict what will happen next in the story. Will one of the suitors end up marrying the cruel Turandot? Will the story have a happy ending? Will the prince be beheaded at the end? A film version of *Turandot* was performed in its original setting, in the Forbidden City of Beijing, with Zubin Mehta as conductor. Based on the Brothers Grimm *Hansel and Gretel* fairy tale, Engelbert Humperdinck's (1999) opera *Hänsel und Gretel* varies slightly from the original fairy tale by providing a less troubling version of how the children end up lost in the woods. The mother in the opera accidentally, rather than intentionally, sends the children into danger. Several of the melodies from the opera are well known and familiar:

> With your feet you tap, tap, tap.
> With your hands you clap, clap, clap.
> First go here, then go there,
> Turn around just anywhere.

Many people also know the prayer melody from this same opera entitled, "Now I Lay Me Down to Sleep." Lines from these melodies are simple and familiar and make this opera particularly accessible to young children.

   La Cenerentola, Turandot, and *Hänsel und Gretel* have enriched our study of fairy tales in different years with different classes. To illustrate the possibilities of an in-depth study and the ways in which opera can enhance reading and writing, our next section will describe our work with *The Magic Flute* by Wolfgang Amadeus Mozart.

The Magic Flute: Bridging Fairy Tales with Opera

The Magic Flute (Die Zauberflote) has several fairy tale elements: a queen, a prince, a dragon, and the important number three. It has engaging characters such as Papageno, the half bird-half man, who does not always tell the truth and has difficulty staying quiet even when he needs to. It also has the Queen of the Night, who appears kind and good at the beginning of the opera but becomes vengeful and mean as the story progresses; her motivations are ambiguous. The strong storyline is filled with quests for a beautiful princess and trials that need to be overcome before everyone, or almost everyone, can live happily ever after. Best of all, *The Magic Flute* contains music that evokes a strong sense of place, character, and mood.

Initially, we ask our students to listen as the three strong chords of the overture to *The Magic Flute* sing out. "There's that important number three," one of our students, Nora, says. Another student, Ashton, starts conducting the music, his arms moving in time to the beat. Ta! Tada! Tada! Our students are drawn into Mozart's music. Isabel tries to get as close to the music as she can, her head almost touching the CD player. Jenmarie sits absolutely still in rapt attention, something that is usually very difficult for her. The words coming out of the speakers are in German, but it does not matter to our students, they are entranced. They hear the emotion behind the words, even if they do not understand what is actually being sung. At the end of the first day, our students cannot get the music out of their heads. The next day, they bring in notes from their parents apprising us of the far-reaching effects of the opera. One parent writes, "Marco has been singing the music at home. What a treat!" Another lets us know, "I try to play piano (very elementary piano, that is) for Rose at bedtime. 'Play something by Mozart,' she asked me tonight." And another says, "Thayer's [her son] been singing the songs from *The Magic Flute* as he plays with his action figures." Howard Gardner (cited in Checkley, 1997), a scholar who has studied the effects of the arts on learning, believes that, "People who have strong musical intelligence don't just remember music easily, they can't get it out of their minds; it's so omnipresent" (p. 12). By immersing ourselves in music, we develop a classroom environment in which students just cannot get the music "out of their minds!"

For several weeks, our students listen to Mozart's opera from the moment they enter the classroom until the end of the day. We play it while we read, and we play it to inspire our own stories and poems during writing workshop time. It calls us to a class meeting, and it leads us to move in the gym as the characters may have moved on the stage. Over time, students become familiar with the music. We talk about what they imagine happening in each scene. While fast arpeggios explode from the speakers, students share how they visualize the huge dragon lumbering onto stage, chasing Prince Tamino, and how they feel the terror he must be experiencing. When Tamino goes through the tests of fire and water, students hear the magic flute and imagine what that scene might look like.

Setting

Listening to the music of *The Magic Flute* helps our students begin to visualize and build a sense of place. To move our students into a deeper understanding of the concept of setting, we add the dimension of the visual arts. We visit the Oberlin Allen Memorial Art Museum in our town with the intention of studying artists' perspectives on landscape. If you are not lucky enough to have an art museum in your neighborhood, consider using the Internet to bring works of art into your classroom. In the museum, we look thoughtfully at paintings by several artists including Nicholas Roerich's *Menhirs in the Himalayas*. As we talk about his painting, we imagine ourselves in this setting, in the empty spaces amid the jagged rocks.

Back at school, our own sketchbooks in hand, we bridge our learning from the museum as viewers of settings in art to artists of our own school's landscape. We gather in the back playground of Eastwood and talk about its trees, its special hill, and its grassy area. We notice the arrival of autumn with a blanket of leaves beginning to cover the green grass. We observe the orange and yellow of the maple and oak leaves and even the drying flowers in Eastwood's garden. We sketch what we notice, our own special landscape. Now our children have moved from imagining setting to a more concrete understanding of setting as landscape.

To help us expand our ideas about setting even further, our art teacher Kathy Hilton, offers us lessons in painting and drawing (Figure 2.2). In teams of four, our students work around table-size sheets of paper to illustrate what they hear as the music of *The Magic Flute* plays once more. Mrs. Hilton asks, "Does the

FIGURE **2.2.** *Student-artists illustrate the music they hear.*

music sound happy? Does the music sound ominous?" The swirls of color and the patterns of paint reveal the mood of the music and the setting the children imagine. Another day, Mrs. Hilton invites our student-artists to add animals, trees, and hills to their imaginary landscapes. Students create creatures that float in a dreamlike place where fairy tales can happen. The integration of story, music, and art helps our students develop a powerful understanding of the need for setting and how it contributes to a musician's, artist's, or author's ability to communicate.

Character Study

Once the scene is set, we shift our focus to character study. The music serves as a strong bridge to our students' understanding of character because music conveys mood, and mood informs characters and their actions. The overture of *The Magic Flute* immediately conveys a mood of anxiety and tension as Tamino runs away from the dragon. In the first scene, Papageno's signature sound is light and playful as he enters, dancing to the music of his panpipe. Later the "star-blazing" Queen of the Night is introduced with thunder and flashes of lightning. The loud crashing music makes students wonder out loud whether she is a mean character. As they continue to listen, the music changes. We hear a melody that makes us think she may be sad and not angry after all. This shift in mood helps children understand a different aspect of the Queen's character and the sorrow she must feel because she has lost her daughter. And yet, in the same aria, the final fast section helps us see the Queen as a person of power.

After listening to the music, several children draw pictures of what they think the Queen of the Night would look like at different times in the opera. Nora's vision (Figure 2.3) has the Queen's mouth open in song, her cape billowing up behind her from the force of her feelings. This artistic rendering indicates Nora's strong understanding of the Queen's character as depicted in the libretto: a long flowing dress, a crown set into a bouffant hairstyle, and a regal posture—an elegant lady surrounded by the stars in the night sky. Seeing pictures of queens from fairy tales we have read earlier also added to Nora's vision of a queen-like character.

As part of their study of operas and fairy tales, our students write their own stories. Isabel writes about a girl who actually meets the Queen of the Night:

> Once unpon a time there lived a girl One day the girl Saw the Queen of the night at her House. She was Vary Kind to her. The Queen of the night Said Wold you like to Sing With me? the girl said yes. So they Saing the magic flut. then they Startd to Sing the part when the Queen of the night got mad. then it Was over so they Saing it agin and agin and agin. Then the Queen of the night disapard.

Gardner's idea of music being "omnipresent" is expressed in Isabel's story (Checkley, 1997). It is not enough for the Queen of the Night to sing her song once. She has to sing it over and over and over again. This song becomes a part of the Queen's everyday life.

Although the dragon has a very small part in the opera, his character intrigues many children. They draw pictures of what they think the dragon might look like. Eli's journal sketch (Figure

FIGURE **2.3.** *Nora's vision of the Queen of the Night.*

FIGURE **2.4.** *Eli's journal sketch of a dragon.*

2.4) visually interprets the dragon as a nice creature with a smile, one with whom he would like to hang out. Eli writes:

> If the dragon from the Magic Flute came to my house I would invite him in. And ride him all around the house. Then we'd whach T.V. The movie would be about a dragon. After that we'd get tirde and take a nap. It would last for a haur. He'd have to go home. Then the next day, he'd come agian and we'd do the same thing.

In their writing about characters, both Isabel and Eli express the desire to do the same activity again and again. Isabel wants to sing a song over and over, while Eli's dragon wants to play day after day. This idea of repetition suggests that students want to keep the characters from the opera with them always.

Like Isabel and Eli, Rose draws her own vision of a favorite character, Tamino (Figure 2.5). Above the prince's head she includes a thought balloon telling us, "The music is coming out. He is getting ready for the tests. He's wondering if he'll see his magic flute again, or hear his friend's bells." Such visual representations enable us to understand our students' interpretation of

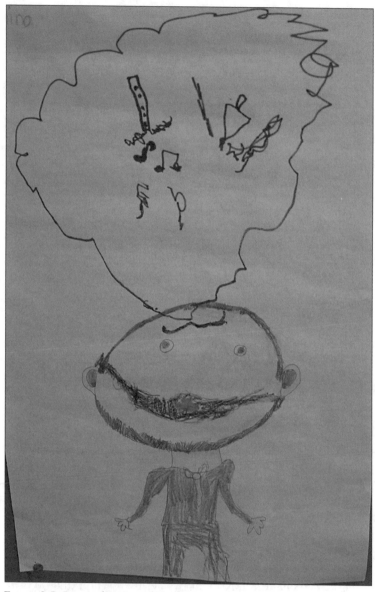

FIGURE 2.5. *Rose's drawing of Tamino.*

character as expressed through art, language, and music. Further, their writing becomes richer with detail because they attend to the story, the music, and the art, all of which help them imagine and interpret the story in more complex ways.

Rose is so enamored with the characters from *The Magic Flute* that she brings in stuffed animals and dolls from home to represent every one of them. Rose lines her creatures up and they all listen with us as we play the music again and again. Surprisingly, little bird-man Papageno sits as quietly as everyone else does.

Our students are now ready to return to the art room and create masks of their favorite characters. They think about the duplicity of the Queen of the Night, the frivolity of Papageno, the bravery of Tamino, and the strength of Sarastro before designing masks that represent these characters' unique traits. A variety of media is available as students once more experience the signature sounds of each character. Their masks are soon ready to display against their landscapes, imagined and painted as they listen to the music of *The Magic Flute* with the art teacher, Mrs. Hilton.

We conclude our work in understanding the story of *The Magic Flute* with movement as a motivating extension of character study. As we play the overture to the opera, we ask, "How would Monostotos move his arms? How would Sarastro walk?" We invite our students to think deeply about the feelings of these characters and to take on their roles. Why would they move in a particular way? What actions or events encourage them to move? To give ourselves more room to move, we go to our school gymnasium, play the music, and we move (Figure 2.6). We are Papageno struggling to be quiet, Tamino running from the dragon, then the Queen of the Night parading with her Three Ladies.

Using Film Versions of *The Magic Flute*

After the students have a chance to think about the story and story elements such as setting and character by listening and moving to the music, we show three movie versions of *The Magic Flute*. In the same way that we read and compare different picture book versions of *Cinderella* tales or *Hansel and Gretel* stories, we watch and compare these movie versions of *The Magic Flute*. Looking for similarities and differences in the productions, we also read the libretto and talk about each scene as it unfolds. These movie versions enable us, as viewers, to enjoy aspects of the production that Mozart's music alone could not.

FIGURE **2.6.** *Students move about the gymnasium to the music.*

Ingmar Bergman's (2000) *The Magic Flute*, sung in Swedish, invites us into the backstage area as the actors change into their costumes. We laugh when we see Tamino and Pamina playing chess during intermission and revel in watching the scary-looking dragon—no longer so fierce—relaxing after his part is finished. We then watch the Metropolitan Opera version conducted by James Levine, so realistic in its production that we feel as if we are actually in the opera house enjoying contemporary artist David Hockney's sets. As teachers, we think that watching two versions of the opera might be enough, but our students want to see more. We end our study by showing Julie Taymor's (2006) production of *The Magic Flute*. This shortened version sung in English includes bears, birds, and a dragon all brought to life through puppetry. It adds another dimension to the richness of our study of this fairy tale and affirms for students that there are many ways to tell a story.

Our inquiry into Mozart's music and movie versions of the opera engage our students in discussions and comparisons of each version, capturing their attention and imagination in ways that just reading it cannot. Jenmarie, a student who seldom raises her hand during class meetings, starts participating in discussions. She actually talks about her favorite lines, giggling as she says, "Papageno said, 'I should be still now.'" She gets the joke. Richard, a student who often finds it difficult to engage in the lessons during class meeting time, starts reading the subtitles as we watch the opera. As Sharon reads just enough of the libretto out loud so the children can understand what is going on, she leaves out some of the words so as not to interfere with the joy of the music. Richard calls her to task. He notices and announces to the class when she does not read everything that is on the screen. The children cannot get enough of *The Magic Flute* and its music. Janae says, "I wish it wasn't time to go home. I want to watch more of *Magic Flute*." Evelyn says, "All night I dreamed about what's coming next in the opera, *Magic Flute*. I couldn't stop it. I was just wondering and wondering. I was dreaming about how Monostatos was going to threaten Pamina."

We find that we take parts of *The Magic Flute* with us wherever we go. Evelyn, thinking about the Queen of the Night, names her toy horses, "Princess of the Night" and "Queen of the Snow." P.K. announces in class that "I told my dad all about *The Magic Flute* yesterday." Zach dresses up as Prince Tamino and prepares to act in our fairy tale theater. Our students are developing the "consciousness of listening" (Ceppi & Zini, 1998, pp. 90–91) that the Reggio Emilia educators talk about. They are gaining "the ability to select sound stimuli, to know them and recognize their sources, in the same way as we recognize an object by its shape and color" (Ceppi & Zini, 1998, p. 91).

The flute itself provides an opportunity for more study. We invite Patrick, a new friend from Oberlin College, to bring his flute into class. What a discovery! He talks about his instrument, how it works, the care it requires, and his studies at the Oberlin Conservatory of Music. Patrick then plays his flute with jaw-dropping skill. He answers our questions and gives in to our students' requests for more! More! More! Patrick's improvisations inspire students in our class who have instruments in their homes to bring them in and share their musical interests and talents. This inquiry into music engages parents as well. In our classrooms, both students and their parents alike participate in informal performances full of music, compliments, questions, and encores.

Our students and parents see each other in new ways through music. Clara's dad, who has taken cello lessons for only one year, performs and tells the story of how he came to play this instrument so late in his life. Janae's dad not only brings in a lute—an unusual and unfamiliar instrument for most of the class—but announces that he made it himself! Eli's dad, who visits our classroom monthly for sing-a-longs, brings and plays an accordion which intrigues the class. Rui, one of our students visiting for the year from Japan (and learning to speak English with the help of all) impresses his peers with his expertise by playing the keyboard. Jordan, who has recently started taking piano lessons from a friend in the community, proudly shows off his new piano book. An accordion, cellos, keyboards, trumpets, violins, recorders—some played with style, others held and admired with wished-for ability. All are shared with enthusiasm. Our class's intense inquiry leads us to support their interest by helping them invent their own instruments and to develop a class orchestra that includes every child.

Music as Inquiry

The study of *The Magic Flute* continues and develops into an inquiry that over time moves our students from listening to music to reading a range of texts. The children discover that Mozart, the composer of *The Magic Flute*, had no formal lessons, and learned to play the piano at the age of four by listening to his sister play. Our students listen to biographies about Mozart's early life and discover that he and his sister, Nannerl, toured Europe and played for kings and queens—a perfect bridge from reading fairy tales to a real person's life! They get to know Wolfie, as his sister called him, and empathize with his desire to play and run and tease, only being still when he was at the piano or composing. They ask questions about other composers who might have known Mozart and begin their research in earnest.

To facilitate their inquiry, we bring in picture books (works of art themselves) that enable our students to partner up and read and talk about composers and musicians. We invite our students to write in their journals what they learn about the lives of people who lived and made music long ago. Students start a class timeline and add names and dates so they can see whose lives overlapped. Their learning is insatiable and contagious. They talk with their families about their desire to learn more and find themselves at the library with parents who are also caught up in the joy of research. Our class library grows both in books and music as parents contribute CDs of Mozart and his contemporaries, whose music now fills our days.

Our students' curiosity about Mozart and *The Magic Flute* is indeed a study, not solely about fairy tales, but inquiry in its truest and most authentic form. Although our genre study of fairy tales and the inclusion of the opera, *The Magic Flute*, help us explore the elements of story, setting/landscape, character, mood, and plot, it is much more. Our initial study of fairy tales and Mozart's opera lead us to read biographies of other composers and musicians. Student questions about the flute bring parents and other members of the community into our classroom to help us study musical instruments. This work inspires a study in the science of sound, the invention of new instruments, and the creation of our own orchestra. Our study of opera does not just afford us an opportunity to study a genre of literature, the fairy tale. Our study also helps us understand how children see an interrelatedness of other disciplines as they ask questions that invite perspectives from science, social studies, history, music, written and oral language, drama, and art.

Implications for Practice: Creating a Multimodal Classroom

This picture of our classroom may seem daunting to teachers who want to work with music and inquiry as we do with our first- and second-grade children, but this work is authentic. It is not separated from the real life of elementary classrooms but integrates music as a central component to support young students' literacy through reading, writing, music, art, and drama. In this section, we offer some ideas for getting started. First, we suggest that a classroom library must include a variety of music and the CD players, iPods, tape players, and/or computers to play that music at a moment's notice. If music is going to be an integral part of the classroom, it needs to be at the teacher's and students' fingertips. Developing a musical library takes time, but it is worth it in order to have music to suit different needs, moods, and projects throughout the year. For example, Barbara Berger's (1990) *Gwinna*, the story of a young girl who wishes she had a harp, was one of our recent read alouds and provided us with the opportunity to listen to harp music. Discoveries about the shape of the instrument, the length and strength of strings, and the quality of the sound contribute to background knowledge that makes the story more meaningful. When our children need to get re-energized, we are able to pluck from our selection Yo-Yo Ma and Bobby McFerrin's (1992) version of Nikolai Rimsky-Korsakov's *Flight of the Bumblebee*. If our students need to reestablish a sense of calm, we play Samuel Barber's *Adagio*. Having an accessible library of music means that we are more likely to integrate music into our curriculum.

As part of students' initial experiences, we invite teachers to consider how music can be used throughout the day. The following are descriptions of opportunities that we provide our students to build musical confidence and to help lay the groundwork for bigger projects such as writing a libretto and composing the music for our own operas.

We celebrate the beginning of fall by listening to Antonio Lucio Vivaldi's (2002) concerto "Autumn" from *The Four Seasons*. Our students move like leaves falling down. We read Leo Lionni's (1967) book, *Frederick*, and collect colors, sunshine, and the breeze like the thoughtful little mouse, Frederick. We listen again to Vivaldi while we draw pictures that convey what we see and hear in our imaginary places on a fall day.

Another day we find ourselves in the gym where we can spread out and move with partners in a mirroring activity inspired by Don McLean's (1980) song, "Vincent," about Vincent Van Gogh. Our empathy for this struggling artist grows as we read biographies and try on his style at our painting center. We read Maurice Sendak's (1963) *Where the Wild Things Are* and then roll paper around our fingers to make claws so we can dance to the music of the opera version of this story. We have our own wild rumpus and then freeze when Max sings out, "Now stop!"

We fill our bodies up with jazz until we have to "cut a rug" with Duke Ellington. His visually exciting biography, *Duke Ellington: The Piano Prince and His Orchestra*, makes us want to move to the sounds that are envisioned by illustrator Brian Pinkney and author Andrea Davis Pinkney (1998). Our study during Black History month of famous musicians continues with the Queen of Scat, Ella Fitzgerald (2004). We watch her perform, *A-Tisket A-Tasket*, courtesy of YouTube and the Internet (http://www.youtube.com/watch?v=XUYpUogn91U). Then we read the book illustrated by Ora Eitan with rhythm and pleasure in "scat."

We observe and sketch a mysterious object on our science table, then listen to a reading of *A Flower Grows* by Ken Robbins (1990); we plant an amaryllis bulb we now know more about and watch it grow. Marilyn Crispell's (2001) music titled "Amaryllis" is the accompaniment to watercolor work at the art table and the writing and reading of poems to share our feelings about the amaryllis.

We study sound waves and invent our own musical instruments. The computer program "Garage Band" is helpful in giving students songwriting time and opportunities to play with patterns and rhythms as they compose. We reinforce patterns in math and reading with musical rhythms. We clap, snap, and tap our way into feeling, understanding, and naming the patterns we create with color, shape, and movement. *Rap a Tap Tap* by Leo and Diane Dillon (2002) about Bill "Bojangles" Robinson, the "man who danced in the street" (p. 1) and "made art with his feet" (p. 5) helps us move to these rhythms.

Whether working with older elementary, middle, or secondary students, teachers can make a number of strong music/literature connections. Scott Joplin's (1992) *Treemonisha* can be part of a study of life in the South after the Civil War. Hans Krása's (1993) opera, *Brundibár*, can help a class envision the horrors of a German concentration camp. Listening to opera can enrich any examination of another country's culture or language. Puccini's (1990a) *Madame Butterfly* is set in Japan; Rossini's (2004) *The Barber of Seville* takes place in Spain; Verdi's (2001) *Aida* is set in Egypt. High school classes studying Shakespeare find Verdi's (1998) *Otello* a match for *Othello*. The possibilities are endless.

Conclusion

Music flows like a river through our classroom. We put our toes in, dabble in the shallow end, dive under and immerse ourselves, swim along on waves of sound, and float under a wider sky with the songs of children. We invite everyone to wade in and tickle their toes, to sing and splash about, to take pleasure in people, places, and learning that have been made more enticing, more energizing through music.

Works Cited

Barber, S. (1990). *Barber's adagio* [Recorded by the New York Philharmonic with L. Bernstein conducting, CD]. New York: Sony.

Berger, B. H. (1990). *Gwinna*. New York: Philomel.

Bergman, I. (Director, Producer). (2000). *Ingmar Bergman's the magic flute* [DVD]. (Original motion picture released 1975)

Ceppi, G., & Zini, M. (Eds.). (1998). *Children, spaces, relations: Metaproject for an environment for young children*. Reggio Emilia, Italy: Reggio Children.

Checkley, K. (1997). The first seven . . . and the eighth: A conversation with Howard Gardner. *Educational Leadership*, 55(1), 8–13.

Crispell, M. (2001). Amaryllis. On *Amaryllis* [CD]. Munich, Germany: ECM Records.

Dillon, L., & Dillon, D. (2002). *Rap a tap tap*. New York: Blue Sky Press.

Eisner, E. W. (2003). The arts and the creation of mind. *Language Arts*, 80(5), 340–344.

Ellington, D. (1990). *Three suites* [CD]. New York: Sony.

Fitzgerald, E. (2004). A-tisket, a-tasket. On *A-tisket, a-tasket* [CD]. New York: Synergy Entertainment.

Fitzgerald, E., & Alexander, V. (2003). *A-tisket, a-tasket*. New York: Philomel Books.

Glyndbourne Festival Opera. (1994). *Where the wild things are* [music by Oliver Knussen, libretti and designs by Maurice Sendak, Videocassette].

Humperdinck, E. (1999). *Hänsel und Gretel* [CD]. New York: RCA.

Joplin, S. (1992). *Treemonisha* [CD]. Hamburg, Germany: Deutsche Grammophon.

Käch, R. (Director), & Käch, H. (Director). *Turandot at the Forbidden City of Beijing* [Z. Mehta conducting, DVD].

Krása, H. (1993). *Brundibár* [CD]. Amsterdam, The Netherlands: Channel Classics.

Large, B. (Director). (1991). *Die zauberflote (The Magic Flute)* [Metropolitan Opera with J. Levine conducting, DVD].

Lionni, L. (1967). *Frederick*. New York: Pantheon.

Ma, Y.-Y., & McFerrin, B. (1992). Flight of the bumblebee. On *Hush* [CD]. New York: Sony Masterworks.

McLean, D. (1980). Vincent. On *American pie* [CD]. Los Angeles: Liberty Records.

Medearis, A. S. (1995). *Treemonisha*. New York: Henry Holt.

Mozart, W. A. (2000). *The magic flute* [CD]. London, UK: EMI Classics.

Pinkney, A. D. (1998). *Duke Ellington: The piano prince and his orchestra*. New York: Hyperion Books for Children.

Puccini, G. (1990a). *Madama butterfly* [H. Von Karajan conducting, CD]. West Hampstead, UK: Decca.

———. (1990b). *Turandot* [Z. Mehton conducting, CD]. West Hampstead, UK: Decca.

Purrington, S., Rinehart, C., & Wilcox, W. (1990). *Music! Words! Opera!* Charlotte, NC: Delmar.

Robbins, K. (1990). *A flower grows*. New York: Dial.

Rossini, G. (1993). *La cenerentola* [CD]. London, UK: Decca.

———. (2004). *The barber of Seville* [Recorded by the London Symphony Orchestra with J. Levine conducting, CD]. London, UK: EMI Classics.

Sendak, M. (1963). *Where the wild things are*. New York: Harper and Row.

Taymor, J. (Director). (2006). *Great performances at the Met: The magic flute* [DVD]. New York: Public Broadcasting Service.

Verdi, G. (1998). *Otello* [J. Levine conducting, CD]. New York: RCA.

———. (2001). *Aida* [Recorded by New Philharmonia Orchestra with R. Muti conducting, CD]. London, UK: EMI Classics.

Vivaldi, A. (2002). *The four seasons* [CD]. London, UK: EMI Classics.

CHAPTER THREE

Opening Doors, Unlocking Writers: A Classroom Exploration of Picture Books with Sound

JOANNA ROBERTSON

Syracuse University

It just opened a whole new door for kids—to look at something differently. And me, not just them, but me! (Interview with Mrs. Winter, August 22, 2007.)

Increasingly, authors of print and electronic media communicate in multiple modes, including linguistic, visual, gestural, spatial, and audio representations as well as representations that combine those modes. In addition to the growing body of research on digital and technological formats that use multiple modes, research is needed that explores the use of other kinds of multimodal texts to help teachers recognize students' existing knowledge regarding multimodality and the use of multimodality as a resource for curriculum and teaching (Siegel, 2006). Although attention has been paid to the interaction between the visual and linguistic modes in picture books, there has been little exploration of the increasing number of children's picture books that use other modes of representation (Nikolajeva & Scott, 2000; Nodelman, 1988; Sipe, 1998). Little is known about how children transact with such multimodal texts. This knowledge may help teachers support students in constructing meaning in multiple modes, and may, in turn, help acknowledge and value all students, including those with poor print literacy skills, who are often marginalized in traditional school settings.

The data presented in this chapter are from a larger classroom case study designed to explore a combined fourth- and fifth-grade classroom's transactions with picture books with multimodal representations, specifically those that represent the audio mode in addition to visual and linguistic modes. The following two research questions were explored in the larger study: (1) What were the teacher's perspectives and practices regarding the inclusion of multimodal picture books in instruction? and (2) How did students respond to multimodal picture books? This chapter focuses on interactions with *What Charlie Heard* by Mordicai Gerstein, one of the ten books presented in the larger study. I discuss the teacher's instructional practices as she included this multimodal picture book in her lessons, as well as some of the ways that students responded to this book both directly and through their own writing.

Theoretical Framework

Trends in Children's Literature

Children's picture books, defined by the way they "tell a story or develop an understanding of a concept through a unique combination of text and art" (Galda & Cullinan, 2002, p. 11), are a widely used instructional tool that can benefit learning at all levels. Many scholars have tied changes in children's literature to changes in social, cultural, and political realms. As Anstey and Bull (2006) explained, contemporary books are a product of changing times, require new understandings about text, and are well suited for preparing students to be multiliterate individuals. Scholars have identified trends in children's picture books relating to postmodernism (Pantaleo, 2004; Serafini, 2005) as well as digital and technological advances (Dresang, 2003). Dresang (2003) claimed that by censoring or by not providing necessary guidance and support for contemporary texts, adults are not educating students to deal with the experiences in their world. This study explores books that are reflective of the trend toward increased multimodality in today's society.

Multiliteracies and Multimodality

One of the earliest and most influential voices on multiple literacies and multimodality in education belongs to Elliot Eisner (1991), who has argued that schools' focus on reading and written language systems marginalizes other forms of expression and, likewise, marginalizes students who have talents and abilities in these other forms. The authors of the multiliteracies theory, the New London Group (1996), similarly argued for broadening the scope of literacy pedagogy to value multiple modes of representation and a variety of text forms, claiming that opportunities have been denied to a wide range of learners because literacy has been "restricted to formalized, monolingual, monocultural, and rule-governed forms of language" (p. 61). Their multiliteracies theory was comprised of the "what"—the design theory, and the "how"—the pedagogical aspect of the theory.

There are three aspects of the multiliteracies design model: *available designs, designing,* and *the redesigned.* Available designs are the resources a person has to make meaning, including audio, spatial, gestural, linguistic, and multimodal designs. When readers transact with a text, the text itself is an available design, as well as the readers' social and cultural contexts and prior knowledge and experiences. Designing is the process of representing and recontextualizing available designs to make new meaning. In the process of reading, readers make meaning using the text and within their own context; this meaning making is an act of designing. The outcome of designing is the redesigned, a new meaning that in turn becomes an available design for subsequent meaning making. Central to the design theory is the idea of interpreting, critiquing, and designing with multiple modes (New London Group, 1996).

The pedagogical aspect of the multiliteracies theory has four components: *situated practice* that immerses learners in designing experiences; *overt instruction* that explicitly describes and interprets designs, including those in different modes; *critical framing* that allows learners to step back and critically analyze designs and their contexts; and *transformed practice* that transfers meaning designed in one context to new contexts (New London Group, 1996). The pedagogical aspect of the multiliteracies theory therefore emphasizes the importance of multiple instructional situations when teaching new designs and working in new or less familiar modes. In the findings and discussion, I will explain how the elements of the multiliteracies design and pedagogical theory looked in practice by highlighting these elements in Mrs. Winter's instruction of a multimodal picture book. As I discuss these elements, I will continue to use the terms introduced by the New London Group as they appear here: *available designs*, *designing*, and *the redesigned*; *situated practice*, *overt instruction*, *critical framing*, and *transformed practice*.

Multimodality is a semiotically grounded theory that recognizes the different systems humans use to communicate (Jewitt & Kress, 2003). According to Jewitt and Kress (2003), each system of communication, or mode, has its own affordances and therefore is better suited for some tasks than others. Knowledge of each mode's affordances and constraints within a cultural context allows individuals to choose the mode or modes that most appropriately express a message. A multimodal text integrates more than one mode to express a message by drawing on the affordances of each mode to create a new meaning.

Picture books depend on multimodality, as they are based on the interaction between at least two modes. A number of researchers have analyzed the complex relationships between words and images that exist in children's picture books using a semiotic framework (Nikolajeva & Scott, 2000; Nodelman, 1988; Sipe, 1998). Further, researchers have explored the concept of multimodality in K–12 settings (Berghoff, 1993; Gallas, 1994; Short, Kauffman, & Kahn, 2000). Although scholars often include sound effects and music in their list of modes that are available for literacy learners, most of the research on multimodality with students focuses on how students respond or create in the visual and linguistic modes (Hull & Nelson, 2005; Jewitt & Kress, 2003). Van Leeuwen (1999) explored the dimensions of the audio mode as a communicative resource, but his framework focused more on fully composed musical pieces and less on isolated sound effects or how audio functions within a multimodal text. There has been little empirical research on students' multimodal meaning making that incorporates audio representations as a mode of communication. Research that addresses how students transact with multimodal representations, and specifically audio representations, in text is needed.

Hybridity

In the field of literacy education, the concept of hybridity is most commonly associated with Bakhtin's (1981) definition and explanation of a hybrid as *"an artistically organized system for bringing different languages in contact with one another"* (p. 361; emphasis in the original). As it relates to multiliteracies theory, The New London Group (1996) discussed hybridity as transformed designs resulting from the relation and combination of all the available designs, including multiple facets of identity, experiences, and discourses. As they described, "People create and innovate by hybridising, that is by articulating, in new ways, established practices and conventions within and between different modes of meaning" (pp. 30–31). In this way, I consider the multimodal picture books to be hybrid texts in that they combine established practices in different modes and discourses. However, the discussion also investigates how the combination of available designs into hybrid texts and practices took place on other levels in the classroom.

Methodology

This chapter describes a small part of a larger classroom case study that explored how a teacher and her students in a combined fourth- and fifth-grade classroom transacted with picture books that used multiple modes, specifically visual, linguistic, and audio modes. The following research questions were explored:

1. What were the teacher's perspectives and practices regarding the inclusion of multimodal picture books in instruction?

2. How did students respond to multimodal picture books?

Case study methodology was appropriate, as the classroom represented a bounded system chosen to help give insight or understanding to the research questions (Stake, 1995).

Participants

The participants in this case study were the teacher and students in an upper elementary classroom in the Northwest region of the United States. This particular school fell in the low- to mid-socioeconomic range for the district, with roughly one-third of the students on free and reduced lunches. The district was part of a diverse working-class community, which was physically isolated from a nearby larger city. The population of the school was 89 percent Caucasian, 4 percent Hispanic, 3 percent Asian, 3 percent African American, and 1 percent American Indian/Alaskan Native (Office of Superintendent of Public Instruction, 2006). There were twenty-four students in this combined fourth- and fifth-grade classroom. Fifteen of those students were in fourth grade and nine were in fifth grade. There were twelve girls and twelve boys in the classroom. The teacher in the selected classroom, Mrs. Winter (all names used are pseudonyms), had taught third through sixth grades at various schools in the district for sixteen years. She received a bachelor's degree in education and began her teaching career after working several years in another profession. She was Caucasian, grew up in the local area, and her own children, now adults, had gone to school in the same district.

Criteria for Selecting Texts

Prior to entering the classroom, I selected fifteen picture books that satisfied criteria for quality of writing and illustrations, avoidance of stereotypes, and age appropriateness (Darigan, Tunnell, & Jacobs, 2002; Kasten, Kristo, & McClure, 2005). In addition to these general criteria, the predominant criteria used to select texts for this study was the presence of design elements that allowed for the possibility of meaning making through the audio mode, in addition to visual and linguistic modes. Texts that represented meaning *through* the modes of visual, linguistic, and audio were sought, rather than texts that merely dealt with or expressed (linguistically) an idea *about* sound. My interpretations were informed by Kress's (2000) claim that modes are related to the sense that is employed in order to make meaning of the represented information. For example, if I fully understand a message because I am employing my sense of hearing, even if

I am just doing so in my head, then I can argue that the audio mode is being used to make meaning.

To this end, I took into account the function of a representation, noting that even visual and linguistic information may serve the primary purpose of representing an audio meaning. For example, while the words *barking dog* on a page primarily represent linguistic meaning, and a picture of a dog primarily represents a visual meaning, the word *arf* in a speech bubble attached to a picture of a dog is meant to represent the sound of a barking dog. Each has its own purpose, and only the third explicitly refers to and represents a sound. The books selected for this study include a range of representations of the audio mode, from the use of linguistic text as a musical or rhythmic element to the inclusion of a musical CD as an integral aspect to making meaning. A table with all fifteen selected texts is shown in the appendix.

This chapter focuses on how Mrs. Winter used one of the picture books, *What Charlie Heard* by Mordicai Gerstein (2002), in her instruction. *What Charlie Heard* is a picture book biography of composer Charles Ives that uses words as visual pictures but also as communicators of sound. Words on each page are set apart in a bordered text box that is always white with black text. These words function like a traditional text and tell the story of the picture book. However, in order to represent the sounds that Charles Ives heard and used to compose his music, the pages of *What Charlie Heard* are covered with sound words that appear in different colors and sizes and are integrated within the design of the illustrations. These words represent sounds and are placed in appropriate places in the illustration itself ("tweet" near the bird, and "clang" near the pots); this suggests that they will support readers not just in comprehending a literal meaning, such as "the sound that a bird makes," but in actually representing the sound itself. The reader is encouraged to *hear* the sound as the word is read and also hear the multiplicity of sounds that Charles Ives heard.

Data Collection and Analysis

I collected data in the classroom for a full school year. The classroom observations consisted of two phases: (1) observing as the teacher and her students shared, discussed, and responded to children's literature activities on a normal basis during language arts; and (2) observing as the class transacted with ten books that the teacher had chosen to present from the fifteen I had previously selected (see appendix). I gathered data by observing classroom instruction, audio and video recording presentations of literature, conducting semi-structured and unstructured interviews with the teacher and students, collecting examples of students' written work as well as artistic or multimodal responses to the texts, and writing memos throughout the data collection process reflecting on the research process as well as emerging themes.

Data were coded with the assistance of the N7 Qualitative Software program that allowed me to code and compile individual segments of data in numerous ways. I analyzed data and created codes using the constant comparative method because this approach allowed for a consistent and comprehensive analysis of data (Glaser & Strauss, 1967). The cycling between data and codes helped ensure an analytical approach to applying and creating categories to describe the data. Some of the categories that emerged under the research question concerning the teacher's pedagogy included "writer's craft," "making connections," and "teacher prompting." Categories that helped answer the question regarding students' responses included "imitating a model," "expressing sound in writing," and "noticing details in illustration." I also made extensive use of analysis memos by writing memos after reading through the data in each coding category and also after reading through all the data connected to each individual book.

Findings

Mrs. Winter's Pedagogy

Mrs. Winter had begun using a writing workshop approach in her classroom a few years before the study took place. Though she had included picture books as instructional materials prior to this, when she started writing workshop, she found that picture books were most helpful in sharing elements of writer's craft to guide students' writing. Fletcher and Portalupi (2001) believe that:

> Picture books have many advantages that make them ideal for
> the writing workshop. The brevity of these books allows you
> to read them in one setting. Since they are so short, they have
> a lovely transparency that often makes it easier for kids to
> grasp the elements of writing—lead, setting, shape of the story,
> climax, ending—than it does when you read a long, complex
> novel. (p. 76)

Mrs. Winter often echoed a similar reasoning for using picture
books as models of writer's craft during her writing workshop
lessons. For example, when sharing *Rap-a-Tap-Tap* by Leo and
Diane Dillon (2002) prior to sharing any multimodal books for the
study, Mrs. Winter read, "He didn't just dance, he made art with
his feet. Rap a tap tap, think of that." Then she commented, "I like
that; he made art with his feet" (Field Notes, May 7, 2007). This
articulation is representative of the writer's craft pedagogy Mrs.
Winter used throughout the year. She often pointed out phrases
in a text to be explicit about what she felt was strong writing, in
this case highlighting what she believed was a successful example
of descriptive writing.

Later, as Mrs. Winter shared the multimodal books, her
instruction demonstrated her belief that the designs in the multimodal books sometimes required explicit attention to how the
author crafted the audio representation as well. In this way, the
multimodal picture books brought new available designs that
Mrs. Winter used in the designing of her pedagogy (New London
Group, 1996). In the presentation of *What Charlie Heard*, Mrs.
Winter shared her interpretation of the audio representations to
help guide the students:

> I *love* how all of the sounds are shown here. Fiddlee-dee-dee,
> diddle-dee-dee. All of that. That was the fiddle. Look at the
> foot tapping. Tap tap tap. Look at here, peep, peep, peep—the
> little chicks . . . But look at the noises. There's the train in the
> background, there's the church bell going off. Interesting. All
> kinds of things going on around us every day. (Field Notes,
> March 23, 2007)

Mrs. Winter started with a simple comment about how she liked
the representations of sounds in the book using the discourse of

modeling powerful writing that she had used throughout the entire year. She then modeled her interpretation of those representations to help students who might be having trouble interpreting this perhaps unknown type of representation. This represents the redesigned aspect of her pedagogy as she explicitly guided students to understand the way the author crafted the audio representations in addition to the print and visual representations (New London Group, 1996). She closed her comment with, "interesting," again pointing out that this was an aspect of the writing that she felt was strong and powerful. This ending statement more directly reflected her original discourse of pointing out aspects of writer's craft.

Another instructional strategy that was part of Mrs. Winter's writer's craft pedagogy was to refer students back to the writing model while they were working on their own writing. Mrs. Winter asked students to use the content from memoir stories they were working on to explore how they might communicate a scene from their own writing through an illustration similar to the model in *What Charlie Heard*. She gave the following direction:

> And I want you to think hard. In the center of your page is the character in your memoir. And around this character after you've drawn whoever it is in the center, you're going to fill this page up with the noises and the music and the sound of that experience, that moment, that time. . . . (Field Notes, March 23, 2007)

This prompt encouraged students to think about their memoir stories in a different way, following the model of *What Charlie Heard*. As the students worked, Mrs. Winter frequently made explicit references to the picture book model. For example:

> Look up here just a minute. His noises kind of came in clusters, some of them. Clang, clang, clang. Fiddle diddle diddle diddle. Bang, and then Blam! Some great big sound that maybe only happened once was huge! And colorful. (Field Notes, March 23, 2007)

This reminder referred specifically to the way that the author crafted the audio representations in the picture book, guiding students as they worked with this mode in their own writing.

This writing assignment drew from the available designs in the multimodal picture books and invited students to use multiple modes. The writing prompt for *What Charlie Heard* included elements of drawing and writing combined. It was modeled directly after the pages of the picture book and encouraged students to combine audio and visual representations. Additionally, this prompt focused students' attention on the way sound was expressed in the book. Mrs. Winter's language acknowledged the fact that the writing would let the reader hear the sound through its words and pictures.

Students' Responses to What Charlie Heard

WRITTEN RESPONSES

The model itself, plus Mrs. Winter's overt instruction related to the available designs and multiple modes in the model text, led to student writing that expressed sound similarly to the representations in *What Charlie Heard* (New London Group, 1996). Elizabeth (Figure 3.1a), Nicole (Figure 3.1b), and Sara's (Figure 3.1c) examples showed a lot of careful thought about how to represent sound. In all of these examples, the students imitated the style of Gerstein's representation in their own work. Though each is a little different in design, each student's response showed a scene or event with sound words placed near the objects or characters from which those sounds originated.

Mrs. Winter constantly encouraged and reminded students of how the model text used the design elements and pushed students to try this on their own. She directed students' attention back to pages in the book as they were working. These were quick reminders, but they were effective. Students could easily determine what Mrs. Winter was asking them to think about. The representations in the model were very specific, and students were successful as they explored this mode of communication. The students' illustrations showed that they understood the concept and representation in *What Charlie Heard* and could adapt that design to fit their own stories and communicative purposes. Students were able to represent their world using different modes of expression.

FIGURE **3.1a.** *Elizabeth's memoir story with audio representation.*
FIGURE **3.1b.** *Nicole's ocean illustration with sound.*
FIGURE **3.1c.** *Sara's dog illustration with sound.*

STUDENTS' REFLECTIONS ON *WHAT CHARLIE HEARD*

Students were attentive to the sound words in *What Charlie Heard* and easily grasped how they represented sound. Mark said that Charlie heard a lot of sounds. I asked him in his interview how the book communicated that, and he replied, "With lots of, uh, words (pause) that were describing the noises (pause); they were all over the page and they're hard not to notice." Elizabeth also talked about the audio representations. She said, "[*What Charlie Heard*] was all about sound. Sound drawn on the paper, expressed in the writing, even on the cover." Finally, Alexandra said in her interview, "Charlie, like when they heard the fire truck, kind of like, beep, beep, it said that, and you could actually hear it if you paid attention and opened your ears, and that's what I liked about it." These responses showed that students clearly understood how the words drawn all over the pages communicated sound.

Although Mrs. Winter shared other books that used sound words, such as *Gabriella's Song* (Fleming, 1997) and *Max Found Two Sticks* (Pinkney, 1994), the students did not always clearly identify the sound words in these other books as representations of audio. The sound words in *What Charlie Heard* were not part of the linguistic text at all, but rather displayed as a prominent part of the illustrations through the use of different design elements such as color, size, and placement. I believe these elements drew attention to the sound words in such a way as to highlight their function as something different than linguistic or visual communication. The function of the sound words was to represent the noises Charlie heard in his life, and this was carried out so well through the design of the book that students easily accepted that these words *were* sounds.

In addition, students' reflections showed their recognition of the opportunities for expression that they were given in their writing workshop classroom. For example, when Chloe discussed the writing prompt for *What Charlie Heard*, she further acknowledged that the opportunity to draw was helpful to her. She said in her interview:

> I liked the illustrations and, if I could, I would want to do those. Like when we did the project in our journal, how we got to do that. If I could just write a story and do that, that would be pretty easy.

Chloe's statement is powerful. She says that if she were given the opportunity to draw regularly it would be "pretty easy," but if we look further, perhaps what Chloe means is that drawing was a mode of communication that felt natural to her. Though we could look at this and say that she just didn't want to write, which she perceived as harder, this kind of thinking is highly privileging of the linguistic mode. Chloe seems to be saying that if she were allowed to communicate through other modes, she would be able to communicate her ideas more easily and perhaps more effectively. And in saying this, she is also appreciating the opportunity she was given to do this in her writing workshop classroom with Mrs. Winter.

Similar to the findings reported by Gallas (1994) and O'Brien (2001, 2003), multiple modes or ways to express themselves helped all learners, especially struggling literacy learners, communicate. Over the course of the larger study, parents, other teachers, principals, and music teachers all noticed differences in the students' attitudes and abilities in writing, which Mrs. Winter attributed to the addition of audio representations as a communicative resource. My analysis of students' writing was consistent with the comments from Mrs. Winter and other teachers. These differences were not only noted in high achieving or gifted students but in struggling readers and writers as well. In Mrs. Winter's words, "All these kids with huge [learning] issues and some of them just stepped up to the plate and really went places with this . . . at some level, everybody in that room grew as a writer." Some of the struggling readers and writers participated more frequently in reading and writing activities, connected easily to the activities, and showed more confidence in their writing. At the same time, some of the more advanced students in the class were able to use the same activities to explore new ideas in their own writing and thinking.

Summary

Since the books were used as models in writer's workshop, students' writing journals reflected not only the content of the books but the patterns of communication in the books. Mrs. Winter wove a theme of music throughout her writing instruction. Early in the study, students began by descriptively writing about sounds and thinking about imagery. As the multimodal picture books were introduced, students worked on writing that represented sound in ways similar to the authors of the multimodal texts. Using these multimodal picture books as models, students experimented with a variety of ways to express themselves through the use of audio representations. Students appreciated the opportunity to communicate and express themselves through multiple modes. As the New London Group's (1996) multiliteracies pedagogy hopes, giving students the opportunity to use multiple modes as they communicate and use all the available designs lets students be active designers of their own social futures. The students were beginning to feel this empowerment as they worked with multiple modes in their writing classroom with Mrs. Winter.

Discussion

The multiliteracies framework helped to understand Mrs. Winter's instructional practices as well as the students' responses to the multimodal picture books. In the multiliteracies theory of design, available designs are the resources for meaning making, designing is the process of making meaning, and the redesigned is the meaning that emerges from designing. The redesigned becomes a new available design for future designing. There were two levels of designing occurring in this classroom example. On the most basic level, students' meaning making with the text—in which they combined the available designs of the text and their own prior knowledge in order to understand and comprehend the text—is an example of designing. Students were also designing as they wrote and communicated. Students used the multimodal designs of the picture book in *What Charlie Heard*, combined with the designs of their past writing of a memoir story, in their own designing process for this writing assignment.

On another level, design theory helped to explain the process that Mrs. Winter encountered as she planned her instruction. Cope and Kalantzis (2000) suggested thinking of pedagogy as design, believing that good teachers use their creative intelligence to continually redesign classroom activities as they teach. Mrs. Winter had many available designs such as her existing instructional strategy of using picture books for writer's craft instruction. In analyzing how Mrs. Winter presented this and other multimodal picture books as models for student writing, it is clear that, while influenced by her past discourse of writer's craft pedagogy, each teaching event used a redesigned approach that highlighted not just linguistic designs, as she had in the past, but also the audio, visual, and even spatial designs specific to each multimodal picture book model. More than just isolated meaning making events, I believe Mrs. Winter's pedagogy was shifted or hybridized throughout the study as she incorporated the new available designs of the multimodal picture books. The New London Group discussed hybridity in their articulation of multiliteracies theory, describing it as transformed designs that are created by combining, or hybridizing, available designs in multiple modes in new ways.

Researchers have begun to consider teachers' pedagogy as hybridized (Kersten & Pardo, 2007; Luke, 2000). Kersten and Pardo described a teacher's pedagogy as hybrid because of the way she "extracted the strengths of her own practice, identified the strengths of the requirements, and then created a unique pedagogy" (p. 151). The lens of hybridity explained how many of Mrs. Winter's practices changed or expanded to incorporate the multimodal representations in the picture books. Mrs. Winter was negotiating her own experiences and pedagogical approaches, district- and state-mandated approaches, and the approaches she perceived as necessary to include the multimodal picture books in her instruction. These approaches were all available designs that she blended, borrowed, and reconfigured into a hybrid pedagogy that served her needs and the needs of her students.

Hybridity also helped me understand students' designing, as they blended available designs from the multimodal books, including audio and visual designs, in addition to linguistic designs in their written communication. Students' literacy practices, both oral and written, have been analyzed as hybrid texts that result from home, community, and school literacy practices and discourses being combined (Solsken, Willett, & Wilson-Keenan, 2000; Tobin, 2000). When viewed as hybrid practices, we can see how the students in this study combined, adopted, and adapted their communication patterns and literacy practices from a variety of sources and from multiple discourses, including the multimodal picture books.

Implications for Research and Practice

Writer's workshop and writer's craft emerged as integral aspects in this study. Though the study was not framed as one that would investigate these instructional approaches, Mrs. Winter's use of the multimodal picture books in her writer's workshop and writer's craft instruction brought these approaches into the spotlight. There has been a plethora of books and articles published specifically for teachers as guides and testaments to writer's workshop and writer's craft (Calkins, 1994; Calkins & Graves, 1980; Ray & Cleaveland, 2004; Dorfman & Cappelli, 2007; Fletcher, 1999; Fletcher & Portalupi, 1998, 2001; Lain, 2007; Sturgell, 2008). Although many of these are based on classroom experiences, there is a need for empirical research that looks at enactments of writer's craft pedagogy in contemporary classrooms, such as the work of Corden (2007). Similar to the findings presented in this chapter, Corden (2007) investigated mentor texts in a study involving eighteen teachers and their students and found that if the texts were supported by the teachers through modeling, demonstrating, and drawing attention to the text features, children developed an awareness of how they, as authors, could similarly construct texts. Although these findings are similar to what was learned in the present study regarding multimodal picture books, more empirical research on writer's craft pedagogy is needed to strengthen and support the use of this instructional strategy in the classroom. As contemporary picture books are changing to reflect today's society, it is especially important to conduct research that examines the use of these alternative texts in writer's craft pedagogy.

As far as implications for teacher's practice, this study points to the potential for student learning through multimodal picture books in the language arts classroom. Students were able to use the audio representations as available designs in their own designing with support and guidance from their teacher. Both overt instruction and situated practice, pedagogical aspects of the multiliteracies framework, were seen in the classroom example of *What Charlie Heard*, as students were able to experiment with the designs of the book in their own writing after Mrs. Winter specifically highlighted, discussed, and explained the new designs. Although students understood and could experiment with the audio mode based on the examples in the multimodal picture books, they struggled for ways to label or discuss the designs in the multimodal picture books or the new designs they were using in their writing work. This struggle points out a need for the third aspect of the multiliteracies theory of pedagogy: critical framing. This is the aspect that addresses the pedagogical need for creating an awareness and language for students to talk about the multiple modes used in texts and in their own communication. Students needed to engage in dialogue about the use of the audio mode, and other modes of meaning, and needed a metalanguage to discuss what they were learning. Much of this language still needs to be developed through research and practice. However, in the classroom in this study, the teacher and students might have been able to more explicitly identify and label the different ways they saw audio designs being used, similar to the ways they are described in the chart in the appendix. Teachers and students can identify and discuss how the author uses sound words integrated in the text, uses sound words in the illustrations, or includes an audio recording to enhance meaning. This would help students explain how authors use audio designs in the texts that they are reading and how they, as authors, can use audio designs in texts they create.

Multimodal picture books can be a way to bring students of all ability levels, even those seen as struggling literacy learners, into a successful and positive learning environment, which is a promising step toward a goal of educating students for the changing global and digital environments. It is important for literacy teachers to ensure that all students have opportunities to transact with texts that communicate through multiple modes and to explore communicating and expressing their own multimodal messages.

Appendix: Bibliographic Information for All Texts Selected for Study

Title	Author	Illustrator	Publisher	Date	Genre	Type of Audio Representation
Bach's Goldberg Variations	Anne Harwell Celenza	JoAnn E. Kitchel	Charlesbridge	2005	Historical Fiction	External audio representation
* Gershwin's Rhapsody in Blue	Anne Harwell Celenza	JoAnn E. Kitchel	Charlesbridge	2006	Historical Fiction	External audio representation
* This Jazz Man	Karen Erhardt	R. G. Roth	Harcourt, Inc.	2006	Fiction/ Poetry	Sound words that extend meaning in text
* Big Talk	Paul Fleischman	Beppe Giacobbe	Candlewick Press	2000	Poetry	Rhythm
* Gabriella's Song	Candace Fleming	Giselle Potter	Aladdin Paperbacks	1997	Realistic Fiction/ Global Literature	Sound words within text
The Wolf Who Loved Music	Christophe Gallaz	Marshall Arisman	Creative Editions	2003	Realistic Fiction International Literature	Musical notation (real)
* What Charlie Heard	Mordicai Gerstein	Mordicai Gerstein	Farrar, Straus, and Giroux	2002	Picture Book Biography	Sound words that extend meaning in text
* Carnival of the Animals	John Lithgow	Boris Kulikov	Simon & Schuster Books for Young Readers	2004	Fantasy	External audio representation
Yellow Umbrella	Jae Soo Liu	(Music by) Dong Il Sheen	Kane/ Miller Book Publishers	2002	Wordless Picture Book/ International Literature	External audio representation
* Max Found Two Sticks	Brian Pinkney	Brian Pinkney	Simon & Schuster Children's Publishing	1994	Realistic Fiction/ Multicultural Literature	Sound words within text
Mysterious Thelonious	Chris Raschka	Chris Raschka	Orchard Books	1997	Picture Book Biography	Musical notation (abstract)
* John Coltrane's Giant Steps	Chris Raschka	Chris Raschka	Atheneum Books for Young Readers	2002	Fiction	Musical notation (abstract)
When Marian Sang	Pam Munoz Ryan	Brian Selznick	Scholastic Press	2002	Picture Book Biography Multicultural Literature	Song lyrics
* The Deaf Musicians	Pete Seeger and Paul Dubois Jacobs	R. Gregory Christie	G. P. Putnam's Sons	2006	Realistic Fiction	Sound words that extend meaning in text
* Tanka Tanka Skunk	Steve Webb	Steve Webb	Orchard Books	2004	Fiction/ Poetry	Rhythm

Note: An asterisk indicates that Mrs. Winter selected the book to read to her students.

Works Cited

Anstey, M., & Bull, G. (2006). *Teaching and learning multiliteracies: Changing times, changing literacies.* Newark, DE: International Reading Association.

Bakhtin, M. M. (1981). Discourse in the novel (C. Emerson & M. Holquist, Trans.). In M. Holquist (Ed.), *The dialogic imagination: Four essays by M.M. Bakhtin* (pp. 259–422). Austin: University of Texas Press.

Berghoff, B. (1993). Moving toward aesthetic literacy in the first grade. In D. J. Leu and C. K. Kinzer (Eds.), *Examining central issues in literacy research, theory, and practice: Forty-second yearbook of the National Reading Conference* (pp. 217–226). Chicago, IL: National Reading Conference.

Calkins, L. M. (1994). *The art of teaching writing.* Portsmouth, NH: Heinemann.

Calkins, L. M., & Graves, D. H. (1980). Research update: Children learn the writer's craft. *Language Arts, 57*(2), 207–213.

Cope, B., & Kalantzis, M. (Eds.) (2000). *Multiliteracies: Literacy learning and the design of social futures.* New York: Routledge.

Corden, R. (2007). Developing reading-writing connections: The impact of explicit instruction of literary devices on the quality of children's narrative writing. *Journal of Research in Childhood Education, 21*(3), 269–290.

Darigan, D. L., Tunnell, M. O., & Jacobs, J. S. (2002). *Children's literature: Engaging teachers and children in good books.* Upper Saddle River, NJ: Merrill.

Dillon, L., & Dillon, D. (2002). *Rap a tap tap.* New York: Blue Sky Press.

Dorfman, L. R., & Cappelli, R. (2007). *Mentor texts: Teaching writing through children's literature, K–6.* Portland, ME: Stenhouse.

Dresang, E. (2003). Controversial books and contemporary children. *Journal of Children's Literature, 29*(1), 20–31.

Eisner, E. W. (1991). Rethinking literacy. *Educational Horizons, 69*(3), 120–128.

Fleming, C. (1997). *Gabriella's song.* New York: Aladdin Paperbacks.

Fletcher, R. (1999). Teaching the craft of writing. *Primary Voices K–6,* *7(4)*, 41–43.

Fletcher, R., & Portalupi, J. (1998). *Craft lessons: Teaching writing K–8.* York, ME: Stenhouse.

———. (2001). *Writing workshop: The essential guide.* Portsmouth, NH: Heinemann.

Galda, L., & Cullinan, B. E. (2002). *Literature and the child* (5th ed.). Belmont, CA: Wadsworth.

Gallas, K. (1994). *The languages of learning: How children talk, write, dance, draw, and sing their understanding of the world.* New York: Teachers College Press.

Gerstein, M. (2002). *What Charlie heard.* New York: Farrar, Straus and Giroux.

Glaser, B. G., & Strauss, A. L. (1967). *The discovery of grounded theory: Strategies for qualitative research.* New York: Aldine de Gruyter.

Hull, G. A., & Nelson, M. E. (2005). Locating the semiotic power of multimodality. *Written Communication, 22(2),* 224–261.

Jewitt, C., & Kress, G. (Eds.). (2003). *Multimodal literacy.* New York: Peter Lang.

Kasten, W. C., Kristo, J. V., & McClure, A. A. (2005). *Living literature: Using children's literature to support reading and language arts.* Upper Saddle River, NJ: Pearson Education.

Kersten, J., & Pardo, L. (2007). Finessing and hybridizing: Innovative literacy practices in reading first classrooms. *The Reading Teacher, 61(2),* 146–154.

Kress, G. (2000). Multimodality. In B. Cope & M. Kalantzis (Eds.), *Multiliteracies: Literacy learning and the design of social futures* (pp. 182–202). New York: Routledge.

Lain, S. (2007). Reaffirming the writing workshop for young adolescents. *Voices from the Middle, 14(3),* 20–28.

Luke, A. (2000). Critical literacy in Australia: A matter of context and standpoint. *Journal of Adolescent and Adult Literacy, 43(5),* 448–461.

New London Group. (1996). A pedagogy of multiliteracies: Designing social futures. *Harvard Educational Review, 66(1),* 60–92.

Nikolajeva, M., & Scott, C. (2000). The dynamics of picturebook communication. *Children's Literature in Education*, 31(4), 225–239.

Nodelman, P. (1988). *Words about pictures: The narrative art of children's picture books*. Athens: University of Georgia Press.

O'Brien, D. (2001). "At-risk" adolescents: Redefining competence through the multiliteracies of intermediality, visual arts, and representation. *Reading Online* 4(11). Retrieved from http://www.readingonline.org/newliteracies/lit_index.asp?HREF=/newliteracies/obrien/index.html

———. (2003). Juxtaposing traditional and intermedial literacies to redefine the competence of struggling adolescents. *Reading Online*, 6(7). Retrieved from http://www.readingonline.org/newliteracies/lit_index.asp?HREF=/newliteracies/obrien2

Office of Superintendent of Public Instruction. (2006). Washington State Report Card. Retrieved from http://reportcard.ospi.k12.wa.us/summary.aspx?schoolId=122&reportLevel=District&orgLinkId=122&yrs=

Pantaleo, S. (2004). The long, long way: Young children explore the fabula and syuzhet of *Shortcut*. *Children's Literature in Education*, 35(1), 1–20.

Pinkney, B. (1994). *Max found two sticks*. New York: Simon and Schuster.

Ray, K. W. (with Cleaveland, L. B.). (2004). *About the authors: Writing workshop with our youngest writers*. Portsmouth, NH: Heinemann.

Serafini, F. (2005). Voices in the park, voices in the classroom: Readers responding to postmodern picture books. *Reading Research and Instruction*, 44(3), 47–64.

Short, K. G., Kauffman, G., & Kahn, L. H. (2000). "I just need to draw": Responding to literature across multiple sign systems. *The Reading Teacher*, 54(2), 160–171.

Siegel, M. (2006). Rereading the signs: Multimodal transformations in the field of literacy education. *Language Arts*, 84(1), 65–77.

Sipe, L. R. (1998). How picture books work: A semiotically framed theory of text-picture relationships. *Children's Literature in Education*, 29(2), 97–108.

Solsken, J., Willett, J., & Wilson-Keenan, J.-A. (2000). Cultivating hybrid texts in multicultural classrooms: Promise and challenge. *Research in the Teaching of English*, 35(2), 179–212.

Stake, R. E. (1995). *The art of case study research*. Thousand Oaks, CA: Sage.

Sturgell, I. (2008). Touchstone texts: Fertile ground for creativity. *The Reading Teacher*, 61(5), 411–414.

Tobin, J. (2000). Imitative violence. In *"Good guys don't wear hats": Children's talk about the media* (pp. 16–30). New York: Teachers College Press.

Van Leeuwen, T. (1999). *Speech, music, sound*. New York: St. Martin's Press.

CHAPTER FOUR

Inventing a Drama World as a Place to Learn: Student Discoveries While Speaking and Writing in Role as Fictional Workers

ESTHER CAPPON GRAY
Western Michigan University

WITH SUSAN A. THETARD
University School/Illinois State University

This chapter captures what two teachers learned from examining nineteen students' spoken and written discourse during a five-week literature unit about the Holocaust in a midwestern high school. My colleague Susan Thetard was a secondary teacher of English and theater, an acclaimed director of high school plays and musicals who was attracted to the idea of implementing improvised drama episodes to foster student understandings of the Holocaust. I was an assistant professor of reading who had just completed a compelling workshop on educational drama taught by Luke Abbot, an advisor to schools in the county of Essex, England. Abbot had worked for decades with British educator Dorothy Heathcote, renowned for her work in process drama. Susan and I planned and implemented our instruction collaboratively. Drawing on Glaser and Strauss's constant comparative method (Bogdan & Biklen, 2006), we collected data and reflected jointly on our lessons as the unit progressed. We were surprised again and again by the imaginative and thought-provoking ways the students positioned themselves. After the unit was over, I reexamined and analyzed the data, discussed it with Susan, and wrote conclusions about the issues and patterns I had found, sharing ideas with Susan and benefiting from her insights.

Teaching about the Holocaust is more than a matter of documenting a history of anti-Semitism or exposing a political system gone bitterly wrong and inhumane. As articulated by Holocaust education specialist Donald Schwartz (1990), such study can offer learners ways to understand "lessons on the darker side of human nature and on the immorality of indifference . . . [lessons] on the effects of peer pressure, individual responsibility, and the process of decision making under the most extreme conditions" (p. 101). Susan and I strived to help our learners reflect thoughtfully on the Holocaust literature they read by supporting their understandings of the social pressures in ordinary lives during this era. This study examined the process of engaging Susan's class of secondary students in a series of not-for-performance drama episodes as a component within her World Literature course. In these episodes the students invented identities and improvised in role as workers in a bakery in Munich during 1930–1942. This research is built on controversial issues educators have raised about the potential of drama for supporting learners' thoughtful engagement in objectives of Holocaust pedagogy, such as examining events in Germany and beyond; learning about systemic racism and anti-Semitism during the era of the Holocaust; remembering the victims; comprehending the force of bullying, threats, and social pressure; and discovering cases of resistance (Dawidowicz, 1990; Robertson, 1997; Rubin, 2000; Schwartz, 1990; Stephens, Brown, & Rubin, 1995; Totten, 2001, 2002; Totten & Feinberg, 2000; Zatzman, 2000).

Before Susan and I collaborated, previous teaching experiences in separate settings had left us each with the concern that our students had studied the Holocaust with the idea that it was an aberration in history. Even after learning about this monumental tragedy, they seemed to regard the Holocaust as remote: a series of terrible events in a time and place far away, a past that had little relevance to current understandings of politics, justice, or human behavior. Though they recognized that there had been terrible deeds, colossal death statistics, and shocking suffering, they distanced such knowledge with classic generalizations, for example, as awful things that "could never be understood," "must never happen again," or "could never happen here." This distancing impeded their ability to engage in truly critical reading and thinking.

We were drawn to Dorothy Heathcote's pedagogy, which suggests that improvising drama episodes can lead students to reflection and new understandings of human experience. As explained by Heathcote's protégée Cecily O'Neill (1994), "In process drama, active identification with and exploration of fictional roles and situations . . . involves participants in active role-taking. . . . The goal is the development of students' insight and understanding about themselves and the world they live in through the exploration of significant dramatic contexts" (p. 407). Heathcote's idea is not producing a play that presents a complete narrative to an audience, but, rather, establishing a drama setting in which teachers and students learn together by assuming fictional identities and co-creating situations and events that are not rehearsed or repeated for an audience. As one of our students wrote, this can support productive reflection:

> I think my favorite part of this unit was the group discussions, not about the bakery [during the drama] but when we were ourselves and we discussed German/Nazi history. These discussions usually took place right after our bakery [drama sessions]. I liked them because it was a chance to reflect on my own personal feelings as well as learn about history, the Nuremberg laws, etc.

Professional Literature on Which Our Project Was Based

Amid prolific publications addressing theoretical issues and pedagogical practices, educational drama has suffered from limited scholarly research analyzing students' behavior and learning (Bolton, 1985; Booth & Neelands, 1998; Heller, 1995; Manley & O'Neill, 1997; Neelands, 1984; O'Neill, Lambert, Linnell, & Warr-Wood, 1976; O'Neill, 1994, 1995; O'Neill & Lambert, 1990; P. Taylor, 1996; Wagner, 1999; Wilhelm, 2002). Precious examples of closely examined drama facilitation, such as the double entry texts in *Drama Guidelines* (O'Neill, Lambert, Linnell, & Warr-Wood, 1976) and *Drama Structures* (O'Neill &

Lambert, 1990), make the improvised events and teacherly thinking in drama episodes visible in rich detail. However, such works have not led to abundant research about the nature of learning in drama classrooms. In a 1998 survey of research examining educational drama in language arts, Betty Jane Wagner (1998) discovered that between 1989 and 1998 only seventy-one drama education dissertations were produced as compared with thousands of dissertations in reading and writing (pp. 2–3). Wagner advocated research to right this imbalance, calling for studies with "richly detailed observations of teacher-led classroom drama, descriptions that capture the immediacy and power of the student's struggle to make meaning" (p. 235). In alignment with this objective, we set out in our Holocaust Literature Unit to closely observe ourselves and our students in order to consider how engaging in drama activities might affect the students' learning. In addition to the pedagogy of Dorothy Heathcote (Bolton, 1985; Heathcote & Bolton, 1995; Heathcote & Herbert, 1985; Wagner, 1999), we were influenced by the research of Jeffrey Wilhelm and Brian Edmiston who have demonstrated the capacity of drama experiences to raise ethical issues for learners (Edmiston, 2000; Wilhelm & Edmiston, 1998).

Poorly conceived simulations and superficial role-playing activities administered during instruction about the Holocaust have earned enactments a bad name in Holocaust education (Dawidowicz, 1990; Totten, 2001, 2002). Samuel Totten (2002) has written

> Whether teachers like to admit it or not, by using simulations to try to provide students with a sense of what the victims of the Nazis were subjected to, they are minimizing, simplifying, distorting, and possibly even denying the horror of the Holocaust. ... *The best advice in regard to simulations intended to provide students with a sense of Holocaust history, including what the victims lived through and/or the choices that both perpetrators and victims made, is to avoid them.* (p. 123, italics in original)

Such criticism of detrimental drama strategies has raised important issues for educators, but it could render teachers afraid to implement some of the very aspects of educational drama that could elevate students' understandings and counter oversimplification. In contrast to those who discourage drama in Holocaust education, teachers such as Belarie Zatzman (2000) and Janet Rubin (2000) advocate educational drama. Rubin values it as an approach in which "[h]istory moves from facts and figures to an intellectually and emotionally engaging set of stories about people. It takes on a more human dimension" (p. 1).

Brian Edmiston also advocates the use of drama to evoke deep thinking on ethical issues:

> Drama is a powerful tool for thinking about what we "ought to do" and uncovering some of the moral complexities of situations. Not only can the students engage in *talk* about action— moral reasoning about what they *might* do if they were people in particular circumstances—in drama students take action and in imagination *do* that which in discussion they might only sketchily contemplate. . . . Drama can create powerful dialogic spaces in which students' "ethical imagination" changes their moral understandings in making their views more multifaceted, interwoven, and complex. (Wilhelm & Edmiston, 1998, p. 59, 61, italics in original)

Susan and I hoped that drama would provide this kind of tool for us and for our students.

The Research Objectives and Setting

We taught eight females and eleven males, all juniors and seniors who had enrolled in Susan's elective World Literature course. The group consisted of seventeen European Americans and two English speakers whose first languages were Spanish and Vietnamese, as well as one physical needs, mainstreamed student. These students lived in a small midwestern city, home to small industries and the corporate headquarters of several large companies. They came primarily from middle- to upper-class households. During our unit the students spent five weeks, starting in February and ending in March, reading and discussing fiction and nonfiction literature, journaling, and participating in drama improvisations. The class met daily for fifty-five minutes. Within the five weeks of the Holocaust unit, we facilitated twelve interconnected drama episodes that included writing in role along with spoken improvisations. The students chose German names for their drama identities. The focus of the Holocaust Literature Unit was on reading and discussing literature; our drama episodes were supplementary experiences that took place during just five of twenty-five classes.

Our three research questions were concrete and practical. If these adolescents chose to respond to our prompts for discourse in role, we wanted to know: (1) "What role perspectives might high school students adopt during improvised drama experiences that involve ethical dilemmas faced by German citizens during the Holocaust era?" (2) "What understandings of the pressures and decision-making of daily life during this era might be revealed in the students' spoken and written discourse?" and (3) "How would these high school students evaluate the experience of improvising drama activities for the purpose of learning?"

Methodology

A strength of participant observation research (Bogdan & Biklen, 2006; Hatch, 2002) is the way that it brings us close to our subjects and enables us to focus on student behaviors and discourse as primary data sources. We hoped that the lenses of literature and drama would enable our students to begin to see the control of the powerful Nazi State as a sturdy fabric woven out of countless tiny threads, the myriad daily incidents and decisions in people's lives. We wanted to document and analyze the process we were planning in order to reflect upon the positive or adverse effects that drama might bring to this pedagogical goal. We collected student writing during the unit and videotaped class drama improvisations and student debriefing discussions outside the classroom after the unit. Satisfaction and dissatisfaction with the drama activities were indicated in the small-group debriefings, evaluative written reflections, and an anonymous survey. These served as data sources. Along with short lectures, fiction and nonfiction readings informed the improvised dramas the students enacted during five classes. Susan and I reflected daily on the events of the classroom as part of our planning discussions. After the unit ended, I participated in small group debriefing sessions, studied the videotaped drama episodes and student debriefings, read and compared transcriptions of classroom drama episodes, and examined transcriptions of the debriefing discussions. I also studied texts the students had authored, including journals and writing in role. Using all these sources, I sought patterns based on Glaser and Strauss's constant comparative method (Bogdan & Biklen, 2006). Although the number of students in the study and the artifacts examined are inadequate for generalization, this project suggests that improvised drama could be effective in other educational settings.

Holocaust Era Literature Studied

We chose both literary and informational texts that we felt would not only expose the racist events of the Holocaust era but also would contribute to our goal of problematizing issues of social pressure and individual and collective responsibility in a time of rigid, unjust policies and threats (Bunting, 1995; K. Taylor, 2001; M. Taylor, 1998; Ten Boom, 1984; Wiesel, 1982). We assigned two fiction books set in the 1930s that demonstrated ways that social and political pressures can destroy cherished relationships (K. Taylor, 2001; M. Taylor, 1998). To establish background knowledge about the Holocaust, we read short nonfiction literature together such as a packet of biographies and portraits of Holocaust victims produced by the U.S. Holocaust Museum in Washington, D.C. and the racist German Nuremberg Laws of 1935. The students related this content to information depicted in longer fiction and nonfiction literature (K. Taylor, 2001; M. Taylor, 1998; Ten Boom, 1984; Wiesel, 1982).

The Students in Role: A Glimpse into the Process Drama Classroom

A short segment from the closing drama episode of the unit illustrates process drama. In the identities they had invented, students spontaneously interacted about an unresolved issue of their workplace, drawing on their developing knowledge. Susan and I prepared fictional problems to open each drama episode.

On this last day, in role as bakery employees, we informed our fellow workers that we had discovered the fictional Braun family, longtime bakery customers, outside the bakery, badly beaten. We explained to the students (in role as our fellow workers) that, unbeknownst to us, our friend Frau Braun had been hiding her Jewish identity from the world, patronizing our bakery after we had felt compelled to display our "No Jews" sign. We told our bakery associates that when we found the Brauns and their young daughter outside our shop, we had not thought about the implications of our actions. We had just brought them into the back of the store where they now remained.

The students rapidly grasped that in the Munich of our drama era we might find no medical care for Jews and no means to deliver such a family to safety, and that because the Brauns were on our premises we, ourselves, could be punished for harboring Jews. Susan and I quickly discovered that we could leave the leadership of the discussion to "Herr Stein," a student whose role as manager of the group's fictional bakery had evolved over four weeks during four drama episodes. Seated in desks in an oval, with each "bakery worker" wearing a name tag identifying the student's chosen German name, the group instinctively turned to Herr Stein, a classmate who prior to this unit had rarely completed homework for this course. He masterfully took the benevolent and humble stance that he had developed in previous episodes. By attentively repeating the diverse, conflicting statements contributed by his peers, Herr Stein evoked ten strikingly varied proposals from the group. The following is an excerpt from this improvised episode in which the group, all in role as bakery workers, addressed the episode's premise and attempted to work out a solution.

> WERNER: [We should] find a place to smuggle them to. Find a safe place for them to hide.
>
> ANNEROSE: How do we do that, though? How do we find those places?
>
> GISELA: I'm willing to hide them in my house until we *can* find a place.
>
> TINA: That's a huge risk, though. If you were caught that would be dangerous to your children.
>
> GISELA: Does anyone else want to do it?

KARL: We're pretty poor from what I know, and I think if we all pull together some money we can get them out of the country.

HANS: I don't want to spend any money on them. I say we just get rid of them. It's not worth getting caught.

FABIAN: What's the extent of our deliveries?

MORITZ: Not very far outside of Munich.

FABIAN: Then it *is* outside of Munich?

HERR STEIN: The trouble is, we could get away with getting a truck outside Munich . . . quite a distance . . . before being noticed, but . . .

LIESEL: Most of our deliveries are for the [Nazi] Party anyway. So we wouldn't seem suspicious.

HANNAH: I don't have any small children at home. You know, this family, they've been really good to me, so I'd be willing to risk a few things—to have them at my house until we find somebody else to take them. . . . if they *were* found there— I'd be willing to just not mention any other names [of bakery employees].

The discussion during the drama episode was serious, influenced by the content of the students' readings and our class presentations, and all comments were improvised in role. The students' proposals ranged from the self-protective stance of turning the Braun family over to Nazi authorities to avoid jeopardizing the future of the bakery, its workers, and their families, to high-risk, personal ways of helping the fictional Braun family. Susan and I noticed with interest that the six males who proposed helping the Braun family all offered impersonal suggestions, referring the Brauns to agencies or to persons who could care for them, while the females proposed direct interventions, varied versions of taking the Brauns home to their own immediate or extended families, thus endangering their private lives. After considerable discussion by the group in role, Herr Stein proposed that each bakery worker needed to take a stand on what the group should do about the Brauns. When he attempted to survey the group, his classmates' responses to his request were so complex that Herr Stein's attempt at closure brought the group into new discussion about possible solutions.

In process drama, the goal is not a resolution of the dramatic tension in an improvised narrative but, rather, an increased understanding of the *issues* that underlie the story. This frustrated some students who wished we could attain closure on each drama episode. Though clear endings in films or novels may be satisfying, arriving at them may not be the best use of class time. After a lifetime of experience with process drama, Cecily O'Neill (1994) wrote:

> [Process drama] involves the careful sequencing and layering of dramatic units or episodes, often in a nonlinear way, which cumulatively extend[s] and enrich[es] a fictional context. . . . This relationship is likely to be much more complex than the linear connections of sequence or chronological narrative, where the segments of the work are strung together like beads on a chain rather than becoming links in a web of meaning. (p. 408)

Susan and I could see that, despite the frustration of unresolved events, our students were developing understandings about how it might have been to establish a business just before Hitler became Chancellor, then cope with the changes that would arise in their enterprise afterwards.

Educational Challenges in Studying the Holocaust

Teaching about the Holocaust presents unique challenges because of its complex history and disturbing emotional content. A sacredness of memory is called for in the study of victims of terrible institutional abuses, such as American slavery, the Trail of Tears, or the Holocaust. Throughout our collaborative teaching, Susan and I evaluated our progress and planned our strategies with the concern that the work must not become trivial.

In addition to avoiding stereotypes, oversimplification, and disrespect of persons and events, teaching about the Holocaust also entails emotional aspects of dealing with historical instances of immeasurable human pain. As we taught the unit, we regularly considered what kind of emotional support we were putting in place. We felt that even discussing atrocities, such as the abuse in Wiesel's (1982) *Night*, could be damaging if we did not monitor class interactions carefully and help students with processing emotional material (Robertson, 1997). Pain cannot be avoided if we are going to address the hard issues of matter such as the Holocaust. Mindful of this, we were deliberate about setting our drama episodes in a place of workers' daily life, a bakery, that was remote from but not immune to the atrocities and pressures of the National Socialist regime. We did not want our students to improvise drama episodes set directly within any situation of raw power or victimization. Also, to protect the students from vulnerability, we employed a Heathcote tactic and told our participants that at any time during an improvisation if they began to feel uncomfortable or overwhelmed, any one of them could call a time-out, and we would all step out of role (Heathcote, unpublished videotape). Though no student called a time-out during the dramas, in a debriefing session one stated that this assurance had enabled her to trust the process.

Student Understandings of the Era Captured in Dialogue and Fictional Letters

To discover patterns in the ways that the nineteen students applied their developing understandings about the era to their discussions and writing in role, I examined videotapes and transcripts of their drama episodes and fictional letters they had written. I found that the roles the students had invented fell into three categories: (1) *compliant with misgivings*, those in role who accepted demands of the status quo but expressed their private opposition to Nazi principles; (2) *defying personal belief systems to study the historical status quo*, those in role who affirmed or advocated Nazi policies; and (3) *acquiescent realists*, those in role who acknowledged events or policies of the time without taking clear positive or negative stances toward them. Susan and I never assigned or suggested any roles or perspectives to the students. What follows next are these three categories of perspectives that the students assumed in role.

Perspective Category 1. *Compliant with misgivings.* In role, class members like Fabian adopted compliant perspectives but revealed opposing beliefs. In a letter written in role in 1935 under the shadow of the newly established, racist Nuremberg Laws, Fabian told his fictional father that he had trouble accepting the governmental policies of racism and eugenics:

> Work is still going fairly well. I am making more than enough money to survive, and our business is prospering. However, lately small things have not been going so well. For example, Sophia, the mentally challenged girl who is working for us, may need to be fired. . . . Also, we have had to put up a "No Jews" sign to avoid any problems with the Nazi Party. This has saddened me since I no longer get to meet with some of my friends, Jewish customers. However, I am still optimistic that these changes are only temporary and things will return to normal soon.

Perspective Category 2. *Defying personal belief systems to study the historical status quo.* Some students adopted perspectives of committed National Socialists to better understand this time in history. Susan and I had stated as our goal that we all would better grasp the complexities of the era by better comprehending varied, unfamiliar perspectives. In debriefing, students who had voiced National Socialist attitudes spoke of how challenging they had found it to articulate "Nazi" viewpoints. Two student examples illustrate this conflicted stance.

"Liesel" left her own real-life perspectives to take a National Socialist position in a drama episode when writing to her fictional father in a 1935 letter after Germany's implementation of the anti-Semitic Nuremberg Laws:

> How busy we have been. . . . We have filled many orders for the Nazi Party, and this has been our main source of profits. Fortunately, my faith in my fellow businessmen has continued to grow. They have made the choice to follow Hitler, to whom I credit all of our success. We have obeyed the laws by burning despicable books, refusing to serve Jews . . . and getting rid of those workers that really are not productive in our society. . . .

Liesel was an interesting case, because later she chose to shift her perspective radically, moving to her own real-life belief system during the classroom vignette described in this article. The group had not seen the previous letter but came to know its recipient indirectly when Liesel described her fictional father whom she had invented, a retired country physician who believed in the National Socialist cause. Though some group members were against assuming risks to aid the Braun family, Liesel announced in role that she cared about the Brauns and would take them to her father to be cared for if Frau Braun's Jewish identity could be hidden from him. Through drama, she enabled herself to examine the challenge one faces when resisting the flow of a group's thinking to champion somebody powerless and also examine the timeless dilemma of whether to endanger one's loved ones in order to protect somebody one values.

In a written evaluation and a debriefing discussion, Liesel's classmate, Otto, described the experience of taking a National Socialist perspective. Otto had found the stance so unnatural that he had developed his identity through letters rather than speaking in class drama episodes:

> I thought that the [drama] was interesting because you can create a character that is not you. However, the character that I created was the exact opposite of my beliefs, and I struggled with the conflicting viewpoints that this created. What I struggled with was—well, if you were actually *in* Germany, well, you would be a Nazi. But then you struggle in the back of your mind: "I'm not this person. I wouldn't do this." I struggled a lot trying to say what my character would actually say. I had trouble discussing [during class dramas] because the character I created . . . conflicted directly with my views.

Perspective Category 3. *The acquiescent realist.* In role, many students acknowledged instances of regime-imposed personal or political circumstances but did not frame their discourse as clear statements of either advocacy for or resistance to National Socialist ideas or policies. For example, in their letters, Hannah, Reinhold, and Annerose did not take a clear stand. Hannah wrote:

> We are gaining more support than ever because of some of our decisions. We stopped making kosher products at first. . . . As of now we don't get any Jewish customers, because we have decided not to serve them any more. These things have really gotten our business off the ground. . . .

Reinhold wrote:

> Munich has been changing in all sorts of ways. I am glad to
> see the library shelves are filling up again, unfortunately there
> is little variety in what there is to read. . . .

Annerose wrote:

> I am having this hand delivered because it is the safest way. I
> have been part of the shop for 5 years and 5 good years at that.
> There has [sic] been some problems though with a [developmen-
> tally disabled] worker we hired, but I try and stay out of that
> stuff. She doesn't bother me in the back [of the bakery shop].
> There is such tension here . . . everyone is nervous.

Students' Comprehension of Historical Content

As part of monitoring the students' comprehension of the era as
shown by their inclusion of historical content in role, I examined
thirty-four fictional letters to loved ones that they had written
during two different parts of our unit. During the very first drama
episode, set in 1930 before the Nazi government had come to
power, they had written sixteen letters, and five years later in our
drama world, in 1935 when anti-Semitic policies had become law,
they had written eighteen letters. References to historical content
in the student writing matched the pattern of increasing insights
that Susan and I observed in class improvisations and discussions. Among the students' sixteen fictional 1930 letters, written
after the introduction to the unit but before the group had read
any literature texts or experienced the pressures of the era in our
drama world, indeed, before Hitler had become Chancellor, just
half (50 percent) of the writers had made reference to the historical "real world" context in which the founding of the bakery had
taken place. In contrast, all but one of the eighteen later 1935
letters (94 percent) had incorporated historical references that
documented students' growing understandings of life during the
National Socialist regime. The purpose of writing the fictional
letters to loved ones was to explore perspectives and pressures of
the Nazi era. There was a range of perspectives among the seventeen students who referred specifically to historical factors in the

later letters: eight mentioned historical realities without comment, four challenged unjust policies, two took stances accepting such policies, and three in role advocated National Socialist policies. These perspectives were the students' personal choices.

Although the numbers showed that all but one of the students alluded to historical content in the later letters, the details of the actual texts showed their sense of the times. Repeatedly Susan and I were struck with how each class member was imaginatively developing a unique, historically feasible drama identity. The students' readiness to write in role suggested that their improvised identities facilitated the writing process for them.

Creative Understanding in Role

Student creativity in using drama to examine this era was seen in the distinctive approaches of two of the students, Elsa and Peter. Along with Liesel and Otto, Elsa and Peter appeared to be instinctively striving for an ideal of Berthold Brecht: rather than finding comfort and taking an easy road by "inhabiting" characters, they were opting instead for the discomfort of "exposing" their characters for themselves and their classmates (O'Neill, 1995, p. 90). Elsa assumed the role of a bakery worker who concealed her Jewish identity. She did not reveal this to the group until after the unit was over. As she reported during debriefing, in her role as a Jew, each class drama interaction seemed to hold an added layer of tension for her. The "No Jews" sign in the store, the book burning, the injuries to the Braun family, atrocious to all of us in the room, were especially sinister for Elsa because of her chosen fictional Jewish identity.

Peter, who lived with physical limitations that in no way affected his sharp insights and expressive speaking, and who did not have any of the intellectual challenges faced by the fictional bakery worker "Sophia," chose in our drama world to assume the identity of a person with the same physical challenges he faced in real life. The debate about Sophia was especially heartfelt for Peter, as he described during a debriefing discussion:

> If I was disabled in that situation, in that time period, what would I have done in the work force? They weren't adapting

to me and they weren't adapting maybe to Sophia, to her needs and her well-being. Maybe that's what my character was feeling. It was difficult [discussing the Nuremberg Laws]. I know what I would have . . . gone through if I had lived during that time period. . . . I picked to be a dough worker. I probably wouldn't get hired [then] as a dough worker!

Conclusion

With regard to our first research question, what role perspectives high school students might adopt during improvised drama experiences involving ethical dilemmas set in Germany during the era of the Holocaust, Susan and I observed a rich diversity of stances and attitudes. We found that the identities the students developed fell into three categories: (1) persons compliant with misgivings who accepted National Socialist expectations while voicing resistant attitudes, (2) persons who adopted National Socialist stances under the pressures of the Holocaust era, and (3) acquiescent realists who went along with the status quo without taking a stand for or against the regime. Speaking and writing in role, the students developed fictional dimensions that exceeded what we had anticipated. Regarding our second research question, the students' growing historical insights were evident in analyses of their improvised conversations and fictional letters written in role.

In our third research question we had asked how the high school students themselves would appraise the experience of improvising drama activities for the purpose of learning. Though we found that the majority of the students' written reflections attributed valuable learning to the dramas, there were students who did not like the experience or who did not find it beneficial to their learning. We read positive comments such as: "I liked the [drama] thing where we were a group of bakery owners who made decisions that mainly had to do with things that happened in the 1930s. I liked the involvement with that where what we did and said affected everything in the future," and "I really enjoyed doing the [dramas]. It was really interesting to see what it felt like to live during that time. It really made me realize that not all Nazis joined the party for the sole purpose of destroying the Jews. . . . I also saw how quickly things can go from good to bad." In contrast, student reservations helped us balance our perspectives: "[The drama] got off to a rocky start. It was confusing in the beginning and most people were unsure what to say or do. I was never sure how far I could go; what were the limits to making things up?" and "The one thing I really didn't get a lot out of or like very much [in the Holocaust unit] was the [drama]. It was hard for me to get into that kind of mindset. . . ." Unenthusiastic participants emphasized how challenging it felt to improvise dramas about unfamiliar and difficult human circumstances.

When the unit was over we administered an anonymous 1–5 Likert scale evaluation survey in which 5 represented "highly valuable learning experience," and 1 represented "experience not useful to my learning." We were pleased to discover that the students had rated the reading of strong nonfiction narratives highest. Most valued of all in the unit was the reading of Wiesel's *Night* (4.89), and second most valued was reading Ten Boom's *The Hiding Place* (4.63). Improvising bakery drama episodes garnered a rating of 4.08, less than reading the nonfiction narratives and slightly higher than the 3.89 rating of a feature film about the era, *Swing Kids* (Manulis & Gordon, 1993). These ratings told us that the dramas had not distracted the students from the profound literature we had read, and that they saw the drama, overall, as valuable to their learning.

Implications for Practice

This project offers evidence that carefully facilitated student-improvised drama activities can enhance literature study at the secondary level. We learned that students can develop skill using drama in as few as five experiences. Our aim for our students was not that they attain high proficiency in elaborate improvisations, but, rather, that they develop the capacity to learn through imagining historical human experiences and generating discourse in role, both orally and in writing. We discovered that adolescents could willingly move from their classroom into a co-created drama world. These students expanded their understandings by producing identities and inventing fictional friends, family members, and workplace events in historical contexts. In their improvisations they synthesized content from literary and historical texts. The success of students in this group whose previous marginal work in the course improved with drama, and students whose heritage languages were not English, would support the use of process drama with students who find reading and writing challenging, including those for whom English is a new language.

Since our collaboration, Susan has developed a writing project for the end of her Holocaust Literature Unit in which the students apply their learning to the world today through the use of topics developed for the National Holocaust Essay competition. Student papers have linked current world racial profiling, atrocities, and genocide in places like Somalia and Kosovo to what the students discovered in the Holocaust unit, both historically and personally.

Works Cited

Bogdan, R. C., & Biklen, S. K. (2006). *Qualitative research for education: An introduction to theory and methods* (5th ed.). Boston: Allyn and Bacon.

Bolton, G. (1985). Changes in thinking about drama in education. *Theory into Practice, 24*(3), 151–157.

Booth, D., & Neelands, J. (Eds.). (1998). *Writing in role: Classroom projects connecting writing and drama.* Hamilton, ON, Canada: Caliburn.

Bunting, E. (1995). *Terrible things: An allegory of the Holocaust.* Philadelphia: Jewish Publication Society.

Dawidowicz, L. (1990). How they teach the Holocaust. *Commentary, 90*(6), 25–32.

Edmiston, B. (2000). Drama as ethical education. *Research in Drama Education, 5*(1), 63–84.

Hatch, J. A. (2002). *Doing qualitative research in education settings.* Albany: State University of New York Press.

Heathcote, D., & Bolton, G. (1995). *Drama for learning: Dorothy Heathcote's mantle of the expert approach to education.* Portsmouth, NH: Heinemann.

Heathcote, D., & Herbert, P. (1985). A drama of learning: Mantle of the expert. *Theory into Practice, 24*(3), 173–180.

Heller, P. G. (1995). *Drama as a way of knowing.* York, ME: Stenhouse.

Manley, A., & O'Neill, C. (Eds.). (1997). *Dreamseekers: Creative approaches to the African American heritage.* Portsmouth, NH: Heinemann.

Manulis, J. B., & Gordon, M. (Producers), Carter, T. (Director). (1993). *Swing kids* [Motion picture]. United States: Hollywood Pictures.

Neelands, J. (1984). *Making sense of drama: A guide to classroom practice.* Portsmouth, NH: Heinemann.

O'Neill, C. (1994). Drama in education. In A. C. Purvis (Ed.), *Encyclopedia of English studies and language arts: A project of the National Council of Teachers of English* (Vol. 1, pp. 405–409). New York: Scholastic.

———. (1995). *Drama worlds: A framework for process drama.* Portsmouth, NH: Heinemann.

O'Neill, C., & Lambert, A. (1990). *Drama structures: A practical handbook for teachers.* Portsmouth, NH: Heinemann.

O'Neill, C., Lambert, A., Linnell, R., & Warr-Wood, J. (1976). *Drama guidelines.* Portsmouth, NH: Heinemann.

Robertson, J. P. (1997). Teaching about worlds of hurt through encounters with literature: Reflections on pedagogy. *Language Arts, 74*(6), 457–466.

Rubin, J. E. (2000). *Teaching about the Holocaust through drama.* Charlottesville, VA: New Plays.

Schwartz, D. (1990). "Who will tell them after we're gone?" Reflections on teaching the Holocaust. *History Teacher, 23*(2), 95–110.

Stephens, E. C., Brown, J. E., & Rubin, J. E. (1995). *Learning about the Holocaust: Literature and other resources for young people.* North Haven, CT: Library Professional.

Taylor, K. (2001). *Address unknown.* New York: Washington Square Press.

Taylor, M. D. (1998). *The friendship.* New York: Puffin Books.

Taylor, P. (Ed.). (1996). *Researching drama and arts education: Paradigms and possibilities.* Bristol, PA: Falmer Press.

Ten Boom, C. (1984). *The hiding place.* New York: Bantam.

Totten, S. (Ed.). (2001). *Teaching Holocaust literature.* Boston: Allyn and Bacon.

————. (2002). *Holocaust education: Issues and approaches.* Boston: Allyn and Bacon.

Totten S., & Feinberg, S. (Eds.). (2000). *Teaching and studying the Holocaust.* Boston: Allyn and Bacon.

Wagner, B. J. (1998). *Educational drama and language arts: What research shows.* Portsmouth, NH: Heinemann.

————. (1999). *Dorothy Heathcote: Drama as a learning medium* (Rev. ed.). Portsmouth, NH: Heinemann.

Wiesel, E. (1982). *Night.* New York: Bantam.

Wilhelm, J. D. (2002). *Action strategies for deepening comprehension: Role plays, text structure tableaux, talking statues, and other enrichment techniques that engage students with text.* New York: Scholastic.

Wilhelm, J. D., & Edmiston, B. (1998). *Imagining to learn: Inquiry, ethics, and integration through drama.* Portsmouth, NH: Heinemann.

Zatzman, B. (2000). Drama activities and the study of the Holocaust. In S. Totten & S. Feinberg (Eds.), *Teaching and studying the Holocaust* (pp. 263–279). Boston: Allyn and Bacon.

CHAPTER FIVE

Relationships between Artistic and Written Composing: A Qualitative Study of Fourth-Grade Students' Composing Experiences

JENNIFER SANDERS

Oklahoma State University

Overview

This chapter explores the intricacies of the relationships between artistic and written composing processes and the potential for art-infused writing curricula. During the 2005–2006 school year, I conducted a qualitative, phenomenological study of the artistic and written composing processes of six diverse fourth graders attending a public arts magnet school in a small, Southeastern community. Several data sources informed this study: extended classroom observations of the students, think-aloud protocols of composing processes, student work samples, and interviews. Inductive, phenomenological analysis methods were used to identify seven composing relationships that developed between students' artistic and written work. The data indicate the potential for students to transfer composing process knowledge from one sign system to another, engaging in transmediation of composing processes between art and writing, which has significant implications for classroom practice.

Motivating Louis: A Look at One Student's Composing Experience

Louis, a creative, quiet, Puerto Rican boy, was an academically resistant student. He struggled to complete his school work and to maintain focus on assigned tasks but loved to draw and create art. He had attended Expressions Academy since the first grade, so he was familiar with the art opportunities afforded by this public arts magnet school, including the practice of keeping a sketchbook. He had strong language skills, as evidenced by his complex written narratives and advanced vocabulary. But Louis did not like to write any more than required and worked very hard, being meticulous with his handwriting and spelling, to avoid having to do a second draft.

In the context of an art-infused writing workshop, part of his fourth-grade classroom instruction, Louis experienced more success than he did in any other subject area. Having the choice of where to begin, Louis always created his artwork first, and his writing was highly dependent on his art. He also often relied on visual images to provide information for his writing. For example, when he wrote an animal report on wolves, Louis said that his three wolf drawings "help[ed] for my writing by giving me ideas and reporting a lot of what the wolf does, how it lives, and what it's doing right now." Information about what a wolf looks like and how it lives was gathered from the visual text, not the written text, of a trade book he was using as a reference. In addition, Louis was willing to do numerous drafts of his art but would not create more than one draft of his writing.

Louis was expelled in January of the school year because he had not completed any of his math homework or science projects for the entire first half of the school year. However, from August to December, he finished five pieces of writing and four pieces of art (not including the numerous drawings and sketchbook entries he made) in the art-infused writing workshop. Although it did take close monitoring by the teacher, Mrs. Berry, to keep Louis progressing on his writing and to keep track of his papers, the point is that he *did* his writing and art, even when he would not complete any of his other schoolwork. Louis's experiences make a compelling argument for the motivating power of arts-integrated curricula, especially for students who struggle with traditional methods of instruction.

This chapter presents a research project designed to explore what happens when children are afforded the opportunity to work within an integrated art and writing curriculum. First, a brief overview of the trends in writing process research, from the 1960s to the current decade, is described to consider how this new research is both built on and extends previous research in the field of composition. Then, the methodological framework, the research setting, and the art-infused writing curriculum will be detailed. The later portion of the chapter presents the research findings, focusing on the various composing relationships that arose inductively from the data.

Trends in Writing Research

The historical chronology of writing process research in the United States began largely in the 1960s when composition became a discipline worthy of federal funding and universities began developing composition programs of study and research (North, 1987). Prior to this time, composition was a subject of study in American public school education but was not recognized as a field requiring its own body of knowledge and research. The work of Janet Emig (1971) and James Britton with colleagues (1975) in the 1970s and significant studies in the 1980s by researchers such as Donald Graves (1982), Lucy Calkins (1980, 1983), Scardamalia and Bereiter, in collaboration with Goelman and Woodruff, (Scardamalia, Bereiter, & Goelman, 1982; Scardamalia, Bereiter, & Woodruff, 1980), and Linda Flowers and John Hayes (1981, 1984, 1986) helped establish a foundational understanding of the stages of the writing process, issues of audience and purpose in writing, the recursive and idiosyncratic nature of writing, the revision process, and the effects of topic knowledge on writing. In the latter half of the 1980s, George Hillocks, Jr. (1987) synthesized approximately 2,000 existing studies on writing in a seminal review of the research that helped researchers and educators reflect on what had been learned from writing research thus far and determine what was still in need of further exploration.

In the 1990s, writing research began to address the influences of gender, race, class, and culture on the writing process (Dyson, 1993; Fu, 1995; Lopez, 1999; Taylor & Dorsey-Gaines, 1988). However, few works specifically studied the connections between literacy (writing, in particular) and the visual arts (Sweet, 1997). A nascent body of research in the 1990s investigated ways to provide both visual and verbal learning experiences through the integration of art and writing (Blecher & Jaffee, 1998; Ernst, 1996; Ehrenworth, 2003; Olshansky, 1994; Olson, 1992; Olson & Wilson, 1979; Rearick, 1995). Researchers noted the presence of a relationship between art and writing, but the nature of that relationship was not fully understood (Hubbard, 1989; Olshansky, 1994; Olson, 1992; Smagorinsky & Coppock, 1993; Sweet, 1997). Studies explicitly investigating this relationship were inconclusive; yet when the research on artistic composing processes and the research on written composing processes are culled, one finds striking similarities between the two mediums: a period of idea germination that may involve rehearsing or planning the composition and gathering either visual or textual information; a process of drafting, revising, and editing the work; and some means of publishing or sharing (at least some) of the products with an audience (Dewey, 1934; Eisner, 2002; Graves, 1982; John-Steiner, 1997; Patrick, 1937). An area still in need of exploration was how these two language systems might work symbiotically, in tandem, with each other, as suggested by Eisner (2002). How might one symbolic system contribute to composition in the other?

As writing research moved into the new millennium, American society and much of the world media was quickly becoming visually saturated. The influences of popular/media culture were coming onto the radar of writing researchers (Dyson, 2003; Newkirk, 2002). Questions arose as to how this new visual culture affected literacy demands (Unsworth, 2001). A new wave of research developed in the area of literacy and arts integration (e.g., Albers, 2007; Cahnmann-Taylor & Siegesmund, 2008; Flood, Heath, & Lapp, 2008, and two themed journal issues, *Language Arts*, 84(1), 2006, and *English Education*, 40(1), 2007).

Writing research in the new millennium has a greater emphasis on integrating language arts with other media, communicative arts, and visual arts. This chapter contributes to the growing body of integration research by exploring the complexities of the relationship between artistic and written composing processes and the instructional potential for art-infused writing curricula.

The Argument for Integrated Learning

Schools unnecessarily compartmentalize learning into separate subjects in a manner that is unnatural to the way humans think and learn (Dewey, 1934; Gardner, 1983). Mathematics and science are taught as separate subjects, although one can rarely engage in a scientific activity without encountering mathematic concepts. Arts education is separated from "regular" or "academic" curricula, as if the arts were not a part of science, social studies, language, or literature. The language arts (focusing on writing, for the purpose of this chapter) and visual arts, although typically taught separately, both fall under the realm of the arts and enable much of the same cognitive work to take place. Elliot Eisner (2002) lists several cognitive benefits that language arts and visual arts have in common: they both "help us learn to notice the world;" they "engage the imagination as a means for exploring new possibilities;" they frequently force us to "tolerate ambiguity" and "to explore what is uncertain;" they require us to evaluate work based on internal criteria and may therefore lead to increased autonomy; and they are both tools for thinking, enabling us to inspect our ideas more carefully once inscribed (Eisner, 2002, pp. 10–11).

The theories of cognitive pluralism and multiple intelligences shape work in multimodal literacies and in arts integration, including the present study. Vera John-Steiner's (1997) seminal study of more than seventy prominent creative thinkers, including mathematicians, scientists, and dancers, resulted in her theory of "cognitive pluralism" in which each individual possesses diverse "languages of the mind," including visual, verbal, and kinesthetic modes of thought (xvi). Cognitive pluralism aligns well with Howard Gardner's theory of multiple intelligences in which he argues for an expanded view of "what counts as human intellect," originally proposing seven "intelligences"—linguistic, musical, logical-mathematical, spatial, bodily-kinesthetic, interpersonal, and intrapersonal intelligence (Gardner, 1983, p. 4). Gardner (1983) notes that all intelligences are present in each person and that one can typically find "complexes of intelligences functioning together smoothly, even seamlessly, in order to execute intricate human activities" (p. 279). Together, the theories of cognitive pluralism and multiple intelligences support the multiple ways of knowing, making meaning, and expressing one's self made possible by integrated-arts curricula.

The Study

Students seldom have the opportunity to experience, learn, and grow within an art-infused writing curriculum. What would happen if students were provided such a space to create both art and writing together? How might art and writing interact for elementary school students? For this study, six fourth-grade students' experiences of written and artistic composing in an art-infused writing curriculum were explored with the following goals: understanding student composing processes in such a context, identifying the kinds of relationships that might exist between artistic and written composing, and investigating the instructional potential of art-infused writing curricula. To be clear, the focus of this investigation was students' composing processes and *not* their artistic or written products, except for where those products gave insight into connections between the two processes. Two main research questions framed the study: (1) What composing elements constitute the participants' experiences in an art-infused writing curriculum? (2) What is the relationship between the composing processes of art and writing?

Methodology

Phenomenology, a social research tradition with deep roots in philosophy and psychology, can be both a theoretical perspective and a methodology and was an ideal framework to use for exploring students' composing experiences. Phenomenologists examine perceptions of or conscious experiences with objects in the world to uncover "knowledge of human experience" (Moustakas, 1994, p. 28).

Participants' individual composing experiences were accessed through a variety of data sources: think-aloud protocols (e.g., Ericsson & Simon, 1984/1993; Hayes & Flower, 1978; Hayes & Flower, 1987) during which students verbalized their thoughts, composing actions, and decisions into an audio recorder; work-shop observations, one hour a day, three days a week; spontane-ous, informal student interviews conducted during the composing processes; semi-structured student interviews conducted at the end of each completed composition set (approximately six per student); and student art and writing artifacts. Since phenom-enological studies seek to describe participants' experiences through their own words, the think-aloud data were essential in documenting students' "on-line" composing thoughts (Flower & Hayes, 1981, 1984). Researchers have rarely used think-aloud protocols, also called verbal protocols (e.g., Pressley & Hilden, 2004), with elementary students' writing or artwork (Fontaine, 1989), yet this technique provided key information about the sequence of students' composing processes, moments of decision making and problem solving, and student interactions that would not likely have been captured otherwise.

According to phenomenological theory, every conscious, intentional experience consists of both noema, a perceived object or experience, and a noesis, the underlying meaning that explains "how it is" (Moustakas, 1994, p. 32). Phenomenological analysis is a process of identifying both the noematic, or textural, dimen-sions of a phenomenon that uncover, describe, and clarify the conscious experience and the noetic, or structural, dimensions that explain the underlying meanings, processes, and dynamics of the experience (Moustakas, 1994). The individual's perceived qualities (textures) of an experience and the structures (hidden dynamics) come together to create a full understanding of the experience (Moustakas, 1994, p. 79). The textural description shows the phenomenon from "many sides, angles, and views, until a sense of fulfillment is reached" (Moustakas, 1994, p. 78). From textural analysis of the data, eight main elements of the students' composing experiences emerged: environment, freedom, sketchbook use, information gathering, new knowledge, variety in depth of composing process, high-stakes testing, and sense of growth.

In phenomenological analysis, the structural description presents "a picture of the conditions that precipitate an experience and connect with it" (Moustakas, 1994, p. 35). Since intentionality, the mind's conscious orientation to its object, is a key component of any phenomenon, I closely examined the participants' intentionality in their written and artistic composing processes during structural analysis. Although at the outset of the study I anticipated the emergence of only one relationship between artistic and written compositions, during data collection and analysis it became clear that participants' intentionality manifested itself on several different levels. The emergence of seven different relationships came as a surprise and highlighted the complexities of art and writing integration.

In what follows, I present the research setting, participants, and a brief description of the textural findings to provide context for the reader and then focus on the composing relationships that arose from the structural analysis. I conclude with a synthesis that highlights the significance of these data and discuss implications for future research and practice.

The Research Setting

The research site was Expressions Academy (all names are pseudonyms), a public elementary school, grades K–5, designated as an art magnet school in the town of McDermott. The school had approximately 540 students with four teachers at each grade level and was situated in a relatively rural community, within a low socioeconomic neighborhood, and an underserved population. McDermott began as a rural farming area and grew through its involvement with the equine industry to a population of approximately 50,000. It was surrounded by a variety of agricultural, horse, and cattle farms, but growing rapidly. It was the largest community within at least a 30-mile radius. Although it was not a typical, small, rural town, the culture and discourse (Gee, 1996) in this community was rural and southern.

Unlike urban or suburban, middle- or upper-class communities that typically have better access to art resources, such as museums, libraries, city art programs, and full-time art instructors, rural communities have unique education challenges, particularly in the arts (Donehower, Hogg, & Schell, 2007; Montgomery, 2004). Much of the literacy and arts integration research has focused on urban or suburban settings, including the studies in this book (Albers, 2010; Berghoff, Borgmann, Helmerick, & Thorne, 2010; Costello, 2010; Damico & Riddle, 2006; Hubbard, 1989; Mahiri, 2006; Ware, 2006). Some of the research and arts initiatives within rural communities have focused on specialized populations such as artistically talented children (Clark & Zimmerman, 1997; Montgomery, 2004). Thus, the present study addresses a need for arts integration research in rural settings and in the regular classroom.

Expressions Academy focused on fine arts education in addition to the traditional core subjects of language arts, math, science, and social studies. They did not screen students for visual or performing art abilities; students of any ability level could apply to attend. Twenty-six percent of students were on free or reduced lunch, and the school was required to maintain a minimum of thirty-five percent minority student enrollment. Mrs. Berry's fourth-grade class had ten males and eleven females, and eight of the twenty-one students were minorities of African American, Latin American, or Hawaiian descent.

Students kept a sketchbook from the time they enrolled in the school until the end of fifth grade. They took trips to a museum (an hour away), learned from visiting artists, and had opportunities to work with quality art materials such as kiln-fired clay. There were two National Board Certified visual arts teachers who split each class in half so that each instructor worked with only eleven or twelve students during the weekly, fifty-minute art period. In addition to visual arts, students could also choose between dance or theater and choir or strings as standard components of the curriculum. As a participant in this study, Mrs. Berry agreed to devote three days a week to an art-infused writing workshop, except during January and February, months spent in preparation for state-mandated standardized tests.

The Participants

Six focal students, three males and three females, ages nine to ten, were selected from the participating class to include a range of individual qualities: a range of verbal ability (oral, writing, and reading skills), a range of artistic interest and ability, a balance of genders, and ethnic diversity. Four of the six focal students were from working-class families or low-income homes and two were from middle-class homes. Keesha, an African American middle-class girl, had strong verbal skills, was outgoing, and interacted well with her peers. She was not particularly strong in visual arts but participated in private dance activities after school. Lilly, a European American from a low-income home, displayed strengths in both language and visual arts. She wrote stories with elaborate plots, drew extensively in her sketchbook at home, and expressed that she enjoyed "abstract art." Janelle, also European American and from a low-income home, displayed uncertainty about her artistic abilities, yet she seemed to enjoy creating art. At the beginning of the year, her visual art and language skills (reading, writing, and speaking) were on grade level, based on the teacher's initial assessments and my observations.

Louis, of Puerto Rican heritage, struggled to complete schoolwork and maintain focus on assigned tasks. He expressed a high interest in and enjoyment of visual arts and was an avid "doodler." He had many creative ideas for his writing but seldom finished a piece, which caused academic troubles. Ronnie, an African American from a low-income home, loved to draw, and demonstrated average language skills (reading, writing, and speaking). Differences between Ronnie's home dialect, African American English, and the school's academic English presented some writing difficulties for Ronnie. Aaron, a European American from a middle-class background, struggled greatly with writing in the beginning of the year. Spelling and mechanics were noticeably difficult for him, and his writing was characteristically short in length. Like Louis, Aaron had very creative ideas for writing but struggled to get them on paper. He enjoyed art-making but was not particularly skilled at art.

The Art-Infused Writing Curriculum

Although the school provided a variety of opportunities for extended learning in the arts, the classroom teacher with whom I worked, Mrs. Berry, incorporated little art in her lessons prior to participating in this research project. As a volunteer for this study, Mrs. Berry agreed to add a focus on art and writing integration by replacing her regular writing instruction with an art-and-writing workshop for one hour, three days a week, over the course of the school year. I assisted Mrs. Berry by helping her to plan the workshop units and collaborate with the school's art teachers. I regularly demonstrated art or writing mini-lessons, such as using the writer's notebook, watercolor techniques, and revision strategies.

During the hour-long art-infused writing workshop sessions, students could move freely between art and writing and could often choose to begin with either their art or writing. Students received both art and writing instruction and typically created a *composition set*—a piece of art and writing that were related in some way (typically closely related in topic). A composition set might take a student several workshop sessions to complete. Since Mrs. Berry was uncomfortable with her art knowledge, we chose to build the art lessons around what the art teachers were already doing in their 2-D and 3-D classes. For example, if the art teachers were working with clay, students used model clay in Mrs. Berry's classroom during the workshop. When the art teachers taught collage techniques, the students also used collage in the regular classroom to reinforce and apply the techniques they were learning. The connections were not always as close as these, but the goal remained to build on art teachers' instruction.

Mrs. Berry had particular units of study planned for the year that shaped the art and writing instruction, and she added an artist study for the purposes of this project. The units of study, in chronological order and with their respective writing and art lessons, were as follows: (1) Sketchbook/Writer's Notebook: Lessons on using the notebook, doing quick sketches, and revisiting entries; (2) The Personal Narrative Genre: Minimum of three narratives required; Lessons on narrative structure, writing strong leads, written revision strategies, collage media with fore-, middle-, and back-ground layers, and visual elements of line, shape, color, and texture; (3) Thematic Unit on Animals: Writing lessons on informational text structures and creating voice in informational writing, and art lessons on viewing and responding to art and clay sculpting; (4) An Artist Study: Writing lessons on topic selection and biography writing, and art lessons on imitating model pieces and identifying and experimenting with media; (5) State History Unit: Writing lessons on topic and genre selection, researching a topic, and perspective and voice, and art lessons on creating texture with watercolors, using ink with watercolor, and point of view; and (6) Poetry Genre: A focus on free verse with writing lessons on elements of poetry, and art lessons on representational versus nonrepresentational or abstract images.

The teacher provided the students with topic choice on approximately 70 percent of their writing and art making. For the workshop units, the genre or a broad topic was teacher selected, but students could choose their focus within that genre/topic. Since this was Ms. Berry's first time implementing writing workshop and her first experience with art integration, she was only able to partially implement workshop components such as peer conferencing, modeling, and teacher conferencing. Writing workshop, and furthermore the infusion of art, was novel for Mrs. Berry, and developing, refining, and managing all of the components of an ideal writing workshop would require additional time and professional development.

Findings: The Essence of the Students' Composing Experiences with Art-Infused Writing

The participants' artistic and written composing experiences included eight essential elements: environment, freedom, sketchbook use, information gathering, new knowledge, variety in depth of composing process, high-stakes testing, and sense of growth. A very brief overview of these eight elements is provided to give the reader a broad sense of the participants' experience (with each element italicized for identification). Any text in quotation marks is the participant's direct words taken from think-aloud or interview transcripts.

The participants expressed that the art-infused writing curriculum was a positive *environment* in which they felt comfortable to create what they wished and to make mistakes without fear of ridicule. They appreciated that their teacher "just tried to help" them "make it better." When students had the *freedom* to choose topics in their art and writing, they were motivated to work on their pieces outside of school, were conscious of their audience and purpose for the work, and expressed appreciation for this freedom. *Sketchbooks* served as a place for students to collect ideas, select topics, rehearse, and draft their work. Some children preferred to draw often in their sketchbooks, including random doodles, "cartoon" characters, or personal experiences; other students preferred to write about their lives recording "ideas that I might use later." Written entries included diary types of entries, narrative stories, speech bubbles for cartoon characters, information copied in art class, and art-related research notes.

In the art-infused writing workshop, there was room for students to employ their *multiple intelligences*, including the use of intrapersonal intelligence (the ability to interact well with others was demonstrated when students used peers as resources and when Ronnie acted as a confidence coach for a classmate), musical intelligence, spatial intelligence (using visual skills to gather information from images), and linguistic intelligence (Gardner, 1983). Two boys also brought popular media/ culture, such as the *Discovery Channel, Animal Planet*, U-Gi-Oh cards, anime comics or cartoons, and how-to-draw books into their composing processes.

Students *developed and applied new knowledge* about art, such as implementing the concept of perspective, learning how to mix certain colors, and the need for painting the background first. They also developed knowledge about different writing genres in a process of writing-to-learn the elements of different genres. The *depth and variety of elements in the students' composing processes* were products of their individual strengths, knowledge, and previous experiences with composing in certain genres or media. Artistic composing processes included conducting visual research, using several media, considering elements of color or line, rehearsing, drafting in and out of the sketchbook, solving artistic problems, and revising in varied ways. The students used a variety of resources during their written composing, such as peer resources and peer models, visual resources, and model texts. Students also added-in or created their own unique sub-processes, including singing or creating vocal rhythms while composing, engaging in associative thinking, or gathering and making use of visual information.

The *high-stakes writing test* environment seemed to influence the students' writing processes and, at times, to stifle their growth as writers. Students often demonstrated a one-shot draft mentality, wanting to get their paragraphs and spelling right the first time. Some students evaluated their writing in terms of the "score" it might receive and evaluated their progress by the increase in their prompt writing scores.

Glimpses of growth also were observed in the ways in which students applied art content knowledge, applied new writing revision strategies, or discovered new techniques in their composing processes ("I did something I didn't even know."). The freedom in Mrs. Berry's curriculum allowed students to sense their own growth and broaden their conceptions of what they could do: "I didn't know I could draw," "I didn't think I could paint," "I used to think I couldn't write stories," or "I never could write, and now I can!" They remarked that it was easier to find topics, that they used better language, and that they wrote more during the workshop. Often, students learned through resolving dissatisfaction in their artwork or writing. For example, when Aaron became upset about the way his paint was mixing when he tried to paint the background last; he then learned to paint the background first. Although each student's work included hastily completed art or one-shot draft writing, students slowly expanded their composing processes to include acts of revision and problem solving.

Seven Relationships between Artistic and Written Composing Processes

Within the structure of the workshop and with the guidance of their teacher, students developed their own idiosyncratic composing processes and relationships between art and writing. The opportunity to do so generated not just one, but seven varied composing relationships between the students' artistic and written composing process. These seven composing relationships form a continuum of degrees of interaction from least interaction to greatest interaction between the students' art and writing (Figure 5.1). At times, the difference between one composing relationship and the adjacent one on the continuum was only slight, but the decision to identify each relationship as distinct was grounded in the data, considering whole composing episodes and the underlying dynamics that were occurring. When examined over the span of several composing episodes, each student appeared to experience a range of relationships between his or her artistic and written processes, and there was often more than one relationship within a particular composing episode. Each relationship is briefly described in the following, in order from least interaction between art and writing to greatest interaction, with illustrative examples from the focal students' composing episodes.

Converse Relationship

In a converse relationship, the art and writing are doing opposite work, or opposite composing processes are occurring in each medium. An example of a converse relationship in a student's art and writing was evident in Aaron's composing processes for

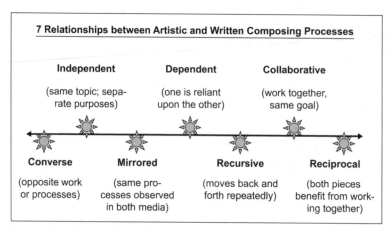

FIGURE 5.1. *Seven relationships between artistic and written composing processes.*

his composition set *Cricket, My Dog.* In this composition set, Aaron's watercolor painting of his dog standing on a dirt mound overlooking a pond was communicating narrative information about his dog, Cricket, falling into a pond at Aaron's father's worksite. Aaron explained, "Like they had like a little pond [where my dad works], and my dad always lets me go swimming in it, cause it's clean. They made it just to cool off the workers, and so [Cricket], she caught the ball and landed in the [pond]." Aaron's writing, on the other hand, was communicating factual, expository information about the breed of dog and its abilities (i.e., "My dog Cricket is a German Short-haired Pointer . . . German Short-haired Pointers are dogs that are trained to point at birds."). The art and writing were related on the level of topic, but appeared to be doing opposite work on the level of genre and specific detail. Based on the data, Aaron intended the writing to be narrative also and was not able to achieve the same degree of narrative quality as he felt he communicated with his art.

Converse relationships also emerged in Lilly's composing processes. She rehearsed and planned for her writing by drawing in her sketchbook, writing entries, and talking to others. But there was little evidence that she drafted or revised her writing beyond the sketchbook rehearsals.

Conversely, Lilly was a flexible composer and a problem-solver in her artwork. She drafted her art by drawing in her sketchbook, making multiple versions of a piece, and revising her artwork. I even observed her cutting out pieces from one painting and incorporating them into a new piece. In Lilly's writing, though, she edited only for sentence fluency and punctuation. In this way, she was doing opposite work in art and in writing, which indicated a converse relationship between the two; the two pieces were related in subject matter and created as a set, even though the composing processes within each piece were opposite.

Independent Relationship

In an independent relationship, the art and writing may be on the same topic, but they may have separate purposes, meanings, and/or goals. Keesha spoke explicitly about how art and writing interacted for her. In our last interview of the school year, I asked her, "How have art and writing worked together for you? Or have they?" She replied with a perceptive analysis, "Sometimes, they never come together, but they're on the same topic. And sometimes they do." Keesha's comment about how her art and writing might be on the same topic but never come together prompted the development of this independent relationship category. Keesha explained that when her writing and art topics were more personally determined, she drew on her everyday life experiences to create her work. But when the topics were more structured or school-determined, she needed to use her writing to create her art (in a dependent nature). She expressed that on expository topics, her art was dependent on her writing and served to directly illustrate her writing. But when the topics were personally determined, her art and writing could have an independent relationship and she drew on her life "outside of school" to create her art; in such cases, her art and writing could be on the same topic but have different purposes or meanings.

Mirrored Relationship

A mirrored relationship is when the same composing processes were observed in both symbolic systems. The presence of this relationship in the students' composing processes confirms the findings of researchers noted earlier. Lilly demonstrated a mirrored relationship between her artistic and written composing processes in the way she used her sketchbook to rehearse both her art and writing; she also viewed all aspects of her life (e.g., going to the hospital, four-wheel riding, horseback riding, Girl Scouts) as potential topics for writing or drawing.

Ronnie's composing process of researching his topic for both his art and his writing when he created his *Milky Way* composition set is another example of a mirrored composing relationship. He visually researched images of the solar system, planets, and night sky when creating a watercolor painting of the solar system. He also researched textual information to draft his writing about outer space, taking notes on factual information about each of the planets. The process of researching before composing was present in both symbolic systems for a particular composing episode and therefore constituted a mirrored composing relationship.

Dependent Relationship

A dependent relationship is one in which a student's work in one symbolic system is reliant on the work in the other, such as when a student's artwork is a straight-forward illustration of the writing and the student depends solely on the writing to determine the content of the illustration; there is no extension or elaboration in the artwork. Louis's writing seemed to be very dependent on his art. He always created his artwork first, which appeared to give Louis time to rehearse, develop his story, think about his topic, or gain information from the images. He often created more than one piece of art before beginning his writing. Doing the art first may also have allowed Louis to become invested in his topic enough to sustain him through the writing process. In this way, Louis's writing was highly dependent on his artwork.

Recursive Relationship

In a recursive composing relationship, the student moves back and forth between the art and writing repeatedly, possibly in order to keep the momentum of composing going in each, or to fuel the student's creative thoughts in each medium. There was a highly recursive relationship between art and writing for Aaron. He continually worked back and forth among his drawing, writing, and painting. He often began by both drawing and writing in his sketchbook. Then while he was writing, he would stop and revisit the drawings in his sketchbook. When Aaron composed his *Castillo de San Marco* work, he wrote in a factual, dry, informational style that lacked voice. Then, he painted two versions of the fort. Afterward, he went back to his writing with the goal of changing the genre to be "more like a journal thing" and engaged in a significant revision. He appeared to move back and forth between media particularly when he met a mental or creative road block, and this recursive movement between media seemed to help him maintain a composing momentum instead of becoming unproductive.

Collaborative Relationship

In a collaborative relationship, the art and writing work together toward the same goal, for example, to tell a story. One example of a collaborative relationship was found in Jannelle's composing episode involving her artist study of Monet. For this composition set, Jannelle took three pages of notes in her sketchbook while gathering information about Monet. Then, she made her painting of one of Monet's *Water Lilly* prints, working carefully to imitate his short, soft brushstrokes and, in her words, "fill the page with mass." Both the written report and Jannelle's imitation of Monet's art collaborated in telling the story of Monet as an artist: the written work provided factual information and included inferences she gained from her experience of imitating his painting (e.g., "[Monet] used a lot of hard brushwork."), while the painting conveyed additional visual information about Monet's artistic style and technique.

Reciprocal Relationship

A reciprocal relationship is a deeper form of the collaborative relationship that occurs when both composing processes (or products) benefit from the interaction. In one of Jannelle's narrative composing episodes, her artistic composing process served as a way for her to rehearse her writing. At the same time, her writing was a tool for digging out more details that Jannelle added to her picture; her writing helped her revise the art. Further, the way Jannelle moved back and forth between art and writing in her narrative composing process also indicated the presence of a recursive relationship between the two and illustrated how more than one composing relationship could be present in a composing episode.

A second instance of a reciprocal relationship in Jannelle's composing process was observed in the way her sketchbook writing about Monet's art seemed to serve as a tool for thinking about and rehearsing her artwork. Reciprocally, viewing, responding to, and creating art in the artist study supported topic development in Jannelle's report writing. Ideas such as Monet's "beautiful pictures," "lovely paintings," and "hard brushwork" that were included in Jannelle's writing came from her experiences with the art. Both her art and writing appeared to have reciprocally benefited from their relationship.

The descriptions in this chapter of the relationships between artistic and written composing provide researchers and educators with foundational information that may assist in future research and curriculum development in the area of writing and art integration and may help teachers better guide students' art and writing development, enhancing learning in both realms.

Potential for Process Knowledge Transfer

The significant implication for the composing relationships discussed previously is the potential for the art-infused writing workshop to mediate students' transfer of process knowledge from one composing process to another. Suhor (1984), in extending semiotic theory, stated that meaningful content can be transferred across sign systems in a semiotic process called transmediation, such as in the case of writing a poem to express the subject of a painting or creating an original work of art to represent a theme in a piece of literature. Although Suhor only mentioned the possibility for content to be transferred across sign systems, the results of this study indicate potential for the transfer of process knowledge as well.

The data revealed that composing processes were often mirrored in art and writing, but at times, composing processes in one symbolic system were richer than in the other, such as in Louis's case described in the vignette at the beginning of this chapter. Louis had a much richer artistic composing process than written composing process. Rehearsal, drafting, research, and revision were all part of his artistic composing process but were seldom found in his written composing processes. In such cases, it would seem beneficial to students if they could be guided in transferring their knowledge of process from one symbolic system to the other. An attentive classroom teacher could help a student like Louis transfer deeper composing processes from the more highly developed communicative system to the less developed system. For example, Louis saw a purpose for revising his artwork and was motivated to do so. Recognizing such a converse relationship between composing processes, a teacher could then hold a process conference with the student to discuss his artistic revision processes and how his writing might benefit from similar kinds of revision.

In another example, the data indicated that Lilly developed a clear sense of audience and purpose in her writing but seldom expressed an audience or purpose in her artwork. Conversely, she revised her art extensively but did not appear to revise her writing much at all. A teacher with a student like Lilly could discuss her composing strengths in each medium and help her to transfer the skill of considering one's audience and purpose to her artwork and the skill of revision to her writing. Therefore, I encourage teachers to explore the instructional potential for transmediation of process, in addition to content, between artistic and written composing processes to develop students' composing abilities. In practical contexts, this might take the form of a "process conference" about students' artistic or written work in which the teacher asks a child to describe his or her composing processes (Calkins, 1994). The teacher would follow up with suggestions for explicit transfer of process knowledge from one medium to the other.

Why Bother?

One could argue that the procedure of process knowledge transfer is too complicated and time consuming to incorporate into instruction. However, just as we know an individual learns a second language easier when already literate in their primary language (Cummins, 1981), it is likely that a student can develop composing proficiency easier when we use what they are already doing well in one symbolic system to strengthen the skills in another. Furthermore, we must revisit the purpose of the art-infused writing workshop in evaluating the significance of process knowledge transfer as a potential instructional strategy. Art instruction is too frequently denied to children in rural and high poverty schools. It is usually the first subject to be cut in a budget crunch. Likewise, pedagogically sound writing instruction is often missing in schools across the United States. An art-infused writing curriculum is full of possibilities and can be a way to incorporate both art and writing instruction in the regular classroom. It can be a way to allow children opportunities to bring their individualities, multiple intelligences, and multiple literacies into the curriculum, and art-infused writing can allow students the freedom to develop their own creative processes and composing relationships. Multimodal literacies instruction such as this enables children to have creative autonomy, to think and act in unique ways, and allows *all* children to have academic access through dynamic paths; this is why we bother.

Works Cited

Albers, P. (2007). *Finding the artist within: Creating and reading visual texts in the English language arts classroom.* Newark, DE: International Reading Association.

———. (2010). Reading art, reading lives: An interpretive study of the visual texts of urban English language arts students. In P. Albers & J. Sanders, (Eds.), *Literacies, the arts, and multimodality.* Urbana, IL: National Council of Teachers of English.

Berghoff, B., Borgmann, C., Helmerick, M., & Thorne, C. (2010). An arts-integrated unit: Learning 21st century literacies while the teachers are on break. In P. Albers & J. Sanders, (Eds.), *Literacies, the arts, and multimodality.* Urbana, IL: National Council of Teachers of English.

Blecher, S., & Jaffee, K. (1998). *Weaving in the arts: Widening the literacy circle.* Portsmouth, NH: Heinemann.

Britton, J., Burgess, T., Martin, N., McLeod, A., & Rosen, H. (1975). *The development of writing abilities (11–18).* London, UK: Macmillan Education.

Cahnmann-Taylor, M., & Siegesmund, R. (2008). *Arts-based research in education: Foundations for practice.* New York: Routledge.

Calkins, L. M. (1980). Children's rewriting strategies. *Research in the Teaching of English, 14*(4), 331–341.

———. (1983). *Lessons from a child: On the teaching and learning of writing.* Portsmouth, NH: Heinemann.

————. (1994). *The art of teaching writing*. Portsmouth, NH: Heine-mann.

Costello, A. M. (2010). Silencing stories: The triumphs and tensions of multimodal teaching and learning in an urban context. In P. Albers & J. Sanders, (Eds.), *Literacies, the arts, and multimodality*. Urbana, IL: National Council of Teachers of English.

Cummins, J. (1981). The role of primary language development in promoting educational success for language minority students. In California State Department of Education (Ed.), *Schooling and language minority students: A theoretical framework* (pp. 3–50). Los Angeles: Evaluation, Dissemination and Assessment Center, California State University.

Damico, J. (with Riddle, R.). (2006). Exploring freedom and leaving a legacy: Enacting new literacies with digital texts in the elementary classroom. *Language Arts, 84*(1), 34–44.

Dewey, J. (1934). *Art as experience*. New York: Minton, Balch.

Donehower, K., Hogg, C., & Schell, E. (2007). *Rural literacies*. Car-bondale: Southern Illinois University Press.

Dyson, A. H. (1993). *Social worlds of children learning to write in an urban primary school*. New York: Teachers College Press.

————. (2003). *The brothers and sisters learn to write: Popular literacies in childhood and school cultures*. New York: Teachers College Press.

Ehrenworth, M. (2003). *Looking to write: Students writing through the visual arts*. Portsmouth, NH: Heinemann.

Eisner, E. W. (2002). *The arts and the creation of mind*. New Haven, CT: Yale University Press.

Emig, J. (1971). *The composing processes of twelfth graders*. Urbana, IL: National Council of Teachers of English.

Enciso, P., Katz, L., Kiefer, B. Z., Price-Dennis, D., & Wilson, M. (Eds.). (2006). Multimodal transformations [themed issue]. *Language Arts, 84*(1).

Ericsson, K. A., & Simon, H. A. (1993). *Protocol analysis: Verbal reports as data* (Rev. ed.). Cambridge, MA: Bradford Books-MIT Press.

Ernst, K. (1996). Widening the frame: Reading, writing, and art in learn-ing. In R. S. Hubbard & K. Ernst (Eds.), *New entries: Learning by writing and drawing* (pp.14–25). Portsmouth, NH: Heinemann.

Flood, J., Heath, S. B., & Lapp, D. (Eds.). (2008). *Handbook of research on teaching literacy through the communicative and visual arts* (Vol. 2). New York, NY: Erlbaum.

Flower, L., & Hayes, J. R. (1981). A cognitive process theory of writing. *College Composition and Communication, 32*(4), 365–387.

———. (1984). Images, plans, and prose: The representation of meaning in writing. *Written Communication, 1*(1), 120–160.

Fontaine, S. I. (1989). Using verbal reports to learn about children's audience awareness in writing. *Educational Research Quarterly, 13*(3), 26–35.

Fu, D. (1995). *"My trouble is my English": Asian students and the American dream.* Portsmouth, NH: Boynton/Cook.

Gardner, H. (1983). *Frames of mind: The theory of multiple intelligences.* New York: Basic Books.

Gee, J. P. (1996). *Social linguistics and literacies: Ideology in discourses* (2nd ed.). London, UK: Taylor and Francis.

Graves, D. H. (1982). *A case study observing the development of primary children's composing, spelling, and motor behaviors during the writing process* (Final Report). Durham: University of New Hampshire, Department of Education.

Harste, J. C., & Albers, P. (Eds.). (2007). The arts, new literacies, and multimodality (themed issue). *English Education, 40*(1), 3–5.

Hayes, J. R., & Flower, L. (1978, March). *Protocol analysis of writing processes.* Paper presented at the annual meeting of the American Education Research Association, Toronto, Canada.

———. (1986). Writing research and the writer. *American Psychologist, 41*(10), 1106–1113.

———. (1987). On the structure of the writing process. *Topics in Language Disorders, 7*(4), 19–30.

Hillocks, G., Jr. (1987). Synthesis of research on teaching writing. *Educational Leadership, 44*(8), 71–82.

Hubbard, R. (1989). *Authors of pictures, draughtsmen of words.* Portsmouth, NH: Heinemann.

John-Steiner, V. (1997). *Notebooks of the mind: Explorations of thinking*. New York: Oxford University Press.

Kress, G., & van Leeuwen, T. (1996). *Reading images: A grammar of visual design*. New York: Routledge.

Lopez, M. E. (1999). *When discourses collide: An ethnography of migrant children at home and in school*. New York: Peter Lang.

Mahiri, J. (2006). Digital DJ-ing: Rhythms of learning in an urban school. *Language Arts, 84*(1), 55–62.

Montgomery, D. (2004). Broadening perspectives to meet the needs of gifted learners in rural schools. *Rural Special Education Quarterly, 23*(1), 3–7.

Moustakas, C. (1994). *Phenomenological research methods*. Thousand Oaks, CA: Sage.

Newkirk, T. (2002). *Misreading masculinity: Boys, literacy, and popular culture*. Portsmouth, NH: Heinemann.

North, S. M. (1987). *The making of knowledge in composition: Portrait of an emerging field*. Upper Montclair, NJ: Boynton/Cook.

Olshansky, B. (1994). Making writing a work of art: Image-making within the writing process. *Language Arts, 71*(5), 350–356.

Olson, J. L. (1992). *Envisioning writing: Toward an integration of drawing and writing*. Portsmouth, NH: Heinemann.

Olson, J. L., & Wilson, B. (1979). A visual narrative program—grades 1–8. *School Arts, 79*(1), 26–33.

Patrick, C. (1937). Creative thought in artists. *Journal of Psychology, 4*, 35–73.

Pressley, M., & Hilden, K. (2004). Verbal protocols of reading. In N. K. Duke and M. H. Mallette (Eds.), *Literacy research methodologies* (pp. 308–321). New York: Guilford Press.

Rearick, M. L. (1995, May). *Improving instruction in the language arts and in the arts through book-making: A collaborative inquiry in a second-grade classroom*. Paper presented at the annual meeting of the New England Educational Research Organization, Portsmouth, NH.

Sanders, J. (2006). *Qualitative study of students' composing experiences in an art-infused writing curriculum* (Unpublished doctoral dissertation), University of Florida.

Scardamalia, M., Bereiter, C., & Goelman, H. (1982). The role of production factors in writing ability. In M. Nystrand (Ed.), *What writers know: The language, process, and structure of written discourse* (pp.173–210). New York: Academic Press.

Scardamalia, M., Bereiter, C., & Woodruff, E. (1980, April). *The effects of content knowledge on writing.* Paper presented at the annual meeting of the American Educational Research Association, Boston, MA.

Smagorinsky, P., & Coppock, J. (1993, April). *Broadening the notion of text: An exploration of an artistic composing process.* Paper presented at the annual meeting of the American Educational Research Association, Atlanta, GA.

Suhor, C. (1984). Towards a semiotics-based curriculum. *Journal of Curriculum Studies, 16*(3), 247–257.

Sweet, A. P. (1997). A national policy perspective on research intersections between literacy and visual/ communicative arts. In J. Flood, S. B. Heath, & D. Lapp (Eds.), *Handbook of research on teaching literacy through the communicative and visual arts* (pp.264–285). New York: Simon and Schuster Macmillan.

Taylor, D., & Dorsey-Gaines, C. (1988). *Growing up literate: Learning from inner-city families.* Portsmouth, NH: Heinemann.

Unsworth, L. (2001). *Teaching multiliteracies across the curriculum: Changing contexts of text of image in classroom practice.* Philadelphia: Open University Press.

Ware, P. D. (2006). From sharing time to showtime! Valuing diverse venues for storytelling in technology-rich classrooms. *Language Arts, 84*(1), 45–54.

Seeing, Writing, and Drawing the Intangible: Teaching with Multiple Literacies

MICHELLE ZOSS
Georgia State University

RICHARD SIEGESMUND
University of Georgia

SHERELLE JONES PATISAUL
Winder-Barrow High School, Winder, Georgia

A s English teachers in the United States face the challenge of teaching students of widely varying language and literacy skills, there is a need to include the visual arts as an important component of a more complete curriculum that will serve all students. Arts-based research (Barone & Eisner, 1997; Siegesmund & Cahnmann-Taylor, 2008) and arts-based curricula provide potentially viable and interesting pathways (Siegesmund, 1999; Zoss, 2009) for students to experience deep structures of meaning where they emotionally connect to content and sustain learning beyond the classroom experience (Stiggins, Arter, Chappuis, & Chappuis, 2004).

One of these pathways is visual learning. It deserves greater attention by English teachers as a pathway to language. Rudolf Arnheim (1969) maintained that visual perception is a cognitive process and involves training the eye to search. Similarly, Elliot Eisner (2002) described writing as a "way of searching in order to see" (p. 89). One must see in order to have something to say. Educators from both the visual arts (Olson, 2005) and language arts (Fleckenstein, 2002) have noted that the two subject areas share a parallel construction of searching to create meaning. This process follows a five-staged pathway: collect, focus, order, draft, and clarify (Murray, 1984). Both Kristie Fleckenstein and Janet Olson argued for constructing classroom lessons that exploit this similarity. Blending these mutual pathways for deep learning provides an example of arts-based curriculum.

This chapter examines part of a longitudinal study that traces the development of a preservice language arts teacher from her initial teacher certification course work through her first years of teaching middle school. In this participatory, multidimensional teacher research study, the two principal participants, Michelle and Sherelle, share changing roles and authority, with Michelle initially serving as Sherelle's teacher and eventually becoming a participant observer in Sherelle's own classroom. This chapter is a small window into the larger qualitative case study and reflects on the second semester of Sherelle's first year of teaching middle school language arts. Data for this study were collected through participant observation field notes, one-on-one interviews with Sherelle, document collection of teacher and student artifacts, and photographs taken in Sherelle's classroom. The data were then analyzed using a coding framework focused on Sherelle's problem solving as a situated activity. Specifically, the interviews with Sherelle were analyzed to shed light on how she used drawing as a tool to bring students into language, how the professional setting in which she worked came into play, and the solutions she developed toward achieving her teaching goals of integrating visual art in her language arts classroom. Our focus here is on a specific drawing and writing event that took place in the spring of Sherelle's first year of teaching.

As strong advocates of arts-based instruction, we, a professor in English education (Michelle), a professor in art education (Richard), and a teacher of language arts and reading (Sherelle), present a portrait of ways in which visual arts, language, and literacy inform each other. This chapter spotlights Sherelle's adaptation of an arts-based composition lesson focusing on writing and visual art in which students draw and then write about material and metaphoric items they carry in their school bags (backpacks). The lesson synthesizes both nonverbal learning objectives found in visual arts and verbal literacy objectives from language arts curricula.

The chapter provides a brief introduction to the creation of an arts-based lesson, "the backpack lesson," which invites students into connecting strong writing with drawing. We then focus on how Sherelle presents this same lesson in her middle school language arts class. Drawings and essays created by students reveal how these students explore perceived sensory relationships, attend to emotional responses, and convert these relationships and responses into personal meaning (Siegesmund, 2005).

The backpack lesson has been a part of our collective research for the last five years, as Michelle explored the connection of drawing and writing in her doctoral research (Zoss, 2007), and Sherelle proceeded through her first years of teaching language arts (Zoss & Jones, 2007). The lesson was first documented and analyzed in Richard's own doctoral dissertation in 2000. As such, the lesson presented here represents an idea that began in one teacher's urban middle school classroom in California and traveled to a rural middle school classroom in Georgia. In between, the ideas have been incubated and nurtured in undergraduate, master's, and doctoral education classes, and applied by language arts and visual arts teachers in several states throughout the elementary, middle, and high school levels.

The History of the Backpack Lesson

Dede Bartels, a California-certified middle school language arts teacher and a National Board Certified teacher in art, created the backpack lesson that emphasizes engaging students in reflective thinking and allowing them to demonstrate their skills and learning through multiple literacies. The lesson initially was prepared for a middle school art class. As is typical in so many middle and high schools, the students in this art class divided about equally into two groups. The first was students with learning and behavior difficulties assigned to the class by the school administration out of its exasperation with them. The second was composed of students with a genuine interest in studying art—some of whom were top academic achievers. An initial tension structures the backpack lesson: on one side, there is a simple systematic approach to observational drawing; on the other is the adolescent and adult fear and self-doubt about one's own ability to competently complete a representational, or realistic, drawing. To navigate the tension between these two poles, there are three "trap doors" in the lesson: points where Ms. Bartels changes the rules and expectations. The pedagogic "surprises" are necessary to keep students on-task while sustaining the high expectations of the lesson, which was completed over two fifty-minute class periods. Not only must Ms. Bartels navigate adolescent resistance to drawing, she must also navigate resistance to writing. She addresses these problems by deeply engaging students in the lesson, so that when challenges for making greater detail in drawing and then attention to detail in writing emerge in the lesson, the students are too invested in the lesson to turn back. These moments in which she "raises the stakes" in the lesson and demands increased concentration are the "trap doors."

The lesson begins with simple exercises in drawing geometric solids: A soda can is a simple cylinder that involves connecting two ovals with straight lines. The forms become slightly more complex (she crumples the soda can) but still there is a high level of confidence by all the students as they follow her examples. Everyone can do it. Then the first trap door opens: Ms. Bartels announces that the task for the day is for students to draw their backpacks. She reassures the students that their successful completion of simple exercises in drawing geometric solids that they have just completed will mean that everyone can succeed in this new drawing task.

She presents the task of drawing their backpacks as simple, yet the students are exhorted to note every line they can see. To emphasize that students need to pay close attention, she introduces a mantra that will be repeated frequently over the next two days: "I want you to draw what you see, not what you think you see."

As their line drawings near completion, Ms. Bartels opens the second trap door: the students are to shade their drawing. There are cries of disbelief and anguish, as a task that the students were relishing as completed now required more work. Calmly, she moves between the students, speaking to the group and guiding individuals into the completion of this next step, all the time repeating, "I want you to draw what you see, not what you think you see." Students work intensely, absorbed in the details of completing their backpacks. As the students finish their work, Ms. Bartels asks that they listen to a short piece of writing, an excerpt from Tim O'Brien's (1992) *The Things They Carried*, which describes items soldiers carried in their backpacks. Ms. Bartels carefully edited the original text so that the language is appropriate for a middle school audience, but she has retained O'Brien's essential point: soldiers carry tangible and intangible objects with them as they move from place to place. The intangible objects, including fear and shame, are the heaviest things they carry.

As they listen to Ms. Bartels's reading, some students continue to draw, but many students put down their chalk. After the reading, Ms. Bartels engages her students in a discussion of what the soldiers carried in their backpacks. The students readily remember and identify the tangible objects, but without mentioning the word *intangible*, she presses the students to remember what else the soldiers carried. Eventually the students begin to make the connection to intangible objects. The soldiers carry their emotions and feelings in their backpacks.

This student response opens the third trap door: understanding the difference between tangible and the intangible objects, that each of them carries around both types at school. This opportunity for personal reflection invites writing—students are invited to extend the visual work with their backpack to write about the contents inside. Like trap doors one and two, this pedagogical move encourages students to consider the details of what their backpacks hold and to use language to develop those details. Ms. Bartels asks the students to take a sheet of notebook paper out of their backpacks and write on this question, "What are the tangible and intangible things that each of you carries?" In their responses, students consider the parts of their backpacks that are real and those that are emotional. Perhaps as an indication of the deep personal investment that the students now feel with their drawings, there are no complaints about this final task. The students eagerly begin to write for the final ten minutes of class and turn their essays in as they leave the room.

In her assessment, Ms. Bartels was amazed at the emotion and intensity in the student writing—particularly in the work by students classified as poor academic performers. She suspected that the drawing of their backpacks together with listening to O'Brien's story had formed an aesthetic connection in the students that allowed them to more fully express themselves emotionally. The drawing exercise forced students to pay close attention to a personal object. Through an intense exercise of gathering nonverbal (visual) and verbal (written) details, the students established a new-felt relationship with an object that was intimately tied to their daily lives. In the specific moment of paying close attention to detail, there is an opportunity to be aware of how one specifically feels. This moment of linking detail and feeling is a first step toward metaphoric thinking (Greene, 2001). In this case, looking at the backpack could raise within a student a sense of anxiety, fear from the high expectations of school. Just as plausibly, the close examination might provoke wonderment and pleasure as the students note the small personal treasures that they have carefully added to adorn their backpacks. Through these small moments of interaction, students may begin to invest the backpack with emotional metonymic and metaphoric significance.

To test this theory that the collection of visual details helped students make the connections between tangible and intangible in their writing, Ms. Bartels brought the writing portion of the backpack lesson to another of her classes, this one a language arts class. In the language arts class, overwhelmingly composed of academically high performing students, Ms. Bartels had them listen only to the O'Brien passage, without going through the backpack drawing experience. The language arts students were exceptional list makers. They catalogued every detail of their backpacks, but none ventured into the emotional or intangible qualities. Yet the art students, particularly those most academically at-risk, spoke with almost heartbreaking clarity and rich metaphor of their fears and hopes of school. The results were startling; here (Figure 6.1) are two examples, one from the visual art class and one from the language arts class (Seigesmund, 2000).

Notice in the essay from the art class student, there are rich references to felt experience, including "my shoulders killing me," as well as the clear metaphoric ability to see the backpack as a potential future that is clearly at risk. In the language arts student example, there is considerable charm in the poetic rhythm and rhyme of the writing, but the student's fears and hopes are masked

Example from Ms. Bartels's Art Class	Example from Ms. Bartels's Language Arts Class

As I walk down this long narrow street with my shoulders killing me I realize I have many things in my backpack. The obvious things like books and a binder are covered in old papers which are already graded. I also have many papers I need to turn in but going through my bag I realize it is nowhere to be found.
 	
One thing which I don't have many of is pencils. I have long, short, broke, and dull pencils. One of the most important things I hold in my backpack is my lunch. I'm not proud to say but the most common thing to find in my bag is detention slips. Every once in a while I will hold my money in my backpack. Most important though is my future. If I can use some of those things in my backpack right I will make a good future for me. Another little thing I carry in my backpack is candy.
	Tour through my backpack
	you will find
	a pen that writes
	a mirror that shines
	to the left is something
	burgundy binder is hiding some-
	    thing?
	binder paper, unfinished homework
	    papers
	tattered catalogs and soda bottles too
	bracelets and ribbons and chapstick
	and hairbrushes nail polish and
	chewing gum.
	playing cards, letters, poems, and
	picture books!
	contacts and cleansing solutions
	    and
	hair from my brush, markers and
	doodles and hair ties too . . .
	    something
	from all my friends, tapes and CD's
	a pager and Walkman that is
	forbidden at school
	things I can't remember are in there
	waiting to be thrown out and
	    discarded.

FIGURE 6.1. Writing samples from the "backpack lesson."

(with the exception of an illegal Walkman that she is carrying). The visual art student makes the connection between the tangible and intangible objects in the backpack; the weight of the future is part of this student's daily journey. In contrast, the language arts student implies possible intangibles: "something from all my friends" and "unfinished homework." These two items imply relationships with peers and potentially unfulfilled expectations in the homework that remains incomplete in the bag. The absence of clear metaphors of intangible things to carry and the fleeting connection to emotions in this second piece of writing only hint at details about this student. The level of specificity of detail that

Ms. Bartels sought in this writing is present, but it lacks the connection to an explicit, possibly deeper meaning that can be seen in the visual art student's writing.

The Backpack Lesson in Sherelle's Class

Sherelle was introduced to the backpack lesson in her preservice training. As she began to teach in a culturally and socioeconomically diverse middle school, helping her students make strong connections and pathways for learning was Sherelle's goal as well. We turn now to her adaptation of the backpack lesson within her own classroom.

Sherelle taught her sixth-grade English language arts/reading classes in a rural school located between a major university town and a large metropolitan area. The students and the lesson we discuss in this section took place in the spring of her first year of teaching in which she taught on an interdisciplinary team that included a math/science teacher and a social studies teacher. During her preservice teacher education program, Sherelle was introduced to inclusive notions of literacy (Gee, 2003; New London Group, 2000) that incorporate visual thinking and arts-based strategies for reading and writing. Her education, which included Richard and Michelle as instructors, anticipated the diversity of students in her classroom. Forty-four percent of the students in her school met the federal standard for living in poverty. Her class was comprised of non-tracked students, of which 36 percent were persons of color and 36 percent spoke a language other than English at home (specifically, the students spoke Green Hmong, White Hmong, Ukrainian, and Spanish). To prepare Sherelle and her classmates for the challenges of working with children from a variety of linguistic backgrounds, her preservice education included explicit instruction in, and opportunities to practice, arts-based literacy activities, including the backpack lesson. For final assessments, Sherelle and her classmates submitted portfolios of their student teaching performance that included artwork together with more traditional language-based essays. Our qualitative study of Sherelle's teaching investigates her integration of these innovative, visual arts strategies into her classroom teaching.

In Sherelle's class, the backpack lesson took place over three days, with each class lasting eighty minutes within a block schedule. For the lesson, students completed both a drawing and an essay, which were then displayed on the walls of the classroom. Michelle acted in the roles of participant observer as a mentor to Sherelle, and as a second teacher, of both visual art and language arts, for the students in Sherelle's class. The lesson unfolded with the same progression of activities found in Ms. Bartels's lesson with Sherelle and Michelle using the same mantra—"Draw what you see, not what you think you see" to help students focus their looking and drawing. With desktops covered with large pieces of drawing paper, the students stood to make their drawings—their backpacks were propped on their chairs on the other side of the desks. Both Sherelle and Michelle helped students find the shapes within their backpacks by drawing in the air with fingers, then on paper with vine charcoal; and the lesson concluded with reading excerpts from O'Brien's (1992) short story and the students writing an essay about the tangible and intangible things they carried. Sherelle made two additions to the lesson. Before starting the drawings of geometric forms, she started by drawing an image on the board of a man stooped with the weight of a very large sack, informed by Shel Silverstein's (1974) poem and drawing "What's in the Sack?" Sherelle read the poem aloud to the class and gestured to the man drawn on the board. The students speculated about what might be in that sack and created a list of possible items the man might be carrying. Then Sherelle said, "Today we're going to think about what we carry in our own bags" and the drawing lesson began.

On day two of the lesson, Sherelle's second addition to the original lesson was a brief discussion about the concepts of tangible and intangible. While students were completing their drawings, she read O'Brien's short story excerpt, and then wrote the words *tangible* and *intangible* next to her drawing of the man with the very large sack. Students set aside their drawings briefly and engaged in Sherelle's brief mini-lesson on the meanings of these two words. She focused on the idea that one word represented "that which one can touch," and the other word is "that which one can perhaps feel but is harder to put a hand on." She asked students to identify tangible things the soldiers carried in the story and then identify two intangible things they carried. The students said love and terror were two things the soldiers carried: love for their sweethearts and families, and the terror of being seen as a coward. With this connection made to the short story, Sherelle then asked her students to generate a list of tangible items they carried in their own backpacks. Several items were listed on the board under the *tangible* word. Next, she asked them to help build a list of intangible ideas and emotions that corresponded with the tangible objects. For example, textbooks were associated with memory, music CDs with "meanings, memories, and songs," photos with love, and "bad letters to parents" with fear. With a completed list of examples on the board, Sherelle told students to take out a sheet of paper and write an essay about the tangible and intangible things they carried, all the while keeping their backpacks in plain sight and their drawings close at hand. The students wrote their essays for the remainder of the period and continued to write and revise the essays during the third day of the lesson.

The Drawing/Writing Compositions

In our study of Sherelle's sixth-grade students' compositions, we found that students were more fully engaged with the activity and wrote longer essays than in the previous term, became more focused in their approach to composing, were excited about this composition, and felt pride in their work. We found that engagement with language improved, especially in enhanced fluency and linguistic elaboration (i.e., ease in exploring and using language as well as developing narrative details). In general, students composed one-page essays, a length superseding any they had produced during the fall. Further, unlike early writing, these essays reflected what Sherelle characterized at the time as descriptive, rich, and personal writing.

For example, when Madison composed her drawing and essay (Figure 6.2) that she declared to be the "best thing I've done in school," she referred to both image and writing. Her essay follows:

In my purse I carry a lot of things. I carry pens, pencils, erasers, and [ ]. I also carry things that make me look nice and smell nice. These things are hair bows, deodorant, lipstick, baby lotion, and chapstick. I also carry love notes, notes from friends, and money in my tinkerbell wallet. Another thing I carry is very important to me. This thing is my cellphone that sits in my pocket, inside my purse.

In this purse I also carry dreams that become memories. Some dreams have come true, and now they can't be considered a dream any more. Now it's a memory that I can cherish for the [rest] of my life. I also carry questions about whose going to act like my friend or what's going to happen in class. I also carry my success and my reputation. I carry my success of being at school every day of the year and making good grades. I also carry my hope with me every where I go, inside my purse. I carry all these tangible and intangible things in my purse that means so much to me.

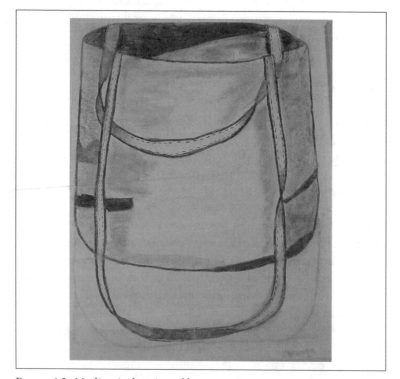

FIGURE 6.2. *Madison's drawing of her purse.*

Like the O'Brien (1992) text, she lists in quick succession the tangible things she carried: "pens, pencils, erasers . . . hair bows, deodorant, lipstick, baby lotion, and chapstick." In this list of tangibles, there is also an intangible quality similar to O'Brien; that is, Madison has included a similar cadence that is evident in O'Brien's listing of things. When O'Brien describes what the men carried, the litany of objects plays out like the march of their feet moving through the jungle. The students in Sherelle's class also put that cadence into their writing. The students began their essays by describing the many objects that had physical weight in their bags. Then they turned to the intangibles they carried: questions, hopes, memories, dreams, and reputations. Rachel wrote, "For every pencil I have a memory of my class and how much fun I had. . . . I have notes of the past and soon to be the future. My hopes and dreams are locked and waiting for the keys."

One of the English learners in the class, Katherine, wrote an essay that had fewer errors and greater complexity than any composition she had produced up to that point. Her essay and backpack drawing follows (Figure 6.3):

> In my backpack I carry my text books, my agenda, and my homework. I also carry a comb and a brush. I also carry chapstick just in case my lips get dry. I carry papers and pens so I can do my home work. In my back pack I carry drinks and snacks when I go in the bus I get hungry and so I eat my snack. In my back pack I carry my binder and my wallet so I can have money when I need some.
>
> In my back pack I carry questions like what we will do in school today, or if something exciting is gonna happen, or if I will get in trouble. In my back pack I carry hopes if we will do something exciting today or if we do a quiz today that I will get an "A" on it. When I come to [school] I carry my back pack with me.

Her essay described how she carried her books, papers, and pens, along with her questions about what she might learn each day, as well as her hopes for success in school. Her construction of both tangible and intangible are similar in construction to O'Brien's lists that include short explanations. For example, Katherine wrote, "I also carry chapstick just in case my lips get dry. I carry papers and pens so I can do my home work." The

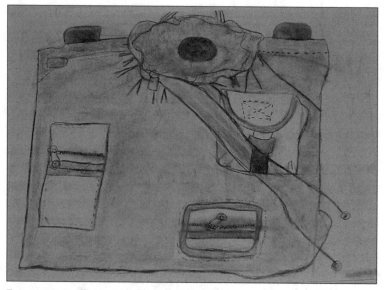

FIGURE 6.3. *Katherine's backpack drawing.*

students thus articulated the tangible and intangible weights they carried through both drawing and writing.

Beginning with a drawing and then moving to an essay provided students with a fresh type of experience for writing. The students had time to visually explore an image on days one and two of the lesson, then verbally explored their backpacks on days two and three of the lesson. The progression of the drawing/writing composition began with the tangible drawing or rendering of the physical object (the backpack), then moved to a discussion about connecting tangibles with intangibles, and finished with writing an essay about these felt objects and weighted ideas and emotions. The writing was based on the object, the drawing, listening to the O'Brien excerpt, the talk about tangible and intangible, and the list the students helped Sherelle to compile on the board. Attention to detail was necessary at every point within this lesson and each detail, whether it was drawn, written, or spoken aloud, was a chance for students to see their backpacks and what they carried through a different medium. Each step invited students to search visually and verbally for more details, to see their backpacks in a different way. This was a rigorous, thoughtful process of articulation.

Sherelle remarked that "No matter how hard [the drawing] was, they just kept going and trying and they created this wonderful thing that sparked them to write." That is, students were challenged, but not discouraged, by the drawing, and their visual accomplishment was a platform from which they then engaged in writing. The students' ability to stay engaged in the art making was due to at least two factors: the unconventional application of a nonlinguistic problem in a classroom where many students struggled with language, and Sherelle's application of Ms. Bartels's progression from tangible to intangible as a concept and as an action. As a result, students did not give up or disengage from the visual art task. Instead, students, with only minimal art instruction provided by Sherelle and Michelle, escalated rapidly into a high level of complexity and technical skill in their drawing. The drawings from Sherelle's class exhibited a level of specificity of detail in line, shape, texture, and shading that one would find in a group of drawings produced in a visual arts course for middle school students. Very few of Sherelle's students in this class were enrolled in visual arts, yet they produced well-developed drawings. This level of quality in the drawings and the concentration on really seeing what was carried led, in turn, to a higher level of rich detail and sophistication in the writing.

Sherelle describes the potential of this lesson to bring focus, pride, and excitement into her classroom:

> This lesson asked my students to do something that was challenging and difficult, but I saw there was a certain confidence within many of them and a willingness to try. Unlike other assignments in class, whether to do some brief writing or to work in their grammar workbooks, or even to work on some of the other arts-based activities we did with drama, this lesson felt different. The students were being asked to do something so different from what is normally expected in a language arts class. Instead of starting an assignment with reading a story or a novel while sitting at a desk and then writing an essay, this lesson started with the students standing up and facing not only their backpacks, but a huge sheet of paper. To draw something that big while using charcoal—a tool my students don't normally have access to in language arts class—was

unexpected. And the students' responses were positive. Like Ms. Bartels's students, some did voice their disbelief. But, they also stood up at their desks and started drawing. That's what I mean by confidence: They continued to try throughout the lesson, even though we kept asking the students to add details of line and shading.

I also saw focus in this lesson that was different from other activities. Throughout the year, I saw the students work on their writing in a focused way, but the backpack lesson stood out in the way the students focused on their work. I watched them as they stood to do their drawing. They were intently watching their book bags and watching their drawings and going back and forth from looking to drawing. And though art teachers may recognize this kind of focus as an everyday occurrence in their classrooms, this was different from all the other activities I taught that year in language arts. This focus that I saw there was amazing.

As the students worked, I also saw a lot of pride. Not only was the task challenging and different, it involved baring yourself on a huge piece of paper. Madison, one of the students, said to me, "This is the best thing I've done all year." I saw other students turn to each other and say, "Yeah, I love that" or "Look at yours!" And they said these things with smiles on their faces. It is this pride and attention that I would want to see them have with every assignment, whether it's drawing or whether it's writing or whether it's talking. This is the level of engagement and achievement that I want them to get to with every piece they write or at least some part of this focus and pride and willingness to step up to a challenge. Maybe students don't have to be proud of everything they write, but at least they can go through some of these steps toward building pride and concentration.

Finally, I saw excitement. They were excited to get started on it again as each day started. When we began the writing, which was not something that we had done a lot of that year, there were no complaints. Unlike other shorter writing assignments I gave, no one said, "How long does it have to be?" I don't think I heard that question because the students knew they were writing about this piece that they had created. They were going to tell as much as they needed to, and they didn't need me tell them how much was necessary.

The result of this willingness to try, focus, pride, and excitement translated into essays with interesting language. I talked with my colleagues and Michelle about the imagery and the sophisticated ways that they wrote. Compared to the writing that preceded it, the backpack essays were better quality writing. Doing the drawing first seemed to help the writing. Whether it was organized well because they had that tangible object to think about: "What is inside here and then what do those things inside relate to me?" or whether because they had focused on the shading or because they had attended to certain details of the backpack, they were able to pull that imagery and that really rich, detailed language into their writing, too. The work in the essay was to describe the thing they had spent so much time staring at and focusing their attention on. In the end, they look at the drawing and the essay as one piece, especially since each was displayed with both parts intact. Each student had a huge drawing and a full page of writing to describe the tangible and the intangible things they carried.

For Sherelle, there is potential for the backpack lesson to motivate students and encourage them to learn in a challenging but achievable activity. The students practiced seeing their backpacks and recording what they saw in both visual and verbal forms. Sherelle watched them look from bag to drawing and back again and then saw them share with their classmates their triumphs in accomplishing this active looking and thinking and feeling. For many of them, the drawing was as large as the backpack they carried to school each day. This process of seeing and re-seeing, drawing and writing, was a means of teaching students Murray's (1984) five-stage pathway of composition: collecting, focusing, and ordering details, then drafting and clarifying those details. Because this lesson moves from drawing to writing, the composition path mirrors the student meaning making path: begin with the tangible and focus on that to render the physical object of the backpack, then move to the intangible and focus on abstract details to render the emotional and metaphorical connections with the backpack.

Moving from Tangible to Intangible

The backpack lesson frames a specific pathway into language. It moves from perceptually tangible to the metaphoric and metonymic intangible. Students begin with the tangible in front of them; they draw the backpack. With the directive in the drawing, "draw what you see, not what you think you see," students become keyed into the details of their backpacks—the bulges of things resting inside the bag, the zippers open and unopened, the pockets empty or full, the straps and handles jutting from this edge or that side. This concrete backpack is the focus of their attention. They pass through the first two trap doors: (1) to draw the backpack in front of them, and (2) to add more details and shading to the drawing. As students work with charcoal, this medium inevitably ends up spreading across their fingers, a very tangible experience. Other tangible elements of this project include how they look at their bag, their practice of the motion of finding lines and shapes in the air with hands and arms, and the retranslation of this motion into those shapes and lines on the paper. Once the drawing is nearly complete, then the third trap door opens to the writing task ahead. Now the intangible can be addressed in these backpacks. As the students think about what they carry in their backpacks, they have two bags in front of them: the original, weighty backpack that they transfer back and forth to school each day, and the drawing of the backpack that they have just spent a couple of hours composing and reworking. The drawings evidence how the students worked through feeling the shape of their bags and paying attention to the minutest of details in those shapes. It is with the weight of these two tangible objects, drawing and bag, that the students then turn to language to explore further the tangibles and intangibles associated with the backpacks.

Implications

For students who struggle with language, an arts-based strategy of moving from the nonlinguistic to the linguistic can be a critical type of pedagogical intervention. Arts-based learning strategies are methods for explicitly teaching the parallel pathways of visual and linguistic thinking. Students learn how to move from the realm of visual thinking to the universe of oral and written language. The backpack lesson involves students thinking first visually about what they carry with them to school each day and then moves that thinking to a language-based thinking with the concepts of tangible and intangible. Furthermore, arts-based strategies can assist all students in reaching deeper and personally significant goals in linguistic composition. To have Madison, as well as another student in Sherelle's class, declare that the backpack drawing and essay represented their best work was to have those students thoughtfully involved with their school work. These two students also said that the drawings were evidence that that they could do something now that they thought they could not do before. The emotional engagement with learning (Intrator, 2003) evident in the essays and drawings constitutes an unintended but potentially more valuable outcome for the lesson: students discovering the excitement of learning and desiring to continue self-directed study in the nonschool hours.

As a lesson grounded in both visual art and language art, the backpack composition affords students two opportunities to collect, focus, order, draft, and clarify (Murray, 1984): first, with the visual information recorded in the drawing, then with the verbal information recorded in the essay. The lesson frames language and nonverbal visual thinking as parallel literacies. Nonverbal visual thinking recognizes that, even as adults, our first experience of the world is the recognition of perceived sensory relationships (Arnheim, 1969; Damasio, 1999; Dewey, 1958).

Nonverbal visual thinking requires attention to observed details of the visual environment, association with emotional responses, development of concepts through sketching, and revision of initial responses into a complete form of nonlinguistic representation. Visual media allows students to inscribe their nonverbal thinking in forms of representation (Dewey, 1934/1989; Eisner, 1994). The backpack lesson creates two parallel pathways for creating meaning—one visual, the other linguistic. By allowing students to link these two pathways in one lesson, there is the potential for deep engagement in writing (Fleckenstein, 2002).

Sherelle noted how the students, while collecting the qualities of shapes and lines, were focused in their looking, and they ordered their drawings to match the curves and valleys of the backpacks. Working with vine charcoal meant that the students could rub out any decision they no longer wanted in their drawing, but it left a trace of that decision. In Madison's drawing, for example, the trace of where she worked through the line of her purse's handle can be seen at the bottom of the image. As they continued to add darker lines and smooth out whiter areas, the students clarified their images. Likewise, the students began their work on the essays by collecting ideas about tangible and intangible in the large group discussion with Sherelle. Next, they focused on their own bags and began ordering the weight first in tangible items, then intangible qualities. In all the iterations of this lesson that we have taught, with students in elementary classrooms to doctoral students in universities, the essays always begin with the tangibles. The move from tangible to intangible, of collecting and ordering the objects and ideas from concrete to abstract is consistently represented in that order: tangible first, intangible second. The essays written in Sherelle's class were drafted on the second day, then clarified with peer-revision and editing on the third day. Thus, the students moved through their visual and linguistic work in similar pathways.

We are excited about the potential for the backpack lesson as a blending of visual and language arts and as a means to give students a hands-on, tangible approach to learning that can lead to improvement in writing. For us, the value of the backpack lesson lies in the conjoined visual and verbal thinking that produces both an image and an essay. This pairing of visual arts and language arts teaching, which balances sensory images with verbal language in ways that are productive for student achievement, helped Sherelle address state curriculum mandates for increasing literacy skills. The emotional and embodied combination of visual art and language promoted dynamic and inclusive cross-disciplinary pedagogical practices that furthered this young teacher's developing understanding of deep structures of knowledge.

Works Cited

Arnheim, R. (1969). *Visual thinking*. Berkeley: University of California Press.

Barone, T., & Eisner, E. W. (1997). Art-based educational research. In R. M. Jaeger (Ed.), *Complementary methods for research in education* (2nd ed., pp. 73–94). Washington, DC: American Educational Research Association.

Damasio, A. R. (1999). *The feeling of what happens: Body and emotion in the making of consciousness.* New York: Harcourt Brace.

Dewey, J. (1958). *Experience and nature.* New York: Dover.

———. (1989). Art as experience. In J. A. Boydston (Series Ed.), *John Dewey: The later works, 1925–1953* (Vol. 10: 1934, pp. 1–400). Carbondale: Southern Illinois University Press. (Original work published 1934)

Eisner, E. W. (1994). *Cognition and curriculum reconsidered* (2nd ed.). New York: Teachers College Press.

———. (2002). *The arts and the creation of mind.* New Haven, CT: Yale University Press.

Fleckenstein, K. S. (2002). Inviting imagery into our classrooms. In K. S. Fleckenstein, L. T. Calendrillo, & D. A. Worley (Eds.), *Language and image in the reading-writing classroom: Teaching vision* (pp. 3–26). Mahwah, NJ: Erlbaum.

Gee, J. P. (2003). *What video games have to teach us about learning and literacy.* New York: Palgrave Macmillan.

Greene, M. (2001). *Variations on a blue guitar: The Lincoln Center Institute lectures on aesthetic education.* New York: Teachers College Press.

Intrator, S. M. (2003). *Tuned in and fired up: How teaching can inspire real learning in the classroom.* New Haven, CT: Yale University Press.

Murray, D. M. (1984). *Write to learn.* New York: Holt, Rinehart, and Winston.

New London Group. (2000). A pedagogy of multiliteracies: Designing social futures. In B. Cope & M. Kalantzis (Eds.), *Multiliteracies: Literacy learning and the design of social futures* (pp. 9–36). New York: Routledge.

O'Brien, T. (1992). The things they carried. In J. C. Oates (Ed.), *The Oxford book of American short stories* (pp. 636–654). New York: Oxford University Press.

Olson, J. L. (2005). Becoming a member of a professional language learning community. In J. Flood, S. B. Heath, & D. Lapp (Eds.), *Handbook of research on teaching literacy through the communicative and visual arts* (pp. 417–427). Mahwah, NJ: Erlbaum.

Siegesmund, R. (1999). Reasoned perception: Aesthetic knowing in pedagogy and learning. *Arts and Learning Research, 15*(1), 35–51.

———. (2000). *Reasoned perception: Art education at the end of art* (Unpublished doctoral dissertation). Stanford University, School of Education, Stanford, CA.

———. (2005). Teaching qualitative reasoning: Portraits of practice. *Phi Delta Kappan, 87*(1), 18–23.

Siegesmund, R., & Cahnmann-Taylor, M. (2008). The tensions of arts-based research reconsidered: The promise for practice. In M. Cahnmann-Taylor & R. Siegesmund (Eds.), *Arts-based research in education: Foundations for practice* (pp. 231–246). New York: Routledge.

Silverstein, S. (1974). *Where the sidewalk ends: The poems and drawings of Shel Silverstein* (1st ed.). New York: Harper and Row.

Stiggins, R., Arter, J., Chappuis, J., & Chappuis, S. (2004). *Classroom assessment for student learning: Doing it right—using it well.* Portland, OR: Assessment Training Institute.

Zoss, M. (2007). *Integrating visual and language arts: A case study of a teacher composing a curriculum* (Unpublished doctoral dissertation). University of Georgia, Athens, GA.

———. (2009). Visual arts and literacy. In L. Christenbury, R. Bomer, & P. Smagorinsky (Eds.), *Handbook of adolescent literacy research* (pp. 183–196). New York: Guilford.

Zoss, M., & Jones, S. (2007). Enhancing literary reading through visual and language arts practices. In A. O. Soter, M. Faust, & T. Rogers (Eds.), *Interpretive play: Using critical perspectives to teach young adult literature* (pp. 191–209). Norwood, MA: Christopher-Gordon.

CHAPTER SEVEN

Reading Art, Reading Lives: An Interpretive Study of the Visual Texts of Urban English Language Arts Students

PEGGY ALBERS
Georgia State University

In one urban first-grade classroom, students sat on the floor in silent anticipation, waiting for their teacher, Ms. Reynolds, to read a picture book. Ms. Reynolds held up the picture book, and on its cover was a beautifully illustrated pirate with a parrot on his shoulder standing aboard his ship. Ms. Reynolds invited students to share their predictions about the book. Wild and waving hands immediately caught Ms. Reynolds's attention; she then called on several students to share their thoughts. Afterward, Ms. Reynolds began reading Mem Fox's (1998) *Tough Boris*, the story of a pirate named Boris who was fearless. Following this reading and a short discussion of the story, Ms. Reynolds invited me to present a mini-workshop in clay with her 6- and 7-year-olds, a medium these children had not yet experienced and one through which they would present their interpretation of Fox's story. Clay was apt for this engagement because it is malleable and one in which their ideas could be worked and reworked.

Holding up her clay sculpture (Figure 7.1), Lashonda demonstrated the intimate relationship between the maker of a visual text, the visual text itself, and other texts that inform this sculpture. At once, Lashonda positioned herself as a maker of signs, objects that reference her interests in and interpretation of *Tough Boris*. At the same time, the clay sculpture itself informed the viewer about Lashonda as a reader. The details in the written text that Lashonda chose to include in her visual text were both intimately related. In her short presentation, Lashonda indicated that she had sculpted Boris's boat and his parrot. By Lashonda's naming the parts of her sculpture, viewers willingly accepted her description of the undulating clay slab as the ship's deck. Older and adult viewers knew that the decks of ships are not made of clay, nor do they undulate. But in her use of clay, by nature a three-dimensional medium, Lashonda captured realistic details of both the deck and the ship in motion. For her, a wobbly slab of clay was an apt signifier, or material form, through which she could visually express the signified, or the meaning, she gleaned. Upon viewing, the viewer was poised to ask questions about this visual text: What do the other objects in this clay text mean (sticks, bits of construction paper)? Why did she create the image that she did? What is the context that shaped this text? Why did she organize the elements in the way that she did? What story or idea is she attempting to describe? Lashonda's text, one of approximately 130 texts, situates this study, which focuses on the analysis of urban students' visual texts created in English language arts (ELA) classrooms. In general, I wanted to understand, "What types of visual texts are created in ELA classrooms, and what can be learned about the literacy practices of students through close readings and analyses of their visual texts?" Since visual texts are common in ELA classes and are rarely, if ever, analyzed from a perspective outside of aesthetics, this study holds strong interest for both educators and researchers.

Relevant Literature

In the past few years, technology, in particular the Internet, has enabled us to present images to anyone, anywhere, and we can now think of ourselves "not just as viewers and consumers of images but as makers and users of them ourselves" (Dillon, 2000). However, too often, nonprint-based data collected in ELA classrooms go unanalyzed because of educators' lack of techniques for analyzing visual texts (Albers, 2006a), and thus, viewers (both teachers and students) often default to a self-constructed aesthetic response in making sense of these data. Visual representations in

FIGURE 7.1. *Lashonda and her pirate ship made of clay.*

ELA classes are commonplace; however, they are often treated superficially or ignored (Hobbs & Frost, 2003). Further, reading and writing continue to be the communication systems valued by ELA teachers, especially with the onslaught of national testing and accountability. When integrated into ELA classrooms, art is often used as a catalyst to develop strong readers and writers (Carger, 2004; Murata, 1997; Piro, 2002), rather than as viewed as a way to understand students' past and present literacy practices.

The role of art as a catalyst in the development of literacy skills has been articulated extensively in the literature.[1] Early work done by Graves (1973, 1975), Calkins (1983, 1986), Dyson (1983, 1984, 1985, 1986, 1987, 1988) and Olshansky (1994a, 1994b, 1994c, 1995, 1997) suggested that the visual arts support the writing process for the emergent writer. In her ethnographic study, Hubbard (1989, 1990) investigated the interrelation between visual and verbal systems. She found that each system informed the other when children constructed meaning and that development in both systems was enhanced. Writing from an arts-advocacy position, a number of researchers recounted how art informed and expanded meaning potential in literacy learning when the arts were a viable catalyst in representation (Albers, 1996, 1997; Albers & Murphy, 2000; Flynn, 2002; Greenway, 1996; Katzive, 1997; Landay et al., 2001; Murray, 1997; Noden & Moss, 1995; Pfannenstiel et al., 2003; Smith & Herring, 1996).

Studies of learners' visual texts as culturally situated visual representations of their thoughts, beliefs, and experiences are scarce, yet those published provide insight into the cognitive role of the arts (Eisner, 2002). The arts often make visible "gender-stereotypical" images in preschool and kindergarten children (Boyatzis & Eades, 1999; Tuman, 1999) and in middle grade students (Albers, 1996). Holloway and LeCompte (2001) found that training middle grade students, especially girls, in the theater and symbolic arts supported their attempt to "try on new ways of being" that then offered them new perspectives on the roles and careers they might imagine (p. 388). In his study of elementary boys, Newkirk (2002) disproved the simplistic stereotype of boys who were primed to imitate the violence they see, but found that boys most often transformed, recombined, and participated in story lines of the texts in popular culture. These studies, as well as others, suggest a direct link between learners' visual renderings and conscious and unconscious cognitive links to learning and their social environment.

In a world dominated by visual texts, it is not surprising that scholars increasingly recognize the importance of studying the visual in literacy research (Kress & van Leeuwen, 2006). Although research cited here positions the visual arts as integral in the study of literature, language, and learners' lives, less work has been done that specifically addresses what types of visual texts learners create in ELA classes. Further, few studies clearly articulate methods for analyzing such texts, but encouragingly, some work is being done. Marsh (1999, 2000) analyzed the significance of popular culture figures on children's understanding of gender and identity. Oppositional readings helped children develop different narratives, especially around popular culture superheroes. In her work with young children, Moss (2001) studied children's photographs of reading in the home, finding significant differences in how boys and girls documented and represented reading. Pahl (2007) studied children's texts as multimodal artifacts that identified "*traces* of practice, and as instantiations of identities" (Pahl,

2007, p. 87) and showed how systematic analysis of these texts indicated *sedimented identities in text* (Rowsell & Pahl, 2007, p. 388). Across this work, researchers and teachers collectively have shown the significance of studying the dynamic and interactive nature of children's image production within classroom contexts as a crucial part of literacy curriculum and a more complex understanding of literacy practices, work that is long overdue in the field of ELA instruction and research.

Social Semiotics: A Theoretical Perspective

To situate the readings of visual texts created in ELA classes theoretically, this study is located in social semiotics, a study of sign-making and its social dimensions (Hodge and Kress, 1988; Kress & van Leeuwen, 2006). Close readings or interpretations of visual representations involve the analysis of the visual text, the discourses that shape it (Gee, 2005), and the cultural experiences that inform them. Social semiotics is derived from the work in semiotics, a theory that explores the nature and function of signs as well as the systems and processes underlying signification, expression, representation, and communication. According to Hodge and Kress, the smallest semiotic unit is the *message* that has directionality—a source and goal, a social context and purpose. Groups of messages pass between objects or signs in a semiotic act. *Text* and *discourse* are generally used to describe this larger unit of semiotics. Hodge and Kress define a text as "a structure of messages or message traces which has a socially ascribed unity" (p. 6), and discourse "refers to the social process in which texts are embedded . . . text is the material object produced in discourse" (p. 6). In opposition to text, another important semiotic concept, *system*, is construed as a collection of signs that operate together and generally is treated as static. However, Hodge and Kress argue that, within systems, signs have value and place and are continually being reproduced and reconstituted in texts. Texts, according to Halliday (1985), are in a dialectal relation with context; the text creates the context as much as the context creates the text. Meaning arises from the friction between the two. Thus, texts can be critically examined to reveal discourses in operation and the contestation of meanings in institutions (Halliday, 1978; Hodge and Kress, 1988; Kress, 1985, 1988).

General forms of texts and discourses are constrained by rules within logonomic systems in which there is a concern for the struggle for control of knowledge (Hodge & Kress, 1988). Such systems, they continue, operate by "specifying *genres* of texts" (p. 7) by which producers of said texts and consumers are controlled by their rules and defined and enforced by a social group. For example, in schools, the five-paragraph essay is taught to all ages of students. The texts that are produced within this genre lay out a set of practices, consideration of audience, and purposes. Within these texts emerge such genres as narrative, memoir, biography, and persuasion, and this genre becomes generative, each with its own coded set of rules and sets of relationships to social participants (Hodge & Kress, 1988). Such rule systems in the five-paragraph genre are clear and have been set by those in dominant positions (Educational Testing Service, textbook authors and publishers, prescriptive writing programs, etc.). Genre, then, becomes a semiotic category that codes the effects of social change and struggle (p. 7), codes that also apply to visual texts created in school settings.

Since many of the visual texts in ELA classes are pictures, Sonesson's (1988, 2004) principles of reading pictures, located in pictorial semiotics, provide a useful tool in analyzing visual texts. Fundamentally, each picture is a sign, and each picture is made up of smaller signs. Sonesson argues that individual signs, like in written language, are meaningless before they are made to form wholes, but unlike written language, the meaning of the whole is redistributed back to the parts (Sonesson, 2004). Kress and van Leeuwen (2006) suggest that pictures reveal different processes: narrative, classificational, analytical, and symbolic. Narrative processes suggest that there is interaction between and among various objects within a visual text and often tell a story. Classificational processes suggest that information is organized in particular ways; a taxonomy in which objects relate to each other with some objects referring to a conceptually broader object. Analytical processes relate objects from part-to-whole; a conceptually broader object is the center of attention, while other objects explain its purpose or its being. Symbolic processes, or what an object or concept means or is, suggest there must be some knowledge of the symbol and its relationship to the concept produced in order for meaning to occur (Sonesson, 2004).

Research Design

This interpretive study took place in seven urban classrooms in a large metropolitan area in the South: two classes in two elementary schools, two classes in two middle schools, and three classes in two high schools; class numbers ranged from fifteen to thirty students. Six schools are located within the perimeter, the freeway that encircles the city; all are racially and economically diverse, although one of the high schools, outside the perimeter, had a significantly larger middle- to upper-class European American population. In all of the schools, especially the elementary and middle schools, little or no time was allotted for "specials" or subjects such as art. If art was a part of the curriculum, it was often limited to less than one hour per week and/or integrated into English language arts curricula. In the high schools, art was an elective. Several specific questions guided this study: (1) What genres emerge in visual texts that learners produce in ELA classes; (2) Using methods of visual analysis, what relationships exist between marks on the canvas and the signmaker; and (3) What insights can be gleaned from students' literacy practices?

Role of the Researcher and Entry into Setting

My interest in literacy and the arts spans thirty-five years and began with my own experience in art, drama, and music at home and school, and evolved with my first teaching position as a drama director and teacher. My dissertation research (Albers, 1996) in a middle school art classroom focused attention on semiotic processes in visual representation. My ongoing study of the visual arts, especially in drawing, painting, and clay, as an artist-writer (Albers, 2001, 2004, 2006a, 2006b, 2007a, 2007b, 2009; Albers & Harste, 2007), continues. My researcher role was that of participant-observer (Glesne & Peshkin, 1992), sometimes in the role of team teacher who demonstrated art techniques. Over the course of the year, I spent at least three consecutive days with the teacher and the participants in their classroom. In each of these classes, I sat with and among both large and small groups of participants as they designed and produced texts and talked, and I engaged them in talk and/or posed questions about their processes and visual elements in their texts.

Classrooms, Teachers, and Participants

All teachers in this study organized their ELA instruction to provide space for the production of visual texts, and they encouraged visual representations as a means by which students could share understanding by incorporating art materials they personally purchased. Teachers in this study worked with a range of students from English learners, struggling readers and writers, and honors students. All art projects were designed around a theme or a core text, and students were asked to respond visually to issues within written texts. Participants in this study (N = 130) are representative of urban students with whom I have worked over the years and fall within a wide range demographically in terms of ethnicity, class, and ability. Less than 5 percent of the participants had art instruction beyond elementary school. One kindergarten class and one sixth-grade class were given approximately twenty minutes and forty minutes of instruction in clay, respectively, which I delivered, prior to their construction of sculptural representations in clay.

Data Collection and Analysis

Although I used a range of interpretive methods to collect data (observation, fieldnotes, interviews, photographs, visual texts), I report only on the analysis of participant-produced visual texts generated from teacher-designed art projects in response to a written narrative and/or expository text or texts (novels, topic or theme, Greek myths). As Bogdan & Biklen (1992) suggest, my analysis of data was ongoing and recursive, and social semiotic in nature, guided by my research questions and literature in the field. Based on earlier studies of students' visual texts (Albers, 1996, 2006, 2007a, 2007b), I entered these settings with more focused questions in mind and designed an analysis that differed from similar research in this area. My analysis, informed by two researcher journals, one with field notes and the other in which I integrated written analysis with image, proved to be generative. Photos of visual texts alongside written analysis (interpretative and structural) generated inter- and intra-modal insights about these data. Neither set of data was completely written or visual. Rather, both types of data necessarily became part of the social semiotic landscape (Kress & van Leeuwen, 2006) that I was interpreting.

Close readings of visual texts implored the use of visual tools of analysis developed by Kress and van Leeuwen (2006), Bang (2000), and Sonesson (2004), in particular. In general, I analyzed texts in light of: (1) common features, organized these features, and identified three genres that emerged time and time again across visual texts; (2) the signified, or the meanings in each text, as well as the signifiers, or forms; (3) literary texts that generated these compositions; and (4) social settings in which visual texts were produced.

Findings and Analysis

Findings from this study suggested that: (1) texts tended to fall into three specific genres: aesthetic, narrative, and metaphoric; (2) texts had schematic, prototypical, and/or metaphoric structures; and (3) messages sent through visual texts located discourses within the context and culture in which they were constructed. Classifying or categorizing visual texts charts new territory in literacy research, and to name genres within visual texts is clearly chancy but initiates a needed discussion in which visual language is integral in studying learners' literacy practices (Albers, 2007a; 2007b).

Aesthetic Texts

Aesthetics is a field in philosophy concerned with perception, sensation, and imagination, and how they relate to knowing, understanding, and feeling about the world (Greene, 2001). The question, "What is art good for?" locates aesthetics in a discussion between its worth as a way of feeling about the world and its impact on cognition (Eisner, 2002). All visual texts in this study fell into this genre of aesthetic texts because each had a significant form, whether it was two- or three-dimensional, and all provoked an emotional response of sorts. However, aesthetic texts differed from narrative and metaphoric in that the signmaker's intention and interest lay primarily in the text as an aesthetic object; these texts were assessed on such characteristics as *creativity, imagination,* and *neatness,* aesthetic terms that guided class discussions and rubrics for evaluation of visual texts.

After reading *Lord of the Flies* (Golding, 1959), a tenth-grade teacher offered her students five different arts-based projects, a practice familiar to her students. The work would be evaluated on terms associated with aesthetics and characteristics listed previously. In Figure 7.2, Jill chose the poetry project and produced pictures that included original poetry as well as design elements to highlight her writing. Jill's use of various media was immediately visible: construction paper, pencil color, white paper, pencil, and cotton, all collectively and physically related through an overlapping technique. In addition, Jill created two fairly realistic original drawings, one in which Ralph, a protagonist in the novel, was figuratively and literally under fire and a dark cloud of smoke, referents to the survival theme, and a pencil drawing in grayscale of two eyes that stared straight ahead with a single teardrop under the right eye. Together these objects formed a complete picture, a sign, one which was located both in her interpretation of Golding's novel and her stated desire to create an aesthetic object. Cognitively, Jill wrote poetry that linked to the theme of survival and supported it with drawings of fire and Ralph's eyes. At the same time, she effectively positioned the viewer to read the poetry and see the drawings and decoratively cut construction paper as an aesthetic object. Consciously, Jill linked the aesthetic with details in the story, yet, overall, Jill intended to create a lovely text, an art object to be enjoyed by the viewer or reader. Close readings of participants' texts indicated that aesthetics most commonly drove their interests and intentions. Visual elements served primarily to evoke aesthetic emotions, and rubrics guided media choices and how media were organized on the canvas. In

FIGURE 7.2. *Jill's poetry project using various media.*

aesthetic texts, participants made visible the predominant school discourse of art as decoration and revealed their perception of art's place in curriculum.

Narrative Texts

Narrative texts, a second genre of texts that emerged, implied an unfolding of events, and the vectors (Kress & van Leeuwen, 2006) between the action and the people were often very strong. In visual narratives, signmakers placed value on particular objects through size, gaze, mass, volume, color, and/or position on the canvas, while shapes of objects gestured toward signmakers' intentions, for example, to show unity in contrast to separation. Participants produced three types of visual narrative structures: graphically organized texts (implicit/explicit), descriptive texts (captured and fixed moments in action), and multi-phasic texts (Sonesson, 1988).

Graphically organized texts, primarily two-dimensional and with the intention of telling a story, were identified by participants' use of connectors such as lines and arrows to link objects explicitly, or those that did not use explicit connectors but implied a link among objects. Descriptive texts, both two- or three-dimensional, visually represented a single recognizable captured moment or action in the literary text and showed a dense relationship between objects. Three-dimensional texts indicated the signmaker's particular interest in spatial relationships among objects. Multi-phasic texts (Sonesson, 1988) were single static pictures containing many individual signs organized together to represent phases or events, actions, and/or details in the literary text. Objects were layered atop, below, alongside, and overlapped in the picture, with the collage representative of its primary structure.

GRAPHICALLY ORGANIZED TEXTS

Figures 7.3 and 7.4 represent graphically organized texts, explicit and implicit, respectively, created by eighth graders in response to *To Kill a Mockingbird* (Lee, 1988) and *Animal Farm* (Orwell, 1996). Participants in Jack's class (Figure 7.3) were directed to visually represent a part of the novel they thought was descriptive and orally present their visual text. Participants in Jordie's class (Figure 7.4) were directed to visually represent their interpretation of the whole novel and describe their visual text in writing.

Jack's visual text (Figure 7.3) *explicitly* connects various magazine cutouts, using arrows, to represent a part of Lee's novel that he wished to present. The size and volume of each of the objects literally carried the "weight" of the overall picture, and pointed to Jack's interests to depict main characters, their hobbies, and the setting. The top three images had strong directionality that moved from left-to-right and top-to-bottom and, collectively, told his story of one event in Lee's novel. Objects in this semiotic system had distinct identities; that is, each could tell a story of its own; yet when Jack joined them with arrows, their separate identities disappeared and narration became visible. To eliminate ambiguity for his viewers, he "fixed" his meaning (Barthes, 1967) through his use of arrows that directed a viewer's reading from

FIGURE 7.3. *Jack's visual text uses magazine clippings to represent parts of* To Kill a Mockingbird.

one specific image to another to create a narrative. Such graphically organized texts suggested a syntactic configuration (Kress & van Leeuwen, 2006) in which visual language was organized and structured grammatically to tell a story.

Jordie's representation of *Animal Farm* (Figure 7.4) is also graphically organized but, unlike Jack, she *implies* the connections among the animals to tell her story. Objects collectively represented a part of the whole of *Animal Farm* while individual objects acted as participants in the whole (Kress & van Leeuwen, 2006). This picture was schematic; Jordie's signs were rendered descriptively (viewers could identify the animals based upon Jordie's marks on the page), but their relationships were not. The viewer must imply the relationships that existed among signs. With equal placement of objects on the canvas, viewers were visually cued to the relationship that existed among the animals; some story was being told. Jordie's writing fixed the picture through language: "This picture means all the animals are living together." This aspect of the picture as a whole created a similarity among the objects, and the overall impression should have been somewhat harmonious. However, particularly noticeable were the animals'

FIGURE 7.4. *Jordie's representation of* Animal Farm.

outward and direct gazes at the viewers. The animals, including the bird in the profile, stared from behind the canvas and straight into the eyes of the viewers, now locked into position on the frontal side of the canvas. In essence, Jordie created disharmony by her use of confrontational stares and indicated that perhaps not all animals were "trying to get along."

DESCRIPTIVE TEXTS

Brittney produced a descriptive narrative text in her depiction of the shooting of a rabid dog scene from *To Kill a Mockingbird* (Lee, 1988) (Figure 7.5). In such texts, participants visually, and clearly, show a recognizable scene from the literary text in which all elements in this prototypical text are densely related. No ob-

FIGURE 7.5. *Brittney's illustration of the rabid dog scene from* To Kill a Mockingbird.

ject can exist outside the other without changing the meaning. Because viewers were familiar with the signs Brittney used (lawn, window, window shade, house, etc.), and if they knew the novel, they could interpret this text without fixing the meaning with written or oral language. Whereas Jack's and Jordie's visual texts were static and conceptual, Brittney's was dynamic and dramatic. The signs in Brittney's picture suggested a close visual rendering of the written text and brought to life this tension-filled scene. Visual elements were brought into directional transaction from Scout to the open yard, the rabid dog and the sheriff and Atticus, and the open yard and the town (see arrows). The locative relation was realized through Brittney's use of color, thin and thick lines, realistic objects, and literal framing of the scene; viewers saw the action from both inside and outside the house. Brittney's use of pencil color and paper, curved lines, and perspective was apt and plausible for her desire to show this horrific scene but visually softened the action in this text. Viewers may be horrified by the necessary action of the sheriff and Atticus, but the curved lines in the road, the curves of the hill, and the distance between inside and outside served to suppress some of a viewers' anxiety. In narrative literary texts, action verbs create drama, whereas in visual texts, vectors, size, and location of objects serve this purpose. The message that Brittney intended to send to the viewers was one that evoked tension and uncertainty. Scout as object had volume and weight, and the eye falls immediately to the bottom right hand side of the picture. Yet the action of smaller objects (Atticus, the sheriff, and the dog) reads left-to-right and top-to-bottom. Scout's size as object and her perspective contributed to the strength of the vector that moved from her to the men in the yard. Visually, her gripped hand on the windowsill dramatically signified the tension of the action outside.

More so than earlier presented texts, Brittney masterfully controlled and positioned the viewer in the same visual space as Scout. She rendered Atticus and the sheriff in the "effective center of attention" (Bang, 2000), and viewers were obligated to look at them. While Jordie's animals (Figure 7.4) looked out from beyond the canvas and locked viewers into position, Brittney's visual text pulled viewers into Scout's space, and viewers, together with the main character, burrow into the surface of the canvas to have a close look at the action. Brittney's use of scale, shown through the large drawing of Scout in relation to other objects, and placement in the bottom right hand corner, anchored, or grounded, this image (Bang, 2000) and made the main character the most significant part of this particular scene in Lee's novel.

MULTI-PHASIC TEXTS

Multi-phasic texts (Sonesson, 1988) are defined as a single static picture containing many individual signs organized together, in both physical construction and message, to represent phases or events, actions, and details in the literary text. Multi-phasic texts primarily take on the structure of collage, with large numbers of objects in a dense relationship to tell a story, and participants always using cut out magazine images as primary signifiers (Albers, 2007a). Multi-phasic texts were frequently evident in participants' responses to themes in literary texts or in redesigns of book covers.

Figure 7.6 represents Soje's multi-phasic text (Albers, 2007a) produced after her reading of *Lord of the Flies* (Golding, 1959). Arrangement, position, and size of the objects on the canvas referenced the higher value Soje afforded to some signs than others. The pattern in her text read top-to-bottom as well as circular and spiral. INDIFFERENCE (at top) TO NATURE (at bottom) was a sign that was intentionally split (seemingly to initiate the circular pattern) that then spiraled clockwise from SURVIVE to EARTH, which then spiraled into the text's center, *danger*. Soje's use of size and perspective in conjunction confirmed the spiral pattern. The viewer's eye perceived an immediate size difference between INDIFFERENCE/TO NATURE and *danger*, and perspective reinforced the great distance between the two objects. The illusion of three-dimension was created from such spiral patterns. Like

FIGURE 7.6. *Soje's multi-phasic text based on* Lord of the Flies.

Jordie's *Animal Farm* text (Figure 7.4) in which vectors created the illusion of three-dimensionality between viewer and text, Soje also created this illusion through her similar use of space around the canvas. The spiral pattern pushed *danger* into the space behind the canvas, likening it to the stretching of plastic with a blunt object. Viewers can recognize the inward movement of this spatial arrangement of cutouts and can sense its three-dimensionality. Through this pattern, Soje represented phases, events, and actions in the novel.

Visual objects that identified the setting of this novel in nature literally covered the canvas surface, each with its own identity yet, paradoxically, stripped of its identity at the same time. Soje's text was and had to be constructed in layers. She cut apart visual images that referenced nature from magazines. These images had some essence of completeness; she then pasted them onto the canvas. Objects once whole before their cutting now collided and overlapped on the canvas, losing part of their initial identity. Yet because of image convergence, these objects collectively and prototypically related to each other and took on new meaning and a more complete message: the destruction of civilization depicted in the novel. Soje's sign-making was multi-phasic both in terms of its construction as well as its intended meaning. Such design was conscious and seemingly referenced Rosenblatt's (1995) transaction theory in which readers of both written and visual texts move between and among phases of interpretation.

Close readings of visual narrative texts indicated that the signmakers wanted to tell a story. They included various aspects of a literary text such as details, themes, characters, and so on. How participants told their stories differed, from schematic to prototypical, and was often dependent on their knowledge of art as a system of communication. Although neither had advanced art training, Brittney and Jordie knew something about the techniques in drawing, which served as apt signifiers to express their meaning. Jack and Soje used magazine images to produce graphically organized and multi-phasic texts, again apt for the messages they wished to convey. Visual objects in narrative texts take on power positions, sometimes interchangeably, especially in terms of size, placement, volume, and color. Written text layered on top of visual objects fixed Soje's meaning. Written language overrode messages conveyed by visual objects. Conversely, the visual positioning of written text objects elicited a spiral pattern, unique to art, threw the text into three-dimension, and enabled Soje to convey her interpretation of the destruction of civilization. Brittney's use of mass, volume, and perspective identified visual language's power to physically and literarily position viewers to take on the same perspective as Scout and Brittney.

METAPHORIC TEXTS

Metaphoric texts are experienced as unified objects or *gestalts* and are understood to be something else due to the visual context in which they are depicted. Forceville (2004) described four different types of pictorial metaphors, but only the *embodied metaphor* emerged in participants' visual texts. The embodied metaphor has a *target* that is represented in a physically possible way so that it resembles another thing, the *source*. The presentation of one object representing another on equal planes usually signals a metaphor and thus links intention of the producer to depict this language convention. That viewers can identify said metaphors in visual texts (or texts produced in any sign system) further realizes the intention of the signmaker to produce such texts. Embodied metaphors emerged in all classes and across all age groups and operated similarly in visual texts as they do linguistic.

Figure 7.7, produced by Elizabeth, a tenth-grade Korean girl who had been in the United States three years, is representative of a metaphoric text. After reading *Lord of the Flies* (Golding, 1959), she signified the meaning of blindness and sight through visual metaphors, the eye and the conch. Elizabeth's intention as a signmaker was clearly metaphorical; absence of context clues around the visual text made it recognizable to those who were familiar with Golding's novel. Elizabeth's target was the conch in the pupil of the eye, while the source was the theme represented, blindness and sight. Metaphoric texts, such as Elizabeth's, were meant to be read as a whole, and were analytical. Knowledge of conventions such as top-to-bottom and left-to-right was not essential. However, the power of an embodied metaphor lay in its potential to elicit from its viewers, who recognized the metaphor's reference, probable meanings that lay beneath the visual

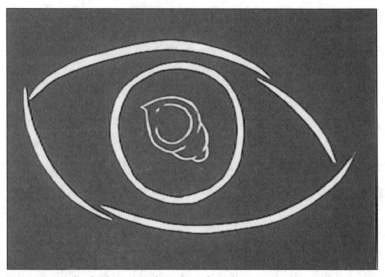

FIGURE 7.7. *Elizabeth's metaphoric text based on* Lord of the Flies.

markings. Unlike narrative texts, embodied metaphors expect that viewers know something about the metaphor's origin and why it was made. All classmates had read this novel, and therefore, Elizabeth's metaphor was transparent and more easily read.

All objects in embodied metaphors must be in relationship to form the complete meaning of the signmaker and, conversely, the whole must reference parts to derive a more complete analysis of the metaphor. Elizabeth's metaphor, read as a whole, led to a discussion of blindness and sight. Yet the meaning of the whole was redistributed to the parts. The eye signaled the capacity for sight, while the conch obstructed the perceived pupil and signaled blindness. Elizabeth's use of the eye, outlined in white against a black backdrop dramatically set up the oppositional forces that drove the protagonists to their doom. The upward turn of the eye gave directionality to the metaphor (Bang, 2000), one that suggested hope within utter chaos. Knowledge of the context in which the embodied metaphor was produced seemed essential to analyze such visual texts: the conch and eye were recognizable objects, and Elizabeth was able to convey her message more clearly and completely.

Discussion

John Dewey (1934) argued many years ago that the study of art objects necessitates a study of the experience and environment in which these objects are produced. Such analyses are just now being done in ELA research. A focus on identification of genre in visual texts lends support to the contention that written language structures and ideological constructs are predominant in all aspects of participants' representations. In ELA classes, children learn to distinguish between and among genres located in written language. They learn how to identify characteristics particular to narrative and expository genres, as well as subgenres such as memoir, biography, and autobiography. Over time, and often to educators' delight, these characteristics are internalized and reconstituted and reproduced in texts, regardless of which semiotic system is referenced. In this study, genres (narrative), structures of representation (implicit/explicit graphically organized texts), and clear visual production of literary terms (metaphor) common to literature emerged in the analysis of visual texts, more predictably than I had anticipated prior to this study.

Analysis of visual texts using visual analytical tools of artists, linguists, and social semioticians reflects the significance of close readings of these texts. Visual texts must be considered in light of what they can visually say or not say. That is the beauty of social semiotic readings. Such readings assume the potential of individual sign systems to say what others are incapable of saying. In this study, participants' visual texts reflected the unique properties of sign systems to carry particular meanings. This sets up art as a sign system in which some things can be expressed only visually. Spiral and circular patterning, power relations among and between objects, perspective, and control of viewers' responses are several of the unique properties that visual language brought to messages conveyed by participants. Cues in visual texts identified both the intention and the interests of the signmaker. To ignore such cues is to ignore the contexts that give rise to such cues. Informed and studied readings offer different and important insights into the signified, or the meaning that learners bring to their representations. Further, signifiers, or the forms of representation, give rise to the importance of medium to express the desired message. Young participants, such as Lashonda, are positioned as unique signmakers especially when given a range of media, familiar and unfamiliar, from which they can choose. Opportunities to represent in a range of media encourage both flexibility and invention in sign-making and sign-interpretation in learners (Albers & Murphy, 2000). Cultural meanings or value placed on media are not yet recognized by young children, and media, therefore, opens up interpretation to more experimental use of form to fit their desired message. Older participants, such as Jill, Jack, Brittney, and Soje, are more aware of the cultural meanings associated with form and media, may be less apt to explore media unfamiliar to them, or may use media about which they have familiarity (paper, pencil color, pencils, cutouts, stencils, and so on) or in which they show some technical skill. That all participants used common classroom media, even in texts constructed outside of classrooms, suggests the domination of certain media as acceptable for representations in classes and may limit learners' flexibility both to create new signs and/or interpret new signs when encountered (Albers & Murphy, 2000). Important to learners' understanding of literacy is the significance of exploration of new and unfamiliar signs, especially in visual texts, and opportunities to use visual analytical tools, such as a grammar of visual design (Kress & van Leeuwen, 2006), to talk about, study, and talk back to visual texts produced in classes. An ability to do close readings of visual texts will apprentice learners, and teachers and researchers alike, into the discourse of art and discourses (Gee, 2000) that emerge in visual texts. Learners will begin to talk about visual texts as they do literary texts. Line, perspective, and color will find an avenue into a range of texts produced in ELA classes, especially multimedia texts that cut across sign systems.

Brought to light in this study is the significance of the signifier and the signified. Soje's use of magazine images, to Brittney's use of pencil color, to Jordie's use of graphite all signal the relationship between what is said to how it is said. Soje's ability to represent the downward spiral in Golding's novel was aptly represented through magazine images. Such representations beg questions like, "What could she have said in watercolor? "What would the difference in message be?" Such links between cognition and sign-making have been fiercely argued by Eisner (2002) and Greene (1995, 2001) as well as others who have studied their relationship.

When invited to respond visually to literature, older participants in this study, in particular, subconsciously defaulted to written language structures and used this knowledge as they made their visual texts. Evident was their use of recognizable conventions such as top-to-bottom and left-to-right organization, in particular. Objects in visual texts such as Jill's aesthetic texts and Jack's graphically organized texts locate arrangement of objects as a reader might find in written language. Such fixing of text (Barthes, 1967), explicit (with language) or implicit (arranged), is internalized by participants, and they know that they must convey certain signs to ensure viewers' correct or intended understanding of the message.

Implications for Practice and Future Research

Art as a system of communication must be more consciously studied in terms of affordance in its potential to communicate. Broudy (1966) wrote about the power of image to evoke feelings and emotions and asserts that the arts express meanings that are not accessible in other symbolic forms, especially when the arts as disciplines are recognized and made significant in learning. If literacy educators and researchers take to heart what Broudy suggests about the critical nature of art in expression, educators and researchers must recognize that the visible marks on a page or canvas are significant and contribute to the viewer's overall understanding of that signmaker's literacy.

Educators and researchers can benefit from this study's identification of genres and their characteristics in visual texts produced in ELA classes. Such readings offer insight into the genres that learners prefer, and also can make visible confusions that learners may have regarding genre. Educators and researchers both can benefit from more intensive study in visual text composition, conventions, and grammatical structures at play in learners' visual texts. Information from such inquiry can lead to more thoughtful and critical discussion of how all texts, visual, musical, linguistic, and so on, inform and shape learners' literacy practices. Critical and social semiotic readings of original visual texts can lead to such readings of visual texts integrated throughout literature anthologies, content area textbooks, picture books, trade books, and so on. An ability to do close readings will encourage learners not only to study a discipline but to read its texts in all their variety. Additionally, they may also become much more reflective about the visual texts they produce. Educators as well as researchers can reflect upon their own beliefs about art as a sign system and consider the purpose of art in their own work. As I have argued in several places (Albers, 1997, 2001; Albers & Murphy, 2000), educators and researchers alike must learn the discipline of art, especially if learners' visual representations are being studied, and especially if they are being graded. Educators and researchers would not think of assessing learners' writing if they knew little about writing. So the same principle holds for art.

Conclusion

The forms through which knowledge and understanding are constructed, remembered, and expressed must be wider than verbal or written language alone. What one can learn and be able to experience through an artwork cannot be known in a discursive form and vice versa. Rather, meaning must be assessed through the lenses through which it is produced. If students are to understand written, visual, musical, and dramatic texts (and so on) and be more able to express what they know through a range of media, they need to have the opportunity both to study structures, purposes, and qualities within their own visual texts and to learn to read said texts. Although art offers a lovely respite from "regular work," like Eisner (2002), I believe there is more to the visual text than meets the eye. When knowledge of art is applied to the analysis of visual texts created in ELA classrooms, richer discussion of learners' literacy practices can emerge.

Note

1. There has been a growing body of anecdotal research (Ernst, 1993,

2001; Frei, 1999; McKay & Kendrick, 2001; Rossi, 1997; Ehrenworth, 2003) and more formal research studies (Cowan, 2001; DuCharme, 1991; Hubbard, 1990; Olshansky, 1994a, 1994b, 1995, 1997; Sadoski & Paivio, 1994) in the visual and verbal connections, or the connections between art and language.

Works Cited

Albers, P. (1996). *Art as literacy: The dynamic interplay of pedagogy and gendered meaning making in sixth grade art classes* (Unpublished doctoral dissertation). Indiana University, Bloomington, IN.

————. (1997). Art as literacy. *Language Arts, 74*(5), 338–350.

————. (2001). Literacy in the arts. *Primary Voices K–6, 9*(4), 3–9.

————. (2004). Literacy in art: A question of responsibility. *Democracy and Education, 15*(3–4), 32–41.

————. (2006a). Imagining the possibilities of multimodal curriculum design. *English Education, 38*(2), 75–101.

————. (2006b, July). *Outsider literacy.* Paper presented at the Whole Language Umbrella Conference, Charlotte, NC.

————. (2007a). *Finding the artist within: Creating and reading visual texts in the English language arts classroom.* Newark, DE: International Reading Association.

————. (2007b). Visual discourse analysis: An introduction to the analysis of school-generated visual texts. In D. W. Rowe, R. T. Jiménez, D. L. Compton, D. K. Dickinson, Y. Kim, K. M. Leander, & V. J. Risko (Eds.), *56th yearbook of the National Reading Conference* (pp. 81–95). Oak Creek, WI: National Reading Conference.

Albers, P., & Frederick, T. (2009). *Literacy (re)marks: A study of seven teachers' visual texts across time.* In V. J. Risko, D. L. Compton, D. K. Dickinson, M. Hundley, R. T. Jiménez, K. M. Leander, D. W. Rowe, & Y. Kim (Eds.), *58th yearbook of the National Reading Conference.* Oak Creek, WI: NRC.

Albers, P., & Harste, J. C. (2007). The arts, new literacies, and multimodality. *English Education, 40*(1), 6–20.

Albers, P., & Murphy, S. (2000). *Telling pieces: Art as literacy in middle school classes.* Mahwah, NJ: Erlbaum.

Bang, M. (2000). *Picture this: Perception and composition*. Boston: Bulfinch Press.

Barthes, R. (1967). *Elements of semiology*. London, UK: Cape.

Bogdan, R. C., & Biklen, S. K. (1992). *Qualitative research for education: An introduction to theory and methods*. Boston: Allyn and Bacon.

Boyatzis, C. J., & Eades, J. (1999). Gender differences in preschoolers' and kindergarteners' artistic production and preference. *Sex Roles*, *41*(7–8), 627–638.

Broudy, H. S. (1966). Aesthetic education in a technological society: The other excuses for art. *Journal of Aesthetic Education*, *1*(1), 13–23.

Calkins, L. M. (1983). *Lessons from a child: On the teaching and learning of writing*. Portsmouth, NH: Heinemann.

———. (1986). *The art of teaching writing*. Portsmouth, NH: Heinemann.

Carger, C. L. (2004). Art and literacy with bilingual children. *Language Arts*, *8*(4), 283–292.

Cowan, K. W. (2001). The arts and emergent literacy. *Primary Voices K–6*, *9*(4), 11–18.

Dewey, J. (1934). *Art as experience*. New York: Minton, Balch.

Dillon, D. R. (2000). *Kids InSight: Reconsidering how to meet the literacy needs of all students*. Newark, DE: International Reading Association.

DuCharme, C. C. (1991, March). *The role of drawing in the writing processes of primary grade children*. Paper presented at the Spring Conference of the National Council of Teachers of English, Indianapolis, IN.

Dyson, A. H. (1983). The role of oral language in early writing processes. *Research in the Teaching of English*, *17*(1), 1–30.

———. (1984). Learning to write/learning to do school: Emergent writers' interpretations of school literacy tasks. *Research in the Teaching of English*, *18*(3), 233–264.

———. (1985). Individual differences in emerging writing. In M. Farr (Ed.), *Advances in writing research, Vol. 1: Children's early writing development* (pp. 59–126). Norwood, NJ: Ablex.

————. (1986). Children's early interpretations of writing: Expanding research perspectives. In D. B. Yaden, Jr. & S. Templeton (Eds.), *Metalinguistic awareness and beginning literacy: Conceptualizing what it means to read and write* (pp. 201–218). Portsmouth, NH: Heinemann.

————. (1987). Individual differences in beginning composing: An orchestral vision of learning to compose. *Written Communication*, 4(4), 411–442.

————. (1988). *Drawing, talking, and writing: Rethinking writing development* (Occasional Paper No. 3). Berkeley: Center for the Study of Writing, University of California.

Ehrenworth, M. (2003). *Looking to write: Students writing through the visual arts.* Portsmouth, NH: Heinemann.

Eisner, E. W. (2002). *The arts and the creation of mind.* New Haven, CT: Yale University Press.

Ernst, K. (1993). *Picturing learning: Artists and writers in the classroom.* Portsmouth, NH: Heinemann.

Ernst da Silva, K. (2001). Drawing on experience: Connecting art and language. *Primary Voices K–6, 10*(2), 2–8.

Flynn, R. M. (2002). Shakespearean slide shows. *English Journal, 92*(1), 62–68.

Forceville, C. (2004). When is something a pictorial metaphor? Retrieved from http://www.chass.utoronto.ca/epc/srb/cyber/cforceville2.html

Fox, M. (1998). *Tough Boris.* New York: Voyager Books.

Frei, R. I. (1999). Making meaning with art: Children's stories. *Language Arts, 76*(5), 386–392.

Gee, J. P. (2000). Discourse and sociocultural studies in reading. *Reading Online, 4*(3). Retrieved from http://www.readingonline.org/articles/handbook/gee/index.html

————. (2005). *An introduction to discourse analysis: Theory and method.* New York: Routledge.

Glesne, C., & Peshkin, A. (1992). *Becoming qualitative researchers: An introduction.* White Plains, NY: Longman.

Golding, W. P. (1954). *Lord of the flies.* New York: Perigee.

Graves, D. H. (1973). Sex differences in children's writing. *Elementary English*, *50*(7), 1101–1106.

———. (1975). An examination of the writing processes of seven-year-old children. *Research in the Teaching of English*, *9*(3), 227–241.

Greene, M. (1995). *Releasing the imagination: Essays on education, the arts, and social change*. San Francisco: Jossey-Bass.

———. (2001). *Variations on a blue guitar: The Lincoln Center Institute lectures on aesthetic education*. New York: Teachers College Press.

Greenway, W. (1996). Poems and paintings: Shades of the prison house. *English Journal*, *85*(3), 42–48.

Halliday, M.A. K. (1978). *Language as social semiotic: The social interpretation of language and meaning*. London, UK: Edward Arnold.

———. (1985). *An introduction to functional grammar*. London, UK: Edward Arnold.

Hobbs, R., & Frost, R. (2003). Measuring the acquisition of media-literacy skills. *Reading Research Quarterly*, *38*(3), 330–355.

Hodge, R., & Kress, G. (1988). *Social semiotics*. Cambridge,UK: Polity Press.

Holloway, D. L., & LeCompte, M. D. (2001). Becoming somebody! How arts programs support positive identity for middle school girls. *Education and Urban Society*, *33*(4), 388–408.

Hubbard, R. (1989). *Authors of pictures, draughtsmen of words*. Portsmouth, NH: Heinemann.

———. (1990). There's more than black and white in literacy's palette: Children's use of color. *Language Arts*, *67*(5), 492–500.

Katzive, B. (1997). Looking, writing, creating. *Voices from the Middle*, *4*(3), 25–29.

Kress, G. (1985). *Linguistic processes in sociocultural practice*. Geelong, VIC, Australia: Deakin University Press.

———. Language as social practice. In G. Kress (Ed.), *Communication and culture: An introduction* (pp. 79–129). Kensington, NSW, Australia: University of New South Wales Press.

Kress, G., & van Leeuwen, T. (2006). *Reading images: The grammar of visual design* (2nd ed.). New York: Routledge.

Landay, E. (with Meehan, M. B., Newman, A. L., Woolton, K., & King, D. W. (2001). "Postcards from America": Linking classroom and community in an ESL class. *English Journal, 90*(5), 66–74.

Lee, H. (1988). *To kill a mockingbird.* New York: Little, Brown. (Original work published 1960)

Marsh, J. (1999). Batman and batwoman go to school: Popular culture in the literacy curriculum. *International Journal of Early Years Education, 7*(2), 117–131.

———. (2000). "But I want to fly too!" Girls and superhero play in the infant classroom. *Gender and Education, 12*(2), 209–220.

McKay, R. A., & Kendrick, M. E. (2001). Children draw their images of reading and writing. *Language Arts, 78*(6), 529–533.

Moss, G. (2001). Seeing with the camera: Analysing children's photographs of literacy in the home. *Journal of Research in Reading, 24*(3), 279–292.

Murata, R. (1997). Connecting the visual and verbal: English and art for high school sophomores. *English Journal, 86*(7), 44–48.

Murray, D. M. (1997). The seeing line. *Voices from the Middle, 4*(3), 3–5.

Newkirk, T. (2002). *Misreading masculinity: Boys, literacy, and popular culture.* Portsmouth, NH: Heinemann.

Noden, H., & Moss, B. (1995). Nurturing artistic images in student reading and writing. *The Reading Teacher, 48*(6), 532–534.

Olshansky, B. (1994a). Image-making. *Instructor, 104*(4), 48–49.

———. (1994b). Making writing a work of art: Image-making within the writing process. *Language Arts, 71*(5), 350–356.

———. (1994c, March). When children become authors/illustrators. *School Arts,* 14–17.

———. (1995). Picture this. *Thrust for Educational Leadership, 25*(2), 14–16.

———. (1997). Picturing story: An irresistible pathway into literacy. *The Reading Teacher, 50*(7), 612–613.

———. (2006). Artists/writers workshop: Focusing in on the ART of writing. *Language Arts, 83*(6), 530–533.

———. (2008). *The power of pictures: Creating pathways to literacy through art, grades K–6*. San Francisco: Jossey-Bass.

Orwell, G. (1996). *Animal farm*. New York: Signet. (Original work published 1946)

Pahl, K. (2007). Creativity in events and practices: A lens for understanding children's multimodal texts. *Literacy, 41*(2), 86–92.

Pfannenstiel, G. (with Dickinson, J., Chandler, S., & Whitney, C. (2003). Journeying through the arts into the Harlem renaissance. *Language Arts, 80*(5), 345–352.

Piro, J. M. (2002). The picture of reading: Deriving meaning in literacy through image. *The Reading Teacher, 56*(2), 126–134.

Rosenblatt, L. M. (1995). *Literature as exploration* (5th ed.). New York: Modern Language Association.

Rossi, P. J. (1997). Having an experience in five acts: Multiple literacies through young children's opera. *Language Arts, 74*(5), 352–367.

Rowsell, J., & Pahl, K. (2007). Sedimented identities in texts: Instances of practice. *Reading Research Quarterly, 42*(3), 388–404.

Sadoski, M., & Paivio, A. (1994). A dual coding view of imagery and verbal processes in reading comprehension. In R. B. Ruddell, M. R. Ruddell, & H. Singer (Eds.), *Theoretical models and processes of reading* (4th ed., pp. 582–601). Newark, DE: International Reading Association.

Smith, J. L., & Herring, J. D. (1996). Literature alive: Connecting to story through the arts. *Reading Horizons, 37*(2), 102–115.

Sonesson, G. (1988). Methods and models of pictorial semiotics. Retrieved from http://www.arthist.lu.se/kultsem/pdf/rapport3.pdf/

———. (2004). The quadrature of the hermeneutic circle. Retrieved from http://filserver.arthist.lu.se/kultsem/sonesson/Quadrature1.html

Tuman, D. (1999). Gender style as form and content: An examination of gender stereotypes in subject preference of children's drawing. *Studies in Art Education, 41*(1), 40–60.

CHAPTER EIGHT

Reading Illustrations: Helping Readers Use Pictorial Text to Construct Meaning in Picturebooks

RAY MARTENS, PRISCA MARTENS, KERI-ANNE CROCE,
AND CATHERINE MADERAZO
Towson University

The illustrations use nice illustrating. The illustration looks like it is using warm and cool colors.
—Kenny's journal entry, January, 2008

In the story "Trapped by the Ice," the illustrator adds meanings by using lines, shapes, and patterns. The illustrations add meaning by using diagonal lines to make it look dangerous. He used neutral colors to make it look cold in Antarctica.
—Kenny's journal entry, April, 2008

Kenny's journal reflection in April on *Trapped by the Ice!* (Mc-Curdy, 2001) shows his growing awareness of how artists represent meaning in illustrations, and how readers integrate that meaning with the written text to understand stories in picturebooks. Although he uses some artistic language (e.g., warm and cool colors), Kenny's entry written in January does not have the language to describe the illustrator's work, let alone acknowledge that an artist created the artwork. However, by April, Kenny speaks with knowledge and conviction about how and why the illustrator used neutral colors, diagonal lines, shapes, and patterns to add meaning to the illustrations.

Kenny and his third-grade classmates were part of a semester-long study that explored how becoming knowledgeable about art language and concepts, and experiencing the techniques and materials artists use to create illustrations, has an impact on how readers' construct meaning. In this chapter, we share the results of this study, how students' comprehension was enhanced by studying art as a language, and what three literacy teachers and one art teacher experienced and learned through this process.

Theoretical Framework

Sign Systems

Semiotics is a theory that explores the nature and function of signs as well as the systems and processes underlying signification, expression, representation, and communication. In brief, it is a study of signs and sign systems, or language systems that have distinct grammars: art, music, language, math, movement, and dance (Albers, 2007b). Sign systems position us differently in our relationship to the world (Berghoff & Harste, 2002), allow us to express meaning in unique non-redundant ways, and offer their own unique perspectives of particular cultural meanings (Kress & van Leeuwen, 2006). Cultures have a variety of mental constructs or signs they use to share meaning (Berghoff & Harste, 2002), and understanding how meaning gets mediated through sign systems offers a way of thinking in which written/oral language and visual texts work in concert, and in which written/oral language is not the primary source through which meaning is mediated and represented (Harste, 1994). In relation to writing and art, John Dewey (1978) stated that sign systems engage the viewer or reader in unique ways of knowing: "Thinking directly in terms of colors, tones, and images is a different operation technically from thinking in words . . . the meaning of paintings . . . cannot be translated into words . . . to ask what [visible qualities] mean in the sense of something that can be put into words is to deny their distinctive existence" (pp. 73–74). Although all sign systems are different but equally valid ways of knowing and communicating, schools generally emphasize language and mathematics to the exclusion of the others (Berghoff & Harste, 2002). However, experiencing and moving across and between sign systems (e.g., visual art and written language) challenges learners intellectually and helps them gain deeper perspectives and insights about particular meanings (Eisner, 1998; Harste, 1994; Kress & van Leeuwen, 2006).

Picturebooks

Picturebooks bring together primarily two sign systems, art and written language, to create a unique experience for readers (Goodman, 1976). Like other researchers, we spell *picturebooks* as one word to reflect this unity. Barbara Bader (1976) describes picturebooks as "text, illustrations, total design; . . . As an art form it hinges on the interdependence of pictures and words" (p. 1). The written text that describes the characters, environment, actions, and developments in the story is dependent and interdependent on the pictorial text. The two texts make sense and can only be understood in the context of the other (Lewis, 2001; Schwarcz, 1982). Nodelman (1988) states that "placing [written and pictorial texts] into relationship with each other inevitably changes the meaning of both, so that good picturebooks as a whole are a richer experience than just the simple sum of their parts" (p. 199). In essence, picturebooks must be read and interpreted through the sign systems of both art and written language.

Many studies show the power of using picturebooks in reading instruction (e.g., Braunger & Lewis, 2006; Hoffman, Baumann, & Afflerbach, 2000). Although the focus of these studies was usually on students' reading of the written text, some studies have also examined readers' responses to illustrations. Sipe (2000) and Sipe and Bauer (2001), for example, studied young children's responses to picturebooks during read-alouds and found that children were more attuned to the illustrations than the verbal text. Arizpe and Styles (2003) studied children ages 4 to 11 in seven schools to learn how they read the visual texts in picturebooks and understood the narrative through the illustrations. They found that the children were "sophisticated readers of visual texts . . . [who] make sense of complex images on literal, visual, and metaphorical levels. They were able to understand different viewpoints, analyze moods, messages and emotions, and articulate personal responses to picturebooks—even when they struggle with the written word" (n.p.). Readers, then, transact with the pictorial text as well as the written text in picturebooks.

Visual Art

The important role visual art plays in education is well documented (Eisner, 1997; Lowenfeld & Brittain, 1970; Read, 1974). For example, Shirley Brice Heath and Shelby Wolf (2004) in a yearlong study in Kent, England, report on a school that provided daily art experiences focused on drawing and details. They found that as the children developed the ability to focus on details that they saw, the depth of their thinking, their attention spans, and their capacity for metaphorical language grew. They also noted that when reading, the children began paying more attention to details.

In his work with Project Zero at Harvard University, David Perkins (1994) discovered that looking at art also enhanced thinking and opens doors for inquiry. He found that looking at art "provides an excellent setting for the development of better thinking, for the cultivation of what might be called the art of intelligence . . . looking at art provides a context especially well suited for . . . helping learners mobilize their mental powers . . . [works of art] demand thoughtful attention to discover what they have to show and say" (pp. 3–4). Arizpe and Styles (2004) also found that as children learned to closely examine illustrations, they gained a sense of the importance of details and internalized the various ways in which details in illustrations deepened the meaning they represented. As works of art, picturebooks provided rich opportunities for children's artistic development and understanding (Nodelman, 1988; Schwarcz, 1982).

Reading

To read, readers use sociocultural, cognitive, and linguistic knowledge and experiences as cues to construct meaning from texts in their sociocultural environments (Goodman, 2003; Halliday, 1975; Rosenblatt, 1978; Vygotsky, 1978). Texts are units of meaning in different forms, including, for our purposes here, written and pictorial (Halliday & Hasan, 1976; Kress & van Leeuwen, 2006). To transact with written texts, readers integrate language cueing systems—the semantic system (meaning cues), the pragmatic system (social and situational context cues), the syntactic system (grammar cues), and the grapho-phonic system (graphic and sound cues)—with their knowledge of the world to infer and predict meaning (Goodman, 1996; Smith, 2004). To transact with artistic texts, readers use comparable cueing systems with visual art components to infer and predict meaning in pictorial texts (Albers, 2007b; Piro, 2002; Pumphrey, 1996). The elements of art (dot, line, value, shape, color, space, form, texture) provide the graphic cues, while the principles of design (balance, emphasis, pattern, rhythm, movement, variety, harmony, contrast, unity) can be understood as the syntactic cues. Together, they are integrated to create meaning, or the semantics.

This body of research describes art and written language as equal, valid, non-redundant ways of representing meaning. They are brought together in picturebooks, where readers integrate and make sense of the written and pictorial texts. We have not found studies, though, that examine how helping students learn to read and integrate the meaning of the pictorial text with the meaning of the written text relates to the meaning they construct while reading picturebooks; it is here that our study is situated.

Context of the Study

Our qualitative study investigated this overarching question: What is the relationship between students' experiences with the elements of art/principles of design and the materials/techniques used by illustrators and the students' meaning making with written and pictorial texts in picturebooks? During the spring of 2008, we worked with Michelle, a third-grade teacher with ten years of teaching experience; Stacy, an art teacher with three years of experience; and Michelle's nineteen third graders who attended school in a large metropolitan area on the East Coast of the United States. Eight students were African American, nine Caucasian, one Asian, and one Hispanic. They all spoke English proficiently and none received special education services. About 19.2 percent of the students received free or reduced-price lunch. Prior to the study, Michelle had no experience with teaching art, and Stacy had no experience teaching with picturebooks.

Reading and Art Curriculum

We met regularly with Michelle and Stacy to develop teaching plans for the integration of art with reading. Michelle was required by her district to use Houghton Mifflin (HM) (2001) materials for reading instruction. The third-grade HM text was an anthology of children's literature picturebooks. Although Stacy had district and state art content standards to meet, she was free to create her own curriculum.

Together, we looked at the story Michelle would be teaching in the HM anthology and decided on specific elements of art (EA) and principles of design (PD) that could be highlighted in the illustrations. Rather than address all of the EA/PD, we decided to primarily focus on a few of them and their associated concepts and continually revisit and weave them into different stories and art experiences. The EA we chose were line, shape, color, space, texture, and the PD were pattern and movement.

In the context of her weekly art curriculum, Stacy designed art experiences that included the EA/PD we selected, and used the illustrations in the HM anthology as examples of the EA/PD. She talked with students about how and why the artists made the decisions they did, the meanings the illustrations represented, and how those meanings related to the story meanings.

In the context of Michelle's daily reading curriculum, she helped students examine the illustrations in the anthology more closely and consider meanings represented through the EA/PD. She also investigated with the students how the illustrations supported or added to the meanings in the written text. Students sketched and wrote reflections and responses to the stories and the illustrations in their journals.

Data Collection and Analysis

The data we collected included observations of reading and art instruction recorded in field notes, informal interviews with the students about their reading, informal interviews with Michelle and Stacy, artwork students created in Michelle's and Stacy's classrooms, students' written reflections on their own artwork, informal follow-up interviews with the students to clarify aspects of their reflections, and students' readings and retellings of a story at the beginning and end of the study. The retellings included questions about the illustrations, such as "Did you notice anything about the illustrations?" and "Is there anything about the illustrations that helped you understand the story? What?" We also asked students to find and comment on their favorite illustrations as well as a preselected one we chose.

We analyzed the readings and retellings using the classroom procedure of miscue analysis (Goodman et al., 2005) and students' comments about the illustrations using discourse analysis (Gee, 2005). Discourse analysis allowed us to examine how students assigned "privilege" to the sign systems of art and written language (Gee, 2005, p. 13).

To create the discourse codes, we independently analyzed the transcript for one student who was chosen at random. As we read the transcript, we each looked for elements that stood out to us (Bakhtin, 1981) and assigned preliminary codes to these elements. Then we met, discussed our initial codings, and made tentative agreements on possible codes to use as we independently analyzed a second random transcript. We followed this process with two additional transcripts, always meeting between codings to share codes, revise and refine our coding system, and build a common perspective for reliability. Once we had a preliminary list of codes, two researchers independently read and coded each transcript and then met to discuss their codings. They discussed any disagreements until consensus was reached. We each had access to all of the data at all times.

How Artists Represent Danger and Fear

To illuminate the collaboration between Michelle and Stacy and how we wove the selected EA/PD throughout the study, we share a curricular snapshot of some of the discussions and experiences we had with the students that focused on how artists represent the concepts of danger and fear.

Artists express the concepts of danger, fear, and uneasiness in a variety of ways using elements of art, such as color and line, and principles of design, such as pattern and repetition. When deciding on color, for example, artists consider color temperature (e.g., warm/cool), contrast of color value (e.g., light/dark), or contrast of color intensity (e.g., saturated/neutral). In thinking about line, artists may use diagonal lines to show tension or action, lines with sharp or pointy edges to signal danger, or repeated lines to create a feeling of violent movement. Patterns are created with repeated elements of art such as lines, shapes, or colors. Repeated shapes with extreme contrast or shapes with many sharp points, in contrast to rounded points or rounded shapes, may express a feeling of uneasiness. For example, teeth with very sharp points, in contrast with teeth that are rounded, feel more dangerous and threatening. In general, lines and shapes with rounded edges are less fearful shapes than those with pointed or sharp joints. In their discussions with the students, Stacy and Michelle found opportunities to highlight EA/PD such as these in the illustrations in the anthology, particularly in stories that involved tension and uneasiness. These stories included *Seal Surfer* (Foreman, 2001), *Across the Wide Dark Sea: The Mayflower Journey* (Van Leeuwen, 2001), and *Trapped by the Ice!* (McCurdy, 2001).

Seal Surfer

The first occasion to highlight for Michelle's students how artists showed danger came in the story, *Seal Surfer*, written and illustrated by Michael Foreman (2001). *Seal Surfer* is the story of a young boy who goes to the beach with his grandfather and finds a mother and baby seal. Over time the boy becomes friends with the seal. Danger occurs in the story when there is a bad winter storm with rough waves that toss the seals around. More danger

FIGURE **8.1.** *Molly's illustration of the sentence, "The fire in the fireplace continued to burn as Sue's mom finished reading her story."*

emerges when the boy, who is handicapped, falls off his surf board and is rescued by the seal. Foreman uses diagonal lines for the waves, the boy heading under water, and the seal diving and rising, and dark-valued (shades) colors for the sky and water bubbles. Michelle and Stacy highlighted elements (e.g., line, shape, color) and principles (e.g., movement, pattern) to show how Foreman represented danger and fear in his illustrations.

In her discussions of the story with the students, Michelle demonstrated how to read the illustrations. She also had the students write reflections on the story and illustrations in their reading logs. These reflections included the students' responses to and feelings about the story, what they noticed in the written and pictorial text, and comments about Foreman's use of elements and principles in the illustrations. In art, Stacy also talked about how Foreman used the medium of watercolor in *Seal Surfer* to create his illustrations. She then had the students use watercolors to illustrate one of several sentences, considering the kinds of colors and lines they would use to represent their meaning. Figure 8.1 represents Molly's illustration of the sentence, "The fire in the fireplace continued to burn as Sue's mom finished reading her story."

In explaining her painting, Molly said,

> My painting was about a girl in a dress laying by the fire so she could be nice and warm and her mother's reading her a story, a fairy tale story, and she's rocking in a rocking chair. . . . The background is a colorful wall in a pattern, like red, purple, blue, green, brown, red, purple, blue, green, black, brown, and blue, purple. . . . I wanted the colors on the wall to be diagonal, because I wanted it to look like it's something that's like moving . . . it's all the colors outside the window in the sky. . . . The arrows are meaning, like so they don't know that it's a plain chair but is rocking. . . .

Molly's comments demonstrated the beginnings of her awareness of how artists represent meaning. She didn't mention her use of warm colors but did talk about the warm scene and feeling by the fireplace. While, in reality, homeowners might not want the pattern on their walls to appear to be moving, Molly revealed that she was thinking about what she represented, also connecting the wall pattern to movement outside the window. She used diagonal lines and arrows to show that the rocking chair was moving, not standing still. Through her comments, Molly showed that she understood the process artists use when they work.

Across the Wide Dark Sea: The Mayflower Journey

The next story in the HM anthology that generated discussions about danger and fear was *Across the Wide Dark Sea: The Mayflower Journey*, written by Jean Van Leeuwen (2001) and illustrated by Thomas Allen. The story describes a boy and his family's difficult journey to America with the other Pilgrims on the Mayflower, along with the challenges they faced to survive the winter at Plymouth Plantation. Stacy used the illustrations to introduce the concept of repeated shapes more generally, without focusing on danger and fear, before Michelle asked the students to read the story. Stacy and the students talked about patterns, for example, in the repeated rectangular shapes and colors in one illustration that showed the passengers waving goodbye as the boat set sail. Since not all repeated shapes indicate danger, she pointed out how these shapes also showed the principles of design of movement, harmony, and contrast. Stacy then had the students individually illustrate one of several sentences she'd written (i.e., "The boat rocked back and forth in the raging storm"), incorporating repeated shapes for a purpose they selected.

Michelle invited Ray to continue this discussion of the illustrations with the students in her classroom before the students read the story. Ray began by reminding the students of what they had talked about with Stacy relative to *Seal Surfer* and *Across the Wide Dark Sea*. As they examined the illustrations, Ray facilitated a discussion with the students that touched on the following:

- the pastel material/medium Thomas Allen used to create the illustrations;

- the types of lines he incorporated: horizontal lines to indicate calm, diagonal lines to indicate movement or danger, and jagged lines to signal danger;

- Allen's use of space to give readers different perspectives (i.e., even though the whole boat wasn't visible, readers knew from the masts and sails the object was a boat);

- Allen's creation of texture through his use of a textured paper and artistic techniques to create an illusion of realism;

- Allen's use of primary colors and how the colors change, depending on the season being depicted; and

- the ways and places Allen used repeated shapes/patterns (e.g., on the boat railing) which create unity but also indicate danger in other places, such as where he has used inverted triangles.

Ray also helped the students infer that Allen selected a beige textured paper rather than white paper to give the feeling of a story from the past.

Following that discussion, Michelle asked the students to reflect on what was said and write several predictions about the story based on the illustrations. Figure 8.2 contains two of these predictions. Third graders responded to both the visual and language elements in the text. Michael wrote, "I predict that a storm came and big waves went on the boat and brushed people away.

LITERACIES, THE ARTS, AND MULTIMODALITY

A. A prediction by Michael

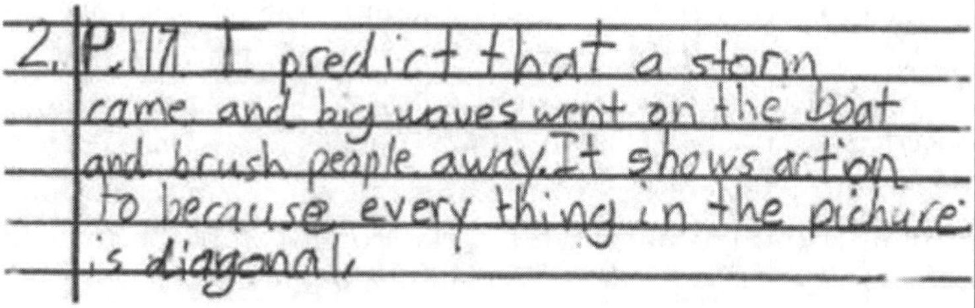

> 2. P.117 I predict that a storm
> came and big waves went on the boat
> and brush people away. It shows action
> to because every thing in the picture
> is diagonal.

B. A prediction by Ben

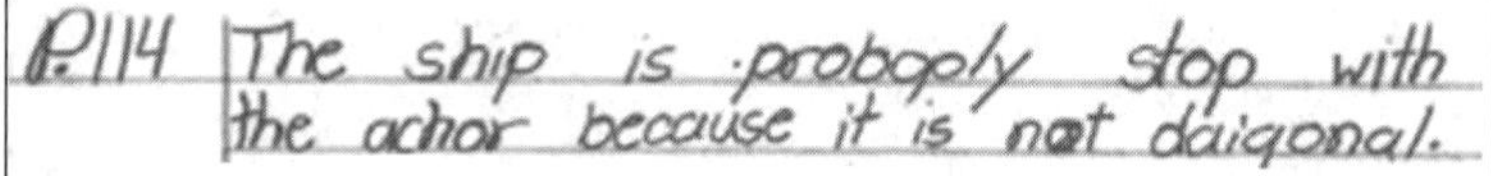

> P.114 The ship is probaly stop with
> the achor because it is not daiqonal.

FIGURE 8.2A. *Michael's prediction.*
FIGURE 8.2B. *Ben's prediction.*

It shows action too because everything in the picture is diagonal"
(see Figure 8.2a). Ben commented, "The ship is probably stopped
with the anchor because it is not diagonal" (see Figure 8.2b).
The comments, focused here on Allen's use of lines, are another
indication that the students understood how artists represent
meaning through image.

Trapped by the Ice!

The last major opportunity to discuss the use of the EA/PD to
represent danger and fear came in *Trapped by the Ice!* written
and illustrated by Michael McCurdy (2001). *Trapped by the Ice!*
is a narrative nonfiction story that describes the 1914 Shackleton Antarctic expedition in which Shackleton and his crew
were trapped and, when their ship was crushed, had to journey
across the frozen sea to safety. The use of neutral (grayed) colors,
emphasizing extreme cold temperatures and a harsh landscape,
shapes with pointed edges, and diagonal lines were particularly
striking in this story.

Stacy first discussed neutral colors with the students, using the illustrations in the story as an example, and then had the students practice making neutral colors with oil pastels. She also talked about McCurdy's use of diagonal lines to show movement, triangular shapes with sharp points such as chunks of ice or the sharp teeth of a giant sea leopard; texture created by his brush strokes that created a feel of ice or snow; and patterns such as repeated triangles in pieces of ice, men pulling a boat, and waves in the ocean. Also highlighted was the element of space conveyed through a range of shape sizes, from small to large, indicating proportional change or overlapping shapes to give the illusion of depth or three-dimensionality.

To represent their learning, Stacy had the students select one of six sentences to illustrate. Kara and Gerald both illustrated "The stormy ocean almost tipped over the small sail boat, as it floated on the waves trying to get to the shore," but interpreted it differently. In an interview about her artwork (Figure 8.3), Kara explained:

> I decided to use gray clouds and trace around them with black to make it dark and stormy. . . . I put blue and I put gray together to make a nice dark blue so it was foggy and the water was messy. . . . I couldn't make the sand bright because that would symbolize everything is calm in that part, so I made it like it's really scary sand. I mixed different colors to make a different kind of brown. . . . I tilted the palm tree to make it look like wind was pushing it . . . the little swirls are wind. I used diagonal lines on the waves to show they're going to crash into the boat and are moving. I used another diagonal for the palm tree. And the water is kind of diagonal on the picture because it looks like it's blowing and it's going really fast and the water is pushing side to side, and I made the wind like move with the diagonal and the swirl to show like it's wind. . . .

Kara showed an understanding of how to produce a certain mood within her picture by using color and line to create movement. She explored the mixing of certain hues to make an entirely new hue that could be used to set the mood she wanted to create. Her use of diagonal and curved lines helped her attain a sense of movement throughout her art piece.

In an interview, Gerald explained his artwork (Figure 8.4):

FIGURE 8.3. *Kara's illustration of the sentence, "The stormy ocean almost tipped over the small sailboat, as it floated on the waves trying to get to the shore."*

The picture shows a boat with men inside of it and a bunch of waves tipped over the boat so men are crying for help. There's danger, like a shark. All their supplies, their lifeboat, their paddles are coming out of it and the people are injured. . . . That's the land down over there, the gray stuff. There is another person but I couldn't draw him because he's underwater drowning. . . . The sky is stormy so it's foggy. You can see some lightning bolts. The waves are crashing down. The tsunamis, like that. . . . There's some fire coming from the boat because that lightning bolt right there struck it. I couldn't find any other colors for fire so I just used that. . . . I used a diagonal line on the boat so it looks like it's tipping over. . . . The waves have diagonal lines too because they're crashing down as hard as possible.

As his interview shows, Gerald was more caught up in the story he created than in explaining how and why he made the decisions he did, although he did talk about color choice and use of diagonal lines to indicate movement. He showed he understood the concept

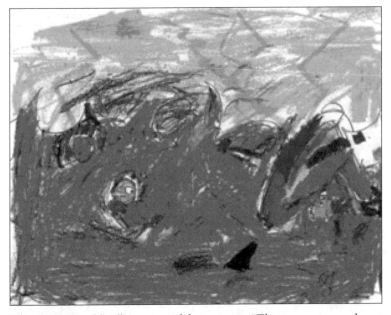

FIGURE **8**.**4**. *Gerald's illustration of the sentence, "The stormy ocean almost tipped over the small sailboat, as it floated on the waves trying to get to the shore."*

of creating a mood or feeling within an illustration by adding the details of sharks, materials coming out of the boat, injured people, lightning bolts, waves crashing, and fire. Gerald's use of color and line helped to heighten the drama of his illustration.

During reading instruction, Michelle built on what the students had discussed with Stacy about McCurdy's use of neutral colors and lines to create mood and feeling of uneasiness as well as other EA/PD. Michelle had the students reflect on the illustrations and what they represented. Josh wrote, "In *Trapped by the Ice* they used diagonal lines and neutral colors to show the dangers of the Arctic. Also they used texture to show how dangerous peaks are and cliffs. Finally they used cool colors to show the cold of the Arctic." Dara said, "In *Trapped by the Ice* the author used diagonal lines and neutral colors to show the danger parts in the story. Like on page 182 he used neutral colors when the man in tent #4 fell in the crevasse." Like Kenny at the beginning of the chapter, Josh and Dara demonstrated knowledge about how and why Foreman made particular decisions to emphasize particular meanings. They both talked about the use of diagonal lines and neutral colors to highlight danger. Josh also commented about the texture of the mountain peaks and cliffs, as well as the use of cool colors to show the frigid temperatures. Their awareness of how artists represent meaning in illustrations enriched the meaning they constructed in the story.

Evidence of Students' Increased Comprehension

This study emphasized for us that picturebooks, the weaving together of a pictorial and written text, are a whole unit that must be respected, valued, and read as such. To look or concentrate on only one part, and not include the other, is not possible. Readers need to read both to get a more complete understanding of the story.

It became increasingly clear to us that the third graders understood this, as the earlier examples we shared demonstrate. At the end of the study we decided to assess the students' comprehension through pictures and words because we wanted to know if our collaborative teaching of art and reading made a difference in what they remembered and how they made sense of a story. We had them read Sally Grindley's (1996) picturebook, *Peter's Place*, illustrated by Michael Foreman, and followed this by having them retell the story. *Peter's Place* is the story of Peter and his love for the ocean and its animal inhabitants near his home. When a tanker spills oil, Peter helps save the animals and cleans the area to restore it.

The students' growth and learning during the study were evident in the depth of their understandings and their appreciation of the relationship between the written and pictorial texts. These were visible in the students' comments about the illustrations during their retellings. As an example of students' growth over the study, Table 8.1 shows excerpts of Kyle's retellings, unaided by the book, of *Seal Surfer* at the beginning of the study in January and *Peter's Place* at the end in June.

TABLE 8.1. Kyle's interpretation of *Seal Surfer* and *Peter's Place*

	Seal Surfer	Peter's Place
Did you notice anything particular about the illustrations?	Yeah, when the text said the water was too cold and the baby hurt a little, it looked like it in the picture.	The first few parts he did it in warm colors because nothing bad was happening. Then when the wave came, he made it at night and he made the waves slanted so it can look like it is hitting the ship and that made the ship break . . .
Is there anything about the illustrations that helped you understand the story?	The last page it said that the baby . . . you didn't see it and in the pictures I didn't see it.	Warm colors, slanted lines . . .
Did you think the words or the illustrations were more interesting?	The words 'cause they had more information from the pictures. They added details.	Illustrations because there's more color. There are colors and it tells you what's really happening. . . .

Excerpts of Brittany's retelling, unaided by the book, offer another example of student learning (see Table 8.2):

In their January reflections of *Seal Surfer*, both Kyle and Brittany talked about what they saw in the illustrations. Brittany, for example, referred to the rocks and the ocean and how Foreman made them look realistic. Kyle also talked about the match between the written text and the illustrations: "when the text said . . . it looked like it in the picture." In January, Kyle and Brittany also both thought the words were more interesting than the illustrations. They said the words "had more information . . . added details" (Kyle) and "the words told you more about the story" (Brittany). They, like Kenny at the beginning of this chapter, showed little understanding of the depth of meanings represented in illustrations.

TABLE 8.2. Brittany's interpretation of *Seal Surfer* and *Peter's Place*

	Seal Surfer	*Peter's Place*
Did you notice anything particular about the illustrations?	I saw a lot of rocks and I saw a lot of the ocean . . . . He draws really good because the seals look realistic and so did the rocks.	Well, in the pictures they usually have warm colors and cool colors. Warm colors because it is happy. In the beginning and the end it was like Peter's land. They cleaned it all up. And in the middle it was all-dark and neutral colors and cold colors because the ship crashed and now everything is all sad because all the animals are dying and all the rocks are fading and all of the ocean is black.
Did you think the words or the illustrations were more interesting?	I thought the words were more interesting because the words told you more about the story and they told you he might have died and there was a seal and it had a baby.	I thought that the illustrations were more interesting because they use warm and cool colors and some neutral colors . . . and it showed in the illustration a lot of texture and a lot of colors. . . .

Kyle's and Brittany's observations in June, however, document the richness of the students' growth and understanding. In contrast to their talk about the objects in the illustrations in January, in June they discussed the use of the graphic and syntactic elements within illustrations as cueing systems for making meaning with picturebooks. Their comments went beyond merely naming particular EA/PD to indicating their understanding of *how* Michael Foreman used the EA/PD to represent meaning. Kyle, for example, stated, "He made the waves slanted so it can look like it is hitting the ship. . . ." and Brittany observed, "The pictures have . . . warm colors because it is happy. . . . And in the

middle it was all dark and neutral colors and cold colors because
the ship crashed and now everything is all sad. . . ." Students'
background and insights into art as a language system formed
across their reading of the other picturebooks, enabled them to
understand Foreman's use of the EA/PD, allowed them to access
another layer of meaning, and enriched their understandings of
the story.

While the students' comprehension, assessed through retellings of the stories, increased from the beginning to the end of the
study, we cannot claim that their more complete readings were
due solely to the experiences the students had during the study.
Comprehension is complex and the numerous other experiences
the students had in and out of school also affected it (Goodman, 2003; Rosenblatt, 1978). However, our analysis showed
sharp increases in the discourse codes for students' comments,
that revealed their understandings of the illustrations and how
the illustrations related to the written text, which was the result
of instruction provided during the study. For example, without
looking back at the illustrations, the students talked about events
shown that were not mentioned in the written text. Charles,
referring to one of the final illustrations, stated, "The dad and
the son were on the boat just sitting there and there were tons
of seagulls flying around," yet there is no mention of people, the
boat, or seagulls in the written text. Students also made many
more inferences from the pictorial text, using information not
stated in the written text. When talking about an illustration that
showed Peter sitting on the shoreline with the ducks after the oil
was cleaned from the area, several students commented on an
image of the tanker sinking in the background. Roy said, "[The
tanker] didn't sink because it is so shallow so it would just stay
there" while Marcie reflected, "Maybe it's not really there and
they just don't want you to forget."

The examples shared throughout this chapter demonstrate
that third-grade students grew in their thinking analytically and
critically about how artists convey pictorial meaning. We, like
Arizpe and Styles 2003, were less concerned about whether the
students' speculations were "correct" than we were that the students understood that pictorial text (illustrations), like written
text, is language that they read and is equally vital to the meaning

of the story. What was made clear to us was that when students are supported in learning to draw on cues in both the written and pictorial texts and helped to consider the meanings each offers to the whole, they expand and enhance their learning, thinking, and meaning making as readers.

Implications

It is evident that art instruction integrated with reading instruction provided students with a larger set of tools by which to make meaning of texts. Using the visual aspects of the pictorial text within picturebooks allowed students to access the graphic cueing system in more depth. Early readers naturally use graphic cues within pictures. It is a tool they inherently turn to as they first make meaning of text. Reading instruction, however, typically focuses readers on the written text. As students develop into adults, they often return to using information within pictures to make meaning of the text (e.g., webpages, newspapers, brochures, billboards). Consider, for example, how looking at the picture on the front page of a newspaper influences adults' opinions of the veracity of the content of the adjacent article or how photographs are seen as evidence of written content. It stands to reason that literacy instruction should involve expanded use of the graphic cueing systems through art instruction. Withholding art instruction from the classroom curriculum limits the meaning students can construct when reading.

We realize that classroom teachers usually do not have a background in art, similar to Michelle's, and that this may discourage them from integrating art instruction within the curriculum. We also realize that not all art teachers may be open to using picturebooks, nor can they work individually with each teacher and create separate curricula for each class. The basic concepts about line, color, shape, space, texture, pattern, and movement in the chapter provide initial background for classroom teachers to begin exploring illustrations more in-depth with their students, and we encourage them to find other resources, including their art teacher. For example, Peggy Albers's (2007a) book is designed to support literacy and language arts teachers to understand the cueing systems within art, and how teachers can integrate basic art elements and principles of design into literacy instruction.

Our point is that art instruction is a necessary component to literacy instruction. Art needs to be valued as a valid sign system that conveys meaning just as written language does (Ohler, 2009). The ability to be able to read the picture in a text and understand how the elements of art and principles of design create meaning within the pictorial texts allows students to understand the whole text as it was designed by both the author and the artist. In this sense, art instruction cannot be ignored within the school curriculum without limiting the amount of information that students are taught to be able to access through text.

Acknowledgments

We thank Michelle Doyle and Stacy Aghalarov (and their students) for inviting us into their classrooms and their eagerness and willingness to be part of this study. Without their participation, the study would not have been possible.

Works Cited

Albers, P. (2007a). *Finding the artist within: Creating and reading visual texts in the English language arts classroom.* Newark, DE: International Reading Association.

———. (2007b). Visual discourse analysis: An introduction to the analysis of school-generated visual texts. In D. W. Rowe, R. T. Jiménez, D. L. Compton, D. K. Dickinson, Y. Kim, K. M. Leander, & V. J. Risko (Eds.), *56th yearbook of the National Reading Conference* (pp. 81–95). Oak Creek, WI: National Reading Conference.

Arizpe, E., & Styles, M. (2003). *Children reading pictures: Interpreting visual texts.* New York: RoutledgeFalmer.

———. (2004). Seeing, thinking, and knowing. In T. Grainger (Ed.), *The RoutledgeFalmer reader in language and literacy* (pp. 185–198). New York: RoutledgeFalmer.

Bader, B. (1976). *American picture books from Noah's ark to the beast within.* New York: Macmillan.

Bakhtin, M. M. (1981). *The dialogic imagination: Four essays by M. M. Bakhtin* (M. Holquist, Ed.; C. Emerson & M. Holquist, Trans.). Austin: University of Texas Press.

Berghoff, B., & Harste, J. C. (2002). Semiotics. In B. J. Guzzetti (Ed.), *Literacy in America: An encyclopedia of history, theory, and practice* (pp. 580–581). Santa Barbara, CA: ABC CLIO.

Braunger, J., & Lewis, J. P. (2006). *Building a knowledge base in reading* (2nd ed.). Newark, DE: International Reading Association; Urbana, IL: National Council of Teachers of English.

Dewey, J. (1978). *Art as experience.* New York: Doubleday.

Eisner, E. W. (1997). *Educating artistic vision.* Reston, VA: National Art Education Association.

———. (1998). *The kind of schools we need: Personal essays.* Portsmouth, NH: Heinemann.

Foreman, M. (2001). Seal surfer. In *Houghton Mifflin reading: A legacy of literacy* (pp. 47–55). Boston: Houghton Mifflin.

Gee, J. P. (2005). *An introduction to discourse analysis: Theory and method.* New York: Routledge.

Goodman, K. S. (1996). *Ken Goodman on reading: A common-sense look at the nature of language and the science of reading.* Portsmouth, NH: Heinemann.

———. (2003). Reading, writing, and written texts: A transactional sociopsycholinguistic view. In A. D. Flurkey & J. Xu (Eds.), *On the revolution of reading: The selected writings of Kenneth S. Goodman* (pp. 3–45). Portsmouth, NH: Heinemann.

Goodman, N. (1976). *Languages of art.* Indianapolis, IN: Hackett.

Goodman, Y. M., Watson, D. J., & Burke, C. L. (2005). *Reading miscue inventory: From evaluation to instruction* (2nd ed.). Katonah, NY: Owen.

Grindley, S. (1996). *Peter's place.* New York: Harcourt Brace.

Halliday, M. A. K. (1975). *Learning how to mean: Explorations in the development of language.* London, UK: Edward Arnold.

Halliday, M. A. K., & Hasan, R. (1976). *Cohesion in English.* London, UK: Longman.

Harste, J. C. (1994). Literacy as curricular conversations about knowledge, inquiry, and morality. In R. B. Ruddell, M. R. Ruddell, & H. Singer (Eds.), *Theoretical models and processes of reading* (4th ed., pp. 1220–1242). Newark, DE: International Reading Association.

Heath, S. B., & Wolf, S. (2004). *Visual learning in the community school.* London, UK: Creative Partnerships.

Hoffman, J. V., Baumann, J. F., & Afflerbach, P. (with Duffy-Hester, A. M., McCarthey, S. J., & Moon, J. R. (2000). *Balancing principles for teaching elementary reading.* Mahwah, NJ: Erlbaum.

Houghton Mifflin. (2001). *Houghton Mifflin reading: A legacy of literacy.* Boston: Author.

Kress, G., & van Leeuwen, T. (2006). *Reading images: The grammar of visual design* (2nd ed.). New York: Routledge.

Lewis, D. (2001). *Reading contemporary picture books: Picturing text.* New York: RoutledgeFalmer.

Lowenfeld, V., & Brittain, W. L. (1970). *Creative and mental growth* (5th ed.). New York: Macmillan.

McCurdy, M. (2001). Trapped by the ice. In *Houghton Mifflin reading: A legacy of literacy* (pp. 171–185). Boston: Houghton Mifflin.

Nodelman, P. (1988). *Words about pictures: The narrative art of children's picture books.* Athens: University of Georgia Press.

Ohler, J. (2009). Orchestrating the media collage. *Educational Leadership, 66*(6), 8–13.

Perkins, D. N. (1994). *The intelligent eye: Learning to think by looking at art.* Los Angeles: Getty Publications.

Piro, J. (2002). The picture of reading: Deriving meaning in literacy through image. *Reading Teacher, 56*(2), 126–134.

Pumphrey, R. (1996). *Elements of art.* Upper Saddle River, NJ: Prentice Hall.

Read, H. (1974). *Education through art.* New York: Random House.

Rosenblatt, L. M. (1978). *The reader, the text, the poem: The transactional theory of the literary work.* Carbondale: Southern Illinois University Press.

Schwarcz, J. (1982). *Ways of the illustrator: Visual communication in children's literature.* Chicago: American Library Association.

Sipe, L. (2000). The construction of literary understanding by first and second graders in oral response to picture storybook read-alouds. *Reading Research Quarterly, 35*(2), 252–275.

Sipe, L., & Bauer, J. (2001). Urban kindergartners' literary understanding of picture storybooks. *New Advocate, 14*(4), 329–342.

Smith, F. (2004). *Understanding reading* (6th ed.). Mahwah, NJ: Erlbaum.

Van Leeuwen, J. (2001). Across the wide dark sea: The Mayflower journey. In J. D. Cooper & J. J. Pikulski, *Houghton Mifflin reading: A legacy of literacy, grade 3, theme 5* (pp. 111–131). Boston: Houghton Mifflin.

Vygotsky, L. S. (1978). *Mind in society: The development of higher psychological processes*. Cambridge, MA: Harvard University Press.

CHAPTER NINE

An Arts-Integrated Unit: Learning 21st Century Literacies While the Teachers Are on Break

BETH BERGHOFF AND CINDY BIXLER BORGMANN
Indiana University–Purdue University at Indianapolis

MELISSA HELMERICK AND CAROL THORNE
Deer Run Elementary School, Indianapolis

Even though the gymnasium at Deer Run Elementary School was filled with four classes of fifth-grade students sitting on the floor, the room was hushed. There were no loud voices, no wrestling or sparring among the students; there was only quiet expectation and the electricity of everyone's excitement as they waited for the exhibition to begin. Artwork created by the students hung on the walls; inquiry projects were displayed on tri-fold boards on the stage; and journals and published writing were laid out on long tables. For the next forty minutes, these students would be performing dances, singing songs, reading myths, and looking at one another's artwork and projects. They would be reflecting on what they had done personally in the process of learning about Native Americans. They would also be adding new images, sounds, information, and emotions to their "imagic stores" (Broudy, 1994) as they enjoyed the rich array of artifacts created to represent the learning undertaken by other students in their school.

Students all turned their attention to the music teacher and the art teacher as they walked to the front of the gym with microphones in hand. "Welcome to our exhibition designed to show what we have learned through our study of Native Americans . . . ."

In this chapter, we recount and theorize the curriculum experiences of the teachers and students at Deer Run Elementary engaged in their first "arts-together" unit of study (Berghoff, Borgmann, & Parr, 2005). We aim to articulate the fundamental premises of arts-based, 21st century literacy learning because our experiences reinforced our belief that a multimodal, arts-infused curriculum better meets the needs of diverse learners than a skill-and-drill, test-prep curriculum.

Seven teachers collaborated to teach this arts-infused unit of study (Consortium, 2002) and to organize this culminating experience for the students. The teaching team included four classroom teachers and three specialists: an art teacher, a music teacher, and a media specialist. The principal encouraged this arts-integration effort because he believed the approach might help the school improve sagging achievement scores. Ten years ago, this K–5 elementary school, situated on the outskirts of Indianapolis, was earning the state's Four Star Award every year for its high test scores. Now the school was under pressure to improve because of its failure to meet Adequate Yearly Progress (AYP). The demographics of the school changed radically during this decade. In 1995, 12 percent of the students received free lunches. Ten years later, 49 percent of the students needed this assistance. In addition, the student body had become more culturally diverse, changing from approximately 50 percent African American and 50 percent Caucasian in 1996 to 30 percent Latino/a, 57 percent African American, and 5 percent Caucasian in 2008 (IDOE, 2009). Meanwhile the teachers involved in the study were Caucasian, except for one African American. Six were women and one had Miami Indian ancestry.

Melissa and Carol are the main characters in this curriculum story. Melissa, at the time of the unit, had been teaching visual arts to elementary students for ten years. Carol had been teaching music for twelve. Their spacious, carpeted classrooms, located at the end of a long hallway, were well equipped and separated by a moveable wall. They saw each other often as they stood outside their classrooms during the exchange of classes. Classes of students, led by their teachers, filed down the hallway to their rooms, coming for forty-five-minute sessions everyone called "specials." Melissa and Carol taught about 650 students each week in their visual arts and music classes, thereby providing the regular classroom teachers with much-needed time to plan and prepare for instruction.

Melissa and Carol were both working on their master's degrees in fine arts education at the Herron School of Art and Design at Indiana University–Purdue University Indianapolis (IUPUI). They were energized by new perspectives they were gaining about the role of the arts in learning (Eisner, 1998). As fine arts teachers, they understood that good instruction in the arts could develop students' cognition in unique and valuable ways (Grumet, 2004). But they also recognized that the visible, audible, and kinesthetic learning that happened in their arts classrooms needed to connect with the important learning going on in the regular classrooms. They wanted to see the arts move to the core of curriculum, but they were uncertain how that could happen when they saw so many children in a week and were viewed more as the means to a break than as teachers who should be substantially impacting student learning.

Melissa and Carol were not steeped in a multiliteracies theoretical framework such as the one explicated by the editors of this book; neither were the fifth-grade teachers with whom they collaborated. But in their first attempt to bring the strengths of the arts to bear on student learning, they achieved thought-provoking results, which we discuss later in the chapter using a 21st century literacy lens. By teaching an arts-integrated unit of study with their general classroom colleagues, these fine arts teachers encouraged the kind of multimodal (linguistic, visual, audio, gestural, and spatial) interactions that typify the new order of communication (New London Group, 1996). They helped students to interpret and create non-linguistic texts and to explore the dynamic relationships between and among texts and modes of meaning making. They led the way in creating innovative curriculum with the potential to teach 21st century literacies.

Generative Experiences

Being inquirers by nature, Melissa and Carol had been exploring the potentials of integrated collaborative units of study. They secured a school district grant to implement an integrated study called "Around the World" and worked with all the special area teachers—music, art, physical education, and media—to help students do computer research and present what they learned about a country in an exhibition. The unit was a success from the standpoint of student learning; the students were highly engaged and produced complex, multimodal projects. But the unit did little to provide the classroom teachers with new insights into the role of the arts in learning because the students did the learning while the classroom teachers were on break.

When Carol and Melissa discovered there was a two-week graduate summer institute focused on arts integration called Arts Together being offered at IUPUI, a university not far from their school, they enrolled. They were hoping to find ways to collaborate with classroom teachers in their school so they could use their knowledge of learning through the arts to accelerate the cognitive development of students at their school (Rabkin & Redmond, 2004). They expected simple solutions, as Carol later reflected: "I came to class with the preconceived idea that I would walk into class on Monday and be handed an instant package of how to integrate my field, music, with other core subjects." The Arts Together class, taught by Beth and Cindy, two education professors with teaching and research experience in arts integration (Berghoff & Borgmann, 2007) did help Carol and Melissa to formulate their next step, but not with a packet of handouts. Instead, Beth, a language arts teacher-educator, and Cindy, a visual arts teacher-educator, collaborated with a music professor and a professional dancer to create a "lived-through" learning experience for these graduate students that was qualitatively different from any they had experienced before (Berghoff, Borgmann, & Parr, 2005). The two-week intensive summer course immersed Carol, Melissa, and other members of their class in an "arts-infused" inquiry. They practiced being artists, writers, musicians, and dancers as they shared in a process of social learning.

The Arts Together class began with a "launch," an introduction that laid the groundwork for the study of immigration. The students were asked to respond to a survey about their personal beliefs about immigration; they explored "invitations," or learning stations (Berghoff, Egawa, Harste, & Hoonan, 2000), that provided a wide variety of perspectives about immigration through selections of literature, video, art, and music. They also viewed contemporary artwork about immigration using the "Visual Thinking Strategy" (Yenawine & Housen, 2000) to encourage critical thinking and communication through the arts and to develop visual arts skills. They made reflection journals and began to consider what they knew about immigration already, what their questions were, and how immigration connected to their lives.

For the next several mornings, the Arts Together sessions were structured so students, who were both classroom and art teachers, were engaged in learning in just one discipline at a time, experiencing what learning is like when the arts disciplines are used in parallel ways to develop cognitive understanding of a complex topic like immigration. Each of the discipline experts on the Arts Together teaching team took Melissa, Carol, and the other students through a learning process that started with interpreting aesthetic/cultural objects from their fields (literature, paintings, songs, or dances) and then shifted to creating personal works of art in the different arts disciplines.

Based on analyses of student learning in previous units of study (Borgmann, Berghoff, & Parr, 2001), Beth and Cindy knew that students who engaged in cycles of interpreting and creating were likely to build positive dispositions toward the arts when they learned like artists, musicians, writers, and dancers. So this immersion in parallel processes was intentional, and class members were asked to reflect on their own experiences as learners at intervals throughout the two weeks of class. Many, such as Melissa, wrote about the challenge of being out of their comfort zone:

> I am experimenting with [sign systems] (music and movement) I would not choose on my own, at least as a participant. Don't get me wrong. I love both these disciplines to listen to and to watch!!! . . . Just learning the elements of music is new to me. I knew they were similar with the arts elements. I see how rhythm and its change effects emotion. Harmonies can create a bold sound or the feeling of unity. The person creating the music is in control of so many things to alter the emotion that comes across. . . . I am finding for myself, I **really** have to concentrate to keep up with the beat when creating music. It is

most certainly out of my comfort zone. I can see how pushing myself to work in this area could help me to retain ideas and the meaning of our subject.

Because learners tend to feel more comfortable with one arts discipline than another, learning in multiple arts disciplines simultaneously involves taking risks and extra focus and attention to the creative work. Learners often feel like they are out of their comfort zone and need the support of the learning community to take risks and stay engaged (Stevenson & Deasy, 2005); this is one insight many students took away from their lived-through experience in the Arts Together Institute. They realized their own students would also feel vulnerable and need the support of positive and attentive peers and teachers.

On the last day of class, every Arts Together student shared in an exhibition of the learning. This culminating event was a chance for everyone to express his or her learning in multiple modalities. The students helped plan the agenda for the exhibition by deciding what they wanted to contribute and figuring out how they might summarize their new knowledge and insights in meaningful displays and performances. After the exhibition, Carol reflected: "I never dreamed that the blueprint I would receive would come in the form of heartfelt stories, emotion-filled music, powerful art, dance, and friendships that touched my life and changed me for the good."

Planning a Unit of Study with the Fifth-Grade Teachers

Melissa and Carol left the summer institute with a plan to continue their teacher inquiry into arts integration. They intended to ask one grade-level team of teachers to collaborate with them to teach an integrated unit. They went back to their school and crafted an email to their principal that explained what they wanted to do. Coincidentally, at the same time as they sent their email, they received one from the principal asking them, as arts teachers, to consider ways to enhance the regular classroom instruction in the coming year. When they met to discuss their plan, they found their principal was especially interested in having an exhibition of the children's learning. He was committed to helping them with funding, resources, or any support needed to get teacher buy-in.

Melissa and Carol knew from their earlier efforts at integration that they would have the support of Carrie, their media specialist. They also knew that Beth and Cindy were eager to support them, as the professors already had committed to attend the planning meetings and to help gather cultural artifacts. A message went out to the teachers, and then everyone waited for school to start up in August. Meanwhile, Carol and Melissa talked about the best way to support the classroom teachers, aiming to make it as easy as possible for the classroom teachers to participate in the unit.

Carol and Melissa felt the first step to planning a unit was to select a theme. They sent an email message to the fifth-grade teachers asking for theme ideas and began to worry when they received only one tentative response. When they met with the fifth-grade team to plan, they discovered the teachers could not offer theme suggestions until everyone knew *when* they would be co-teaching. When Carol and Melissa suggested October, the classroom teachers knew exactly what they wanted to study— Native Americans. This was a unit they did every year at this time, so choosing a theme became easy. To start the planning process, the teachers discussed their past experiences with the Native Americans unit and agreed on the importance of helping students move beyond stereotypical views of Native Americans. They reviewed the social studies standards they were expected to teach and agreed to a focus on teaching about the diversity of tribal nations that populated the United States long ago. They also wanted the students to learn that many of these tribes still exist today. In an attempt to keep the planning process streamlined for the teachers, Carol and Melissa created a cognitive ladder (Gabler & Schroeder, 2002) for the unit based on this planning conversation. This instructional organizer outlined the learning objectives for the unit, while leaving room for each individual teacher to contribute in his or her own way (see Figure 9.1).

In addition to the cognitive ladder, Carol and Melissa also started working on a week-by-week timeline outlining the key learning engagements to be taught during the four-week unit by each specials teacher. In art, Melissa planned to have the children

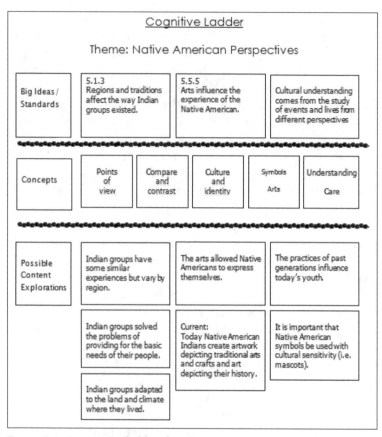

FIGURE 9.1. *A cognitive ladder about Native American perspectives.*

make calendar robes or personal symbol shields; in music, Carol would teach each class a song from a different Native American tribe and help the students create a group dance; and the media specialist wanted to have the students read myths and write stories to explain natural phenomena. When these ideas were shared and discussed one more time with the fifth-grade teachers in a meeting near the end of September, it was also decided that each class would study the tribes indigenous to one of four regions in the United States: the Eastern Woodlands, the Northwest Coast, the Plains, or the Desert Southwest. The final exhibition would provide a glimpse of the rich variety of Native American tribes' customs, stories, artwork, and songs.

Melissa and Carol willingly took the lead in the planning process because they knew the classroom teachers were already overwhelmed with demands placed on them by other programs and initiatives. They sensed the unit of study would be a good first experience for everyone if they could make the planning and implementation easy for the teachers. By the beginning of October, the media specialist had selected library resources and stocked a rolling cart with nonfiction books and Native American myths and legends from each of the four regions, featuring myths from tribes like the Abenaki, the Sioux, the Zuni, and the Snohomish. Beth and Cindy, knowing the importance of resourcing a unit with high-impact artwork, also collected and delivered reproductions of contemporary paintings and images, assorted literature and poetry selections, music CDs featuring Carlos Nakai (1995), a flute player who draws on his Navajo-Ute heritage, and resource kits from the Indiana Museum of Art, the Eiteljorg Museum of American Indians and Western Art, and the Indianapolis Children's Museum. Melissa and Carol studied the fifth-grade social studies textbook, and Melissa took photos of artwork in the textbook and blew them up to poster size to help children see connections between their learning in the arts classrooms and their own classrooms.

Teaching the Unit

The fifth-grade integrated unit about Native American perspectives began on the second day of October, and the final exhibition was scheduled exactly one month later. Each of the classroom teachers fit the unit of study into their scheduled instruction according to their own plans and needs. The teachers studied the chapter about Native Americans in their social studies text with their classes and did additional research about the lives of Native American tribes in their specific regions. Based on their inquiries about regional groups, the classes created artifacts such as tri-fold inquiry boards about the homes, weapons, and clothing of the Eastern Woodland Indians; strings of beads; and drawings of cooking utensils and clay pots to display at the exhibition.

The schedule for the arts classes was somewhat complicated by being a six-day rotation, but for the most part, each of the fifth-grade classes had one forty-five-minute art, music, and media class each week. During the unit of study, the classroom teachers were too busy to stay with their students during the specials classes, but the teachers did touch base with each other and exchange snippets of information about what was happening in their respective classes. They also talked with the children about what they were learning in each context and tried to help them make connections.

For Carol, the music teacher, the weekly lesson plan was repeated with each of the four fifth-grade classes. During Week One, she reinforced the idea that the Native Americans lived in accordance with their natural environments and that tribes and customs varied in different parts of the country. Then she taught each class a chant or song from their music book that originated in the region that their class was going to study. During Week Two, Carol invited students to share what they were learning about the lives of people in the tribes in their region by asking them to create dance movements to represent important features of the region's environment or to show daily activities carried out by the tribe members. To help the students feel comfortable moving their bodies, Carol had the students first create their own personal shapes with their bodies (see Figure 9.2). Then they worked in small groups to represent different ideas. Finally, Carol helped the students sum up what they knew to be essential aspects of the lives of people living in their region. With her help, each class chose one of these significant life experiences to represent in dance. Then Carol encouraged class members to suggest possible movements and positioning, as they choreographed a dance as a whole class. The classes that studied the Eastern Woodlands and the Desert Southwest both created their own versions of a Corn Dance that showed how the elements of weather and peoples' planting efforts helped corn to grow. The class that studied the Northwest Coast had ravens swooping in and out of their dance circle, and the class focused on the Plains depicted parts of a buffalo hunt.

During Week Three, the students discussed what they wanted to share at the exhibition, continued to work on their songs and dances, and explored a set of musical instruments collected from a

FIGURE **9.2.** *A student creates a shape with her body.*

variety of different tribes. Finally in Week Four, the music classes listened to a story about some contemporary Native American teenagers who struggled with their dual membership in the Native American culture of their families and the mainstream culture of their school. Carol invited the students to sketch their responses to the cultural identity struggles of the children in the story. The students were intent while working on their sketches and during the discussion that ensued as they shared their sketches (see Figure 9.3). They empathized with the characters in the story who were being asked to choose between following a Native American custom and acting like all their peers at school. Carol had the classes

FIGURE 9.3. *Students share their sketches with the rest of the class.*

do one last practice of their group dance after the conversations, and then she asked each class to decide whether they wanted to do the dance as part of the final exhibition.

Carol noted a change in the students' attitudes as the unit unfolded. When she mentioned doing a dance as a group the first week, the students had all moaned, but by the fourth week, each of the classes voted to perform their dance at the exhibition. The depth of their engagement with the dance showed in their bodies. They kept time with the beat of the Navajo flute and drum as they practiced movements imitating farmers or rain clouds or birds. In the final practices, students offered suggestions to make the dances more meaningful such as, "We should spread our fingers on the floor to represent our roots."

Meanwhile in art class the first week, the students made sketch journals to use for their personal reflections in all the classes. These small blank books went with the students from art class to the music class to the media center and back to their classrooms. In these personal pages, they wrote thoughts and ideas and drew pictures about what they had seen, read, and heard. A peek inside the pages helped the teachers to see the multiple strands of learning going on and gave the students opportunities to make connections.

Melissa grounded her teaching in images and symbols she borrowed from the students' social studies textbook and the local art museum. She hung poster-sized artworks, both contemporary and historical, all around the room to stimulate visual thinking and to present some carefully selected perspectives of tribal cultures. She introduced the unit by having children look closely at the enlarged image of a traditional Dakota Indian calendar robe. She invited the students to interpret the meaning of the symbols on the calendar robe and discussed why it was important for people to record historical events. Then she had the students start to draw symbols in their sketchbooks to signify important things that had happened in their lives. After this first lesson, she noted in her journal that the children really seemed interested in the traditional calendar robe and were coming up with some great ideas. She particularly enjoyed a conversation she had with a third-grade girl who was trying to figure out how to symbolize the time she learned right from wrong. "Wonderful!" Melissa had penciled next to the notes about the conversation in her journal.

Melissa ended the calendar robe lesson with a discussion of a contemporary artwork by Norman Akers (Osage/Pawnee) entitled *Result of New Contact* (2000). To help the students interpret this painting, she followed the *Visual Thinking Strategy* (Yenawine & Housen, 2000) by asking, "What is going on in this painting?" and "What in the painting makes you say that?" Then she intently listened to their comments, paraphrased them for the class, and pointed out the features of the painting different children noticed so everyone could think about the observations. These interpretive activities helped the students to see more in the images and to better understand the possible meanings of the painting.

In the next lesson, students progressed from interpreting cultural artifacts to creating their own artwork. Melissa helped the students start work on one of two different, but similar, projects. Two classes created symbol shields (Figure 9.4) and two created calendar robes (Figure 9.5); both of these projects invited the students to create their own symbols to record important aspects of their lives.

At the final exhibition in the gym, all the symbol shields and calendar robes were displayed, along with the students' sketch journals, the myths and illustrations they created with the guid-

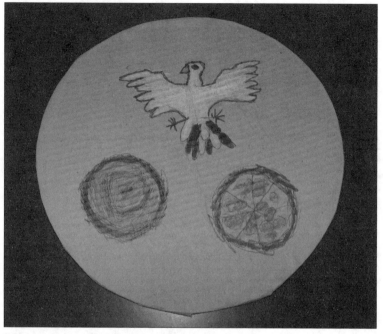

FIGURE **9.4.** *An example of a symbol shield.*

FIGURE **9.5.** *An example of a calendar robe.*

FIGURE **9.6.** *An illustration of a myth.*

ance of the media specialist (Figure 9.6), and the projects they created in different classrooms (inquiry displays, bead necklaces, and drawings). The forty-five-minute exhibition began with several students reading their myths into the microphone. Then the classes performed their dances and sang their songs. The session ended with time for the students to browse all the artifacts.

Reflection

When the teachers discussed the cognitive ladder for this unit of study, they agreed on some big ideas. They wanted the students to understand that Native American culture is often thought of in stereotypic ways when it is really a wonderful example of diversity. They wanted students to recognize that Native Americans lived and live in a variety of contexts, and each tribe or regional group has unique histories, customs, and beliefs. The teachers also wanted the students to know that they could better understand this diverse group of people by studying their lives from different perspectives, including the arts. Since Native American tribes were the first to populate the United States, their lives and perspectives shaped and continue to shape this country; teachers wanted their students to consider and be respectful of the contributions of Native Americans.

It was easy to see in all the artifacts laid out for the exhibition that the children had moved beyond a simplistic view of Native Americans as one cultural group. They did not hear one song, but four songs with different instruments and languages. They saw four different dances and heard many different stories. They saw many different forms of representation and showed deep respect for the Native American cultures in the ways they took up these forms of representation to record events from their own lives. Since the study lasted just four weeks, it was impossible for students to have a complete historical knowledge, but the exhibition showed an understanding that Native Americans were and are diverse in their lifestyles and expressions. The student work displayed in the gym also provided evidence of the connections students made between new information they were learning and their own lives and cultural experiences. Students had gone beyond paper-and-ink ways of knowing to explore their own cultural identities with visual symbols, gestures, and musical expressions borrowed from various Native Americans. They learned in embodied and multimodal ways, and as a result, they were highly engaged and willing to share. During the exhibition, everyone felt the solidarity and excitement that came from being a member of a highly productive learning community. Even the teachers shared a few high-fives as the students finished browsing the artifacts.

It is also significant to note that the arts teachers and the media specialist orchestrated inquiry processes that started with opportunities for the children to learn more about interpreting cultural artifacts created by artists, musicians, and writers. These teachers introduced their students to carefully chosen aesthetic objects to help deepen students' understanding of the ways of knowing made possible by the questions and tools of the disciplines of visual arts, music, and language arts. In other words, they taught aspects of their disciplines while teaching the knowledge constructs of the Native American unit. This set up the next part of the inquiry in which the children used the new additions to their imagic stores to create their own expressions of meaning. Even though their time with the children was extremely limited, these arts teachers focused on working through the generative cycles of interpreting and creating. The students were active participants in using visual images, sound, and movement, not simply for entertainment or decoration, but for learning.

When the unit was completed, the arts teachers engaged in reflective journaling, and they also asked the classroom teachers to answer written questions about the planning process, their observations of student learning, challenges of the unit, the final exhibition, and the teachers' willingness to collaborate on such a unit again. From Carol's perspective, the integrated study of Native American tribes and cultures was a huge step forward for the staff at Deer Run because it was the first effort at collaboration between the classroom teachers and specials teachers to teach shared standards. The arts teachers noticed that the students were cognizant of the connections between what they were learning in their regular classrooms and the arts classes. Melissa noticed specifically that the students tapped into the knowledge base developed with their classroom teachers when thinking about the symbols and images in the traditional and contemporary artwork. The classroom teachers noticed continuity and engagement as well. One teacher commented, "I feel like [the students] were more immersed in their projects. By doing this in the classroom and getting it in music and art, they were seeing the links and getting a holistic picture of what we wanted them to learn." Another teacher reflected:

> I loved seeing them come to my class with their sketchbooks. We didn't always add to them, but they loved sharing them and talking about their activities in class or other specials. They seemed to be more engaged and understanding of how the different classes were reinforcing the study of their region and blending all aspects of their life.

After the exhibition, Melissa provided questions to help the fifth graders reflect on the unit, and she found that students' perspectives mirrored those of the teachers. The students liked the connections from one class to the next and were anxious to be involved in another integrated unit of study. The teachers and students also noted that the exhibition had a positive effect on the students' sense of community and pride in their own learning. The teachers suggested ways the next exhibition might be a little more effective, mentioning more time to browse the artwork and stories, more students talking about their artwork, better microphones and vocal projection, a PowerPoint presentation of pictures taken in classes during the unit of study, and a time frame that would allow additional teachers and classes to attend.

For the most part, the fifth-grade teachers were enthusiastic about replicating the unit, but they expressed some concerns about the balance between their own autonomy as curriculum planners and the demands of collaborating on a unit of study across so many levels. Even though the planning was kept to a minimum by the effective and efficient teamwork of the arts teachers, planning at multiple levels took more time, complicated their decisions, and introduced new time frames and constraints.

Implications for Practice

If the goal of schools is to produce students with 21st century literacies, the arts need to play a more central role. This story describes a first attempt to bring the power of the arts alive, and the results are very interesting when viewed through the lens of changing literacies practices. These teachers created a curriculum that involved designing, creating, and producing multimodal texts (Anstey & Bull, 2006) that developed their students' 21st century literacy skills.

It is worth noting that Carol and Melissa "lived through" an arts-infused unit of study before teaching one themselves. They sought professional development so they would know what to do, and they implemented the Arts Together model as they facilitated the Native Americans unit. They designed their instruction to move from *interpretation* (looking at artwork and discussing its meaning, listening to music or songs, and thinking about what they communicate) to *creation* (making symbol shields and calendar robes, choreographing a dance) to *sharing* at the exhibition. Students were engaged in a social learning process that introduced cultural artifacts that represented meanings in visual and aural ways, and the arts teachers helped the students work together to interpret the meanings of these artworks. Then, they encouraged the students to express their own meanings relative to the unit of study using these sign systems. Students reflected on their learning in journals and created multiple artworks of their own. When these creations were displayed and shared in the gym, everyone experienced the richness of learning that comes from arts disciplines being stacked in parallel ways. By making it possible for the students to shift from one form of literacy to another—to shift from reading and writing to visual arts to singing and dancing—the arts teachers heightened the learners' engagement; both the specials teachers and the classroom teachers noticed this change.

Research in the arts helps to explain this high level of engagement. For one thing, the arts are the most embodied of the disciplines (Dewey, 1934; Efland, 2002; Eisner, 2002). Learners are called on to use all five senses and their emotions when working in the varied art forms (Egan, 1992). Researcher Damasio (2003) shows that individuals who view an artwork have autonomic responses, meaning they have a physical response to the art, such as a constriction in their stomach or an impulse to touch a sculpture. The brain maps these physical responses and uses the nervous system to help *read* the art for meaning. When it comes to dance, the body is totally involved in creating and communicating meaning, and these meanings are rich in emotion. The arts, by making demands on the cognitive, emotional, and physical systems of the body, take learners to high levels of engagement—full of resonance, intentionality, social imagination, and sense of community (Berghoff & Borgmann, 2007; Green, 2003).

When learners are challenged to understand a situation, they generally access as many modes of information as they can to gain a better grasp of what is happening. According to the New London Group (1996), the modes of information can be linguistic, visual, audio, gestural, and spatial. This is nothing new for learners because they use all these modalities in the course of their everyday encounters with the world. Sociocultural language researchers have helped us to see that humans are well-suited to this level of complexity (Lewis, Enciso, & Moje, 2007). Gee (2008), for example, points out that literacy, in its full range, is cognitive, social, cultural, political, institutional, economic, moral, and historic. Given this complexity, it makes perfect sense that learners can more fully engage when the learning context is enriched with multiple perspectives provided by the different arts disciplines.

Melissa and Carol helped students, especially minority and second language learners, to develop the concept of cultural identity by starting the study with discussions of authentic Native American artifacts, music, and artwork. They helped the students explore ways their own lives were similar to or different from the lives of diverse Native American groups. Then they invited the students to try out various cultural forms of representation to express personal and community messages. During this process, the students were reassured that they were not expected to be experts, but rather that they should give being an artist or a dancer a go. This is exactly what they did, and because the work was done primarily in sign systems other than language, even the newest English learners were fully engaged and proud of their work.

Clearly, the arts integration was beneficial for the students in many ways, but the unit of study was not perfect nor did it come together without some struggle and compromising on the parts of various team members. As Carol mentioned early in the planning process, there was no "playbook" available to guide this type of collaboration and teaching. She and Melissa had to be willing to take a risk, to step forward with their best understanding of integrated curriculum, and to try to make it work. The classroom teachers were accustomed to teaching according to standards, but they did not typically think of the arts standards as part of their instruction. It took Melissa and Carol suggesting big ideas that could tie the unit together and creating the cognitive ladder to help the team members see how their individual instruction could be complemented by the arts instruction. This shared focus and coherence is critical to effective integrated instruction. All the teachers needed to buy into the focus and commit to actively helping students make interdisciplinary connections. For teachers at Deer Run, these were new demands that were layered onto teaching jobs that were already very complex, and it was difficult for this team to even find forty minutes to meet and plan or debrief.

Time was perhaps the most daunting obstacle for Carol and Melissa. They both mentioned that they needed more time to do their teaching. Getting through a whole inquiry cycle in four sessions was terribly rushed. In the future, they want to start on a unit of study a couple weeks before the classroom teachers, because they only see the children one period a week. This extra time might help, but clearly there are deeper issues to be solved in the scheduling practices of schools if arts teachers are going to reach their potential in supporting 21st century literacies. The current use of the arts teachers to provide teacher release time is not a structural arrangement conducive to supporting integrated instruction. Two additional obstacles for this team were the challenges of assessing student learning when it took on complex dimensions and of resourcing arts-based units of study. Schools are not typically equipped with arts resources designed to augment the content learning of the curriculum. Schools that want arts teachers to team with classroom teachers to provide multiliteracies instruction will have to invent new ways of organizing for the work.

In closing, we assert that this case study is evidence that elementary schools need to rethink the role of arts teachers if they are at the margins of curriculum rather than at the center. Arts teachers can make 21st century literacies part of the learning culture of a school if they understand inquiry-based cycles of social learning, are able to conceptualize meaningful units, and engage in collaborative planning. Arts teachers can open the door to 21st century literacies by working in coordination with classroom teachers to teach arts-based learning processes that help students unpack the content and concepts of a study. Collaborating in this way, teaching teams can create learning contexts rich with multiple avenues of cognition so that learners can think and express themselves flexibly across sign systems and disciplines, potentially making the learning community more inclusive. Spaces can be created where marginalized students do not have to know and use the mainstream discourse to be successful learners. Finally, good arts teachers know the difference between doing crafts and teaching students to understand, critique, and appropriate cultural representations of meaning. When it comes to 21st century literacies, arts teachers, including language arts teachers, need to lead the way.

Works Cited

Anstey, M., & Bull, G. (2006). *Teaching and learning multiliteracies: Changing times, changing literacies.* Newark, DE: International Reading Association.

Berghoff, B., & Borgmann, C. B. (2007). Imagining new possibilities with our partners in the arts. *English Education, 40*(1), 21–40.

Berghoff, B., Borgmann, C. B., & Parr, N. C. (2001). Dispositional change in preservice classroom teachers through the aesthetic experience and parallel processes of inquiry in arts integration. *Arts and Learning Research, 17*(1), 61–77.

———. (2005). *Arts together: Steps toward transformative teacher education.* Reston, VA: National Art Education Association.

Berghoff, B., Egawa, K. A., Harste, J. C., & Hoonan, B. T. (2000). *Beyond reading and writing: Inquiry, curriculum, and multiple ways of knowing.* Urbana, IL: National Council of Teachers of English.

Broudy, H. S. (1994). *Enlightened cherishing: An essay on aesthetic education.* Urbana: University of Illinois Press.

Consortium of National Arts Education Associations. (2002). *Authentic connections: Interdisciplinary work in the arts.* Reston, VA: National Art Education Association.

Damasio, A. (2003). *Looking for Spinoza: Joy, sorrow, and the feeling brain.* New York: Harcourt.

Dewey, J. (1934). *Art as experience.* New York: Perigee Books.

Efland, A. D. (2002). *Art and cognition: Integrating the visual arts in the curriculum.* New York: Teachers College Press.

Egan, K. (1992). *Imagination in teaching and learning: The middle school years.* Chicago: University of Chicago Press.

Eisner, E. W. (1998). *The kind of schools we need: Personal essays.* Portsmouth, NH: Heinemann.

———. (2002). *The arts and the creation of mind.* New Haven, CT: Yale University Press.

Gabler, I. C., & Schroeder, M. (2002). *Constructivist methods for the secondary classroom: Engaged minds.* Boston: Allyn and Bacon.

Gee, J. P. (2008). *Social linguistics and literacies: Ideology in discourses.* (3rd ed.). New York: Routledge.

Grumet, M. (2004). No one learns alone. In N. Rabkin and R. Redmond (Eds.), *Putting the arts in the picture: Reframing education in the 21st century.* Chicago: Columbia College Chicago.

IDOE. (2009). Indiana Department of Education—School data. Retrieved from http://mustang.doe.state.in.us/SEARCH/snapshot.cfm?schl=5352

Lewis, C., Enciso, P. E., & Moje, E. B. (2007). *Reframing sociocultural research on literacy: Identity, agency, and power.* Mahwah, NJ: Erlbaum.

New London Group. (1996). A pedagogy of multiliteracies: Designing social futures. *Harvard Educational Review, 66*(1), 60–92.

Rabkin, N., & Redmond, R. (2004). *Putting the arts in the picture: Reframing education in the 21st century.* Chicago: Columbia College Chicago.

Stevenson, L. M., & Deasy, R. J. (2005). *Third space: When learning matters.* Washington, DC: Arts Education Partnership.

Yenawine, P., & Housen, A. (2000). *Visual thinking strategies: Understanding the basics.* New York: Visual Understanding in Education.

Artwork and Music

Akers, Norman. (2000). *Result of new contact* [Oil on canvas]. Indianapolis: Eiteljorg Museum of American Indians and Western Art.

Nakai, R. C., Eaton, W., & Clipman, W. (1995). *Feather, stone and light* [CD]. Phoenix: Canyon Records.

CHAPTER TEN

Silencing Stories: The Triumphs and Tensions of Multimodal Teaching and Learning in an Urban Context

ADRIENNE M. COSTELLO
Buffalo State College

When something appears on the educational horizon that is as liberating and transformational as multimodal teaching and learning have been for me and for so many teachers and researchers, it is hard to imagine such innovative practice might be accompanied by specific, daunting challenges. I embarked on a study of digital video composing and informal classroom drama in an urban school and imagined that, while I would not be able to offer it as a panacea to all of the challenges of urban schooling and literacy education, I would be wading through relatively smooth waters. I wanted to be able to tell the world what multimodal teaching and learning did and can do for students in urban schools, for students of color, and for English teachers who seek both to empower their students' voices while engaging in valuable literacy-learning activity. I wanted to explore the potential for multimodal teaching practice to act as a positive pedagogical force, particularly for African American students, who face specific challenges with school curricula that often fail to acknowledge their lived experiences and subjectivities or to empower them as critical members of the societies in which they live (Butchart, 1994; Fecho, 2004; Gordon, 1994; Heath, 1983). When that effort was complicated by some troubling findings and outcomes, I was thrown. I was thrown as a researcher against an unexpected tide of teacher choices and institutional challenges. I realized that, once again, I had to regain my footing in the ever-shifting sand.

This chapter tells a delicate yet important story. Amid the promise that 21st century literacies hold for students and teachers, we cannot overlook the challenges teachers still face in complicated contexts as they attempt to adopt transformational teaching practices, and the personal and pedagogical choices they make in the face of such challenges.

Relevant Research and Theory

This study and discussion is grounded in sociocultural theory (Vygotsky, 1978) and is informed by epistemologies of new literacies studies and multimodal literacy (Albers & Harste, 2007; Alvermann, 2002; Kalantzis & Cope, 2000; Gee, 2003; Kress, 2000; Lankshear & Knobel, 2003; New London Group, 1996). I view digital video composing in the classroom as a literacy learning *supertool* (Miller & Borowicz, 2005) and as an example of multimodal literacy practice (Miller, 2007). I wondered about the potential for digital video composing and informal classroom drama (NCTE, 1982) to work together to create meaningful literacy learning opportunities for students. Informal classroom drama as pedagogical practice draws from the work of Dorothy Heathcote (1984) and other proponents of "process" drama that position improvisational drama activity as a learning tool (Wilhelm & Edmiston, 1998). Viewing informal classroom drama as a reader-response endeavor (Rosenblatt, 1978), I worked with an eighth-grade English teacher to explore the possibility of integrating informal classroom drama and digital video composing into his eighth-grade English classrooms' study of literature.

I pursued an ethnographic case study (Creswell, 1998) in two urban eighth-grade English classrooms taught by the same teacher. While findings from the larger study include the effects of engaging in drama and digital video activities on students' literacy learning (Costello, 2006), this chapter focuses specifically on the classroom teacher and the pedagogical choices he made during one major drama/video project toward the end of the school year. Three major research questions guided the study, and one question is taken up in this chapter: What happens when a middle-grades

English teacher introduces process drama and digital video production to his students as part of the English curriculum?

Although this study was originally aimed at filling a gap in current research literature on the relationship between informal classroom drama and digital video composing, the inquiry took a drastic and unexpected turn in one of the two classrooms studied. Although one classroom had a largely positive experience with a dramatic video project, the other classroom had a significantly different experience. This chapter takes up the story of this second classroom, its students, and the struggle faced by its creative but conflicted teacher.

Methodology, Context, and Researcher's Role

Context of the Study: The School, Its Students, Their Teacher

Neighborhood School (names of people and places in this study are pseudonyms) is located in the urban center of a medium-sized city in the Northeast of the United States. It is a community school in that all of its student population comes from the area surrounding the school; none of the students are bussed in from other areas of the city. In fact, most of the students walk to school each day, except for a small number of students with special needs.

The vast majority (99.3 percent) of students at Neighborhood School are racially identified on the state education website as "Black." The school is located in a section of the city that is predominantly African American in its ethnic makeup. This has created a sort of closeness among students who walk to and from school in large groups, are well acquainted with each other's families, and have known each other for much of their lives. Seventy-six percent of the student body during the time of the study was eligible for free lunch, with another 9.8 percent eligible for reduced lunch. Dylan Bradley, the classroom teacher, is a white man, and the only middle-grades English teacher at the school. On his shoulders rested the sole responsibility for preparing students for the state eighth-grade English language arts assessment, as well as the end of the year city exam, which was a determining factor in whether students moved on to high school. Dylan did not take that responsibility lightly. He came in at least an hour early every morning and stayed after school an extra hour almost every day of the week, offering help and extra support to students.

I came to know Dylan as a graduate student at the university where I had just begun my work as a doctoral student. During this study, he had recently completed his master's degree and had settled into his fourth year of teaching at Neighborhood School. I came to know his enthusiasm for teaching and his innovative and thoughtful ideas after we had, as a class, attended a politically charged lecture by educational researcher Jean Anyon (1981, 2005). We were asked to share our impressions of the lecture to which Dylan raised a clenched fist, and loudly stated, "It's time for a revolution!" The class cheered; I knew that I wanted to work as a researcher with him in his class.

Dylan explained, in an interview with me, that he considered himself a student-centered teacher and shared his teaching philosophy:

> I always believe in putting my students right in the middle. I guess student-centered teaching. I try to get after what's the best practice, the best technique for the students themselves to get the most out of the lesson. I don't believe in standing in front of the class and lecturing or getting into that kind of format. . . . I always like to give the kids, whenever possible, a chance to work in small groups or in partners, and then to share what they came across with those experiences with the larger group. I think kids will learn a lot more from each other than they can learn from me.

Dylan embraced digital video composing in his teaching practice, and used it during several projects with his students throughout the school year. Amid constant administrative pressure to prepare his students for two major high-stakes tests in eighth grade, Dylan repeatedly showed commitment to innovative practice.

Overview of Study

My role in this one-year case study was that of a participant-collaborator; I was committed to offering assistance when needed in an effort to promote reciprocity in the research process (Flinders, 1992; Zigo, 2001). I participated in Dylan's two eighth-grade English classrooms two to three days a week from September to December, three to four days a week from January to March (sometimes every day depending on the activity), and every day from April to early May.

Participants included Dylan, as primary participant, and both classes of eighth-grade students, all of whom were African American. I named the two classrooms "The Outsiders Homeroom" and "Freak the Mighty Homeroom" based on the novel each focused on for the final project. With input by Dylan and my own observations throughout the year, six focal students were selected in an effort to provide data on a range of students who were diverse in both academic standing and classroom behavior, and to provide depth to my examination of the final dramatic video project.

Field notes and daily entries in a researcher's journal (Ely, 1991) were integral components of the data set. Artifacts included storyboards, writing, assignment sheets and rubrics, and digital video iMovie products, and were collected from all students as relevant data. Informal and semi-structured interviews were conducted with Dylan and focal students. These interviews offered me insight into participants' thinking as they constructed various digital projects.

Analysis of the data record was an evolutionary process (Lincoln & Guba, 1985) that was recursive and ongoing (LeCompte & Preissle, 1993) and comprised of two phases. During Phase I of data collection (September through December), I formed some preliminary impressions of what I noticed in the classroom that connected to the research questions. During Phase II (January through May), I more systematically collected and analyzed data through pure immersion. Daily, I listened to audiotapes focused on the six focal participants and typed up and summarized key findings in my field notes. By systematically reading and studying these documents, I was able to refine my data collection strategies as I noticed a gap or a need. Once data collection was complete and I had a complete data set, Phase III of analysis commenced. I repeatedly read my field notes and transcripts and carefully studied and examined all artifacts. I then began initial and final coding of data that aimed to identify the ways in which video production and process drama activity transacted to serve as mediational tools (Vygotsky, 1978) that facilitated participants' literacy learning. This led to the uncovering of important evidence and themes.

The Dramatic Video Project

Part of a larger study, this chapter focuses specifically on the experiences of one classroom throughout the process of working on the dramatic video project, a culminating multimodal experience that included written language, digital video, and drama, and took place toward the end of the school year. Three components comprised this project. First, and primary, were student-improvised "confessionals" in which, as a character from their novel—Philbrick's *Freak the Mighty* (1993) or Hinton's *The Outsiders* (1967)—they shared their inner thoughts and feelings to the camera. Second, Dylan and I asked students, in pairs, to identify a specific theme or "life lesson" that they found to be a focus of the chapter. This theme drove both the title and the character-confessional that the pair developed and performed in a short digital video created in iMovie. And, third, each student-pair's movie included a tableaux, or frozen dramatic pose. Tableaux allowed students to perform two scenes from the chapter, make thoughtful decisions about how to distill multiple events into one revealing frozen scene (Wilhelm & Edmiston, 1998), and work together to make aesthetic choices about the composition of the picture that would result in a powerful visual image. Each digital project did not exceed ninety seconds and would be edited together with those from the rest of the class to produce one whole-class movie about the book.

Findings

Positioning Digital Video as Privilege, not Pedagogy

The two classrooms that engaged in the dramatic video (DV) project had two profoundly different experiences. The Outsiders Homeroom (OH) had largely positive and successful experiences with the project. Conversely, the Freak the Mighty Homeroom

(FH) had a more complicated experience. Throughout the year, Dylan was frustrated by FH's disruptive behavior. Students were continually reprimanded for not completing homework or talking too much, and Dylan expressed that he had serious reservations about their involvement in this project. Two students, Curtis and Raymond, were known throughout the school as "troublemakers" or "thugs." They were often fodder for discussion by teachers in the teachers' lounge where I ate lunch, and it was widely suspected throughout the school that they were involved in neighborhood drug and gang activity. Their relationship with Dylan throughout the year was contentious, and often their disruptions, such as talking sarcastically out of turn and swearing under their breath, would get them removed from the classroom by Dylan and placed in suspension. When Dylan requested that Curtis and Raymond be permanently removed from the classroom for the rest of the year, they were placed in suspension only to return to the classroom several days later with no reasons given for this decision. With Curtis and Raymond as part of the class, Dylan became more and more frustrated with FH, and repeatedly told me that he actually looked forward to the days when he would not have to see this class.

In spite of Dylan's admittedly low expectations for FH, the students began the project enthusiastically. He repeatedly reminded them that the DV project was a privilege, and that they were invited to participate because I had convinced him:

> iMovie is something special. Very few teachers in the city get to use these cameras. Not every student can handle the responsibility, so not every class gets the privilege of participating in iMovie[,] . . . and if you can't behave yourselves, I will cut off the project completely.

After this warning, in a manner that was distant and technical, Dylan introduced the project's requirements, focusing primarily on its timetable and rubric. He then showed a sample digital video we had created around a fight in *The Outsiders*, a book they had read earlier in the year. Every student watched it attentively. No heads rested on folded arms, no eyes stared out the window or at the clock. Every student seemed interested in the movie. However, when the video ended and students began chatting with one another about it, Dylan immediately quieted their comments and responses, in striking contrast with the OH class who were engaged by Dylan in conversations regarding their observations or questions. The FH, now near-silent, listened as Dylan went through each expectation, explaining how our sample video fit the criteria of the rubric. Dylan stopped only momentarily at one point to quiet Curtis and Raymond, who were talking to one another, then organized the FH students into pairs to work. I helped him to distribute blank storyboards, and Dylan instructed students to work on rough drafts and on formulating ideas for their movies based on directions for this day's tasks written on the board.

Passive Students Repositioned as Makers of Meaning

Watching students work together in the early stages of the dramatic video project in the FH was invigorating. All students were working on a chapter from Rodman Philbrick's (1993) young adult novel, *Freak the Mighty*, upon which they would design their confessionals. Philbrick's novel addresses the friendship of two middle-school-aged boys, both outcasts and both who suffer serious medical conditions. Max, the narrator, is extremely large for his age, developmentally delayed, and struggles academically. Freak, who is unusually small, is profoundly intelligent. Like flowers toward the sun, students looked up, opened up, and began to show a level of engagement that was not typical for the class. As students pulled their desks together, shuffled materials around, and started working on the project, I began circulating with my camera to alternate between filming my own research footage and offering assistance to students in need. An excerpt from my reflective notes reads,

> Kids just kept on calling me over. I didn't have a moment to stop and write notes. The students' questions ranged from detailed, logistical/technical questions to artistic and thematic choices. While some groups were more on track than others, most students were progressing really nicely. I even had a few productive exchanges with Curtis and Raymond.

Curtis and Raymond, whom Dylan had paired with one another, sat with their desks turned to face each other. Each time I stopped to check on their work, they had made some progress, from filling in three panels in their storyboard to discussing what they would say in their confessionals. Curtis and Raymond were working on a chapter in *Freak the Mighty* in which Freak starts teaching Max new words. While Max finds this task difficult, he eventually conquers his fears and has success with the dictionary. I stopped at Curtis and Raymond's desks at one point to chat.

ADRIENNE: Can you tell me a little bit about what you're doing?

CURTIS: We're just doin' this stuff for English, you know, so we can pass. A little iMovie.

ADRIENNE: What about your storyboard here? Can you tell me a little bit about that?

CURTIS: It's about how, you know, my man Max here never thought he could learn a new word out the dictionary. So, you know, I teach him a little somethin'.

ADRIENNE: So you're gonna be Freak?

CURTIS: Yeah, I teach him something new about the dictionary. Now he know how to read out of a dictionary and look up words and things like that.

ADRIENNE: Great. So what's the lesson? What's the theme?

CURTIS: You never know until you try!

ADRIENNE: Excellent.

Even though Curtis was a bit sarcastic in his response to my first question, he offered answers to my continuing questions that showed a genuine analysis of this moment in the text. By looking at the text from the character's point of view, Curtis was able to come up with a theme which, in keeping with the demands of Dylan's rubric, "matched the chapter's scene appropriately." The theme Curtis came up with, "You never know until you try," is both an important life-lesson and a thematic representation of the ideas of the chapter.

In the midst of this energy of writing and discussing, Dylan explained his expectations for these confessionals. In written form, they needed to be polished and grammatically correct, while on camera they could use "slang" and must be done "off the cuff," without notes in front of them. When some students voiced confusion over this point and questioned how they would perform their confessionals, Curtis offered this clarification to the class, "It's like you freestylin'!" I remember thinking that I could not have explained it better. The students responded with similar affirmation, such as, "Yeah! Freestylin'! Yeah, it's like a rap." As Dylan continued to explain how students should speak as the character, Curtis interrupted, loudly stating, "I'm gonna rip it!" Drawing on their implicit media and performance knowledge seemed to energize the activity for students like Curtis. Dylan seemed responsive to this positive energy. Instead of reprimanding Curtis, Dylan replied with a smile, "Yes. Please rip it."

"Your Movie's Gone": A Teacher in Conflict Reaches His Breaking Point

Into the next class session, students remained engaged, but their engagement threatened Dylan's need for an orderly classroom; his displeasure with the FH class rose incrementally alongside their more vocal, boisterous behavior. He continually informed the class of his frustration that the classroom was not as orderly and efficient as the Outsiders Homeroom and repeatedly threatened to cut off the project. As students began filming their tableaux and confessionals, Dylan reached his breaking point. The students were out of their seats, bustling around the room, and talking loudly while working on their filming. While I was out in the hallway helping a group of girls with a camera, someone in the classroom threw a book across the room. Dylan was never able to identify who had thrown the book, or why. This was the one pivotal moment that became the proverbial last straw for Dylan, and his many threats to end the dramatic video project for the Freak the Mighty Homeroom became a reality. Dylan repeatedly chastised the class in a twenty-five-minute lecture that began:

> I've always tried to treat you like adults, and all you've done is try to act like little kids. One person in this room ruined iMovie for the rest of you. So what do you expect from me? How many times am I gonna give up more of my energy, more

of my class time to do something for you that you don't care about anyways? How many more times do you honestly expect me to do this this year? That's right, because the answer is zero.

Hearing Dylan reach this point of utter dejection was painful. I felt sympathy both for him and for his students. It was clear that the stress and pressure of the day-to-day dealings with this class had taken their toll on Dylan, and he now needed to let it all out. But as the students stared into the space in front of them, few of them looking directly at him, most of them shaking their heads, I could sense their frustration, as well. Dylan continued:

> From now on, you're done. Every day you come in, it will be the boring class I described to you. If that's the only way you can sit and hopefully learn for yourselves, that's the way we'll do it. On Monday you'll come in we'll start *Anne Frank*. Your movie's gone. You'll have two weeks to read *Anne Frank* to yourself. Every day you'll have little quizzes to make sure you're keeping up with the reading. If you're reading, you'll pass and get hundreds. If you don't, you'll get zeroes and fail. And I don't think that's gonna be a big deal for this class. You've pretty much done that the entire year.

Dylan had decided, essentially, that the pedagogical tools of drama and digital video composing were superfluous. Unlike an educational necessity such as a textbook, these multimodal experiences could be taken away from students as punishment. The Outsiders Homeroom, who created their DV without as much rambunctious disruption as the FH, got to continue their project and created a finished, whole-class movie. The FH, instead, would spend the next two weeks silently reading a play. Dylan had proven to the students that what he said upon introducing the project was true: that digital video was a privilege that could be taken away.

As Dylan went on with his lecture, never looking at me while talking, I became more and more dismayed. It became clear to me that, for all of my attempts at reciprocity and all of my ethical ideals, the relationship between researcher and teacher had become complicated and filled with tension I had never expected. Dylan was clearly frustrated, not only with the students but with himself and with my presence as a researcher in his classroom. He later suggested that I no longer return to the FH, and I respected and complied with his wish.

Discussion

Socially Constructed Identities in an Urban School Context

In order to work through the murky and difficult dynamics that led to the demise of the dramatic video in the Freak the Mighty Homeroom, the sociocultural context of the whole school must be considered. I argue here that the context of the urban school and the resulting construction of teacher and student identities influenced the fate of the innovative approaches to literacy in Dylan's classrooms.

Neighborhood School is an institution that can be characterized as a "tight ship." Students move to and from classes in straight lines and sit in their classrooms in straight rows. Students are told when to get up from their tables for lunch and when to sit down. The culture of the school is one of rigid order, with constant emphasis on controlling student behavior. Weiner (2000), in her synthesis of research on urban teacher preparation, recognizes that most urban schools can be characterized by isolated bureaucracy, chronic underfunding, limited definitions of "intelligence," and a disconnection between school and students. My observations of life at Neighborhood School revealed the presence of these factors, and I was able to see the ways in which they played out in Dylan's classroom.

In first getting to know Dylan as a classmate in a graduate course, I came to see him as a revolutionary, progressive educator who embraced ideas of empowering literacy (Finn, 1999) for his students. In the reality of day-to-day life at Neighborhood School, however, Dylan presented a different teaching identity (Vinz, 1996). His persona became that of an authoritarian, complaining about students in the lunchroom and keeping them in line in the classroom. Dylan was able to switch back and forth between these two very different, socially situated identities depending on the context. Sociocultural theory helps to provide a potential explanation for this shift. Similar to Gee's (1996) discussion of discourse as a situated form of language use involving the meaning-making processes and identities of a particular social group, Bakhtin (1981) recognizes social languages as culturally situated ways of using language shared by a particular community. As the social situation dictates, Dylan is able to take up words from "other people's mouths, in other people's contexts, serving other people's intentions," (Bakhtin, 1981, p. 293) and use them as his own. The messages communicated to Dylan by the administrative organization of the school community as well as the statements of other teachers in school spaces, such as the faculty lunchroom, seem to have affected the way Dylan relates to students in his classroom and manifested themselves in his outward speech. When Dylan is at work, specifically when faced with a challenge, the power of the social language of the school community trumps the discourse of graduate school. In the classroom setting, Dylan reverts to the "deep grammar of schooling" (Lankshear & Knobel, 2003) that is reflected in the speech and controlling social practices of his colleagues and superiors.

A telling example of Dylan's shift in persona was observed in his introduction of the dramatic video project to the two different classrooms. In the Outsiders Homeroom, Dylan began the project by showing a sample movie we had made and welcoming student questions and feedback; he began the project in the Freak the Mighty Homeroom with a lecture about how iMovie is a privilege that could be taken away at any time. After showing the sample video to the Freak the Mighty Homeroom, Dylan did not allow any opportunity for students to contribute comments or questions about the video. When he decided to end the project for that class, he did not allow students an opportunity to express their feelings of dissatisfaction with the decision. Fine and Weis (2003) asserted, ". . . schools are profoundly contradictory spaces. They can be repressive and toxic, and they can challenge social (in)justices by opening the doors that race and class hierarchies have glued shut" (p. 3). I watched as the forces that push against each other to create such contradiction in schools played out in the theater of Dylan's classroom. What resulted were moments of brilliant success, and moments of stifling silence.

What Teachers Need: Social Support and a Reflective Researcher's Stance

I did not expect to witness the type of difficulties that arose in the class, as my previous experiences and interviews with Dylan had shown him to be an empathetic and progressive-minded educator who rarely "lost his cool." Although the event, like so many qualitative research experiences, has uncovered more questions than answers for me, watching Dylan's journey with this class has illuminated several potential issues to be grappled with surrounding urban education and the difficulties associated with the integration of multimodal literacy learning in the urban classroom. In living through the day-to-day struggles of teaching at an underfunded, racially segregated school in which the administration and staff appeared to value controlling students' behavior and raising students' test scores above all else, Dylan's willingness to disrupt the traditional paradigm of teaching quiet students in straight rows with the student-centered, multimodal endeavor of digital video is admirable. But Dylan's willingness to deviate from the traditional "transmission" model of teaching in order to create spaces for students to become "active designers of meaning" (New London Group, 1996) was abandoned when control issues in the class threatened to disrupt the power balance between students and teacher to the point where he felt that to continue the project would be unsafe, unproductive, or simply unacceptable.

In interviews, Dylan "talks the talk" of a culturally sensitive educator. His actions in the classroom, however, reveal an adherence to the traditional mindset that learning through multimodality is a privilege rather than an integral component of an English curriculum. The dichotomy Dylan presents, the disparity between what he *says* (and appears to truly believe) about the nature of teaching and learning and what he *does*, sometimes, in the tensions and realities of the classroom setting, is striking. I could only reflect on this dichotomy and realize, as a field, the truly delicate and difficult undertaking it is to teach every day in contexts like Dylan's. It should be recognized that when teachers like Dylan take steps in the direction of embracing 21st century literacies in their curricula, doing so may go against everything that surrounds them, influences them, and directs them in their daily lives.

Implications for Practice

The implications for the field of teacher education are compelling. When considering the ways in which multiliteracies can complicate traditional teaching practices and classroom power structures, I hesitate to emphasize one true lesson to be learned or one specific set of conclusions based within this story of Dylan's teaching. Rather, I pose certain suggestions and possibilities as a starting place for future discussion and exploration of these tensions. Teachers like Dylan need as much professional support as possible in order to successfully integrate multimodal literacies in their classrooms in the face of the daily challenges to their contexts. Even with the support of a researcher who helped with the teaching, Dylan struggled. It should be recognized that his specific teaching situation was a difficult one: Dylan was the only English teacher for seventh and eighth grade, the only person responsible for preparing students for the exams, and the only person planning the middle-grades language arts curriculum at Neighborhood School. It can be suggested that teachers like Dylan would benefit greatly from continued opportunities to meet and talk with other teachers in his discipline throughout the year, to continue to support and guide him in his teaching, and to give him a chance to address and work through the day-to-day realities of his position. I also suggest that teachers such as Dylan would benefit from adopting the reflective stance of a teacher-researcher. So often when engaged in action research in their classrooms, teachers' eyes are opened to moments that would otherwise go unnoticed. Moments like Curtis and Raymond's conversations about their confessionals, for example, are so often like falling trees in the empty woods to many teachers. When looking at the classroom through the lens of an action researcher, teachers can achieve a heightened awareness of student learning, while at the same time reflecting on the ways in which classroom practice can be strengthened. Teachers such as Dylan can begin to see and hear students such as Curtis and Raymond, as well as themselves, in new ways.

The Road Ahead

Teacher educators must not take lightly the difficulties and challenges associated with the integration of 21st century literacies into classroom contexts, and those complexities need to be brought to light and explored in education courses. It should be acknowledged that when teachers such as Dylan attempt to embrace innovative process, such as improvisational drama and digital video composing, which disrupts and challenges the dominant culture and discourse of the school, it is a brave and bold task filled with moments of promising success and fraught with moments of difficult challenge. Dylan's journey into the integration of multimodal literacies in his teaching, therefore, is an important story that helps us to appreciate all of the complexity that accompanies such an ambitious attempt: the risk taking, the high hopes, the apprehensions, the successes, and the failures. Dylan was willing to take the difficult step of integrating multimodality into his teaching, but his actions in removing the dramatic video project from the Freak the Mighty Homeroom suggest that he views endeavors like drama and video as supplemental learning activities to be used as a reward for good behavior, rather than much-needed pedagogical tools with the potential to transform the everyday life of his classroom. I suggest, then, that 21st century literacies as pedagogical tools should be integrated in preparatory courses for English teachers, such as methods and strategies courses taken prior to certification. I offer such suggestions as a starting point, not a solution. It is important to avoid the temptation to simply label Dylan or his students as deficient or the teaching approach as ineffective. Rather, this story should motivate us to examine multimodality in nuanced and critical ways that take into consideration the broader challenges that stifle innovation and perpetuate inequities in American schools.

Although the story of the Freak the Mighty Homeroom is a complex and difficult one, it is an important one in that it helps to recognize the challenges faced by students and teachers in urban contexts and to consider the ways in which we can disrupt negative trends and empower students in twenty-first century urban classrooms. Fine and Weis (2003) articulate the complexity and potential of urban classrooms and their students:

> Marginalized youth, particularly youth of color, don't expect very much from schools. They don't ask for much, and usually they're not disappointed. But these young men and women know well how to use that momentary contradiction, when a teacher stretches toward, when a classroom comes alive, when brilliance floods the room from all corners. With such a moment, we are delighted to tell you, even the most disengaged youth may just fly. (p. 8)

In considering both the successes and the struggles of Dylan and his students with the integration of drama and digital video, it becomes clear that more research and work is needed to further our understanding of these complexities and to continue to illuminate the possibilities for 21st century literacies in the English classroom. The needs and experiences of teachers and students in urban schools, specifically, need to continue to be explored. There is great potential for students in urban settings to apply their own rich and complex experiences and backgrounds to the type of empowering meaning-making activity afforded by multimodal endeavors like improvisational drama and digital video. At the same time, though, the power structure and ethos of urban schools pose certain challenges to the integration of innovative teaching approaches by teachers that require further exploration and study in order to be more fully conceptualized. It is the responsibility of the field of education to continue to explore teaching and learning through multimodal literacies in complicated contexts, and to continue to search for ways of helping teachers and students in such contexts to take such a bold and spirited step.

Works Cited

Albers, P., & Harste, J. C. (2007). The arts, new literacies, and multimodality. *English Education*, 40(1), 6–20.

Alvermann, D. E. (Ed.). (2002). *Adolescents and literacies in a digital world*. New York: Peter Lang.

Anyon, J. (1981). Social class and school knowledge. *Curriculum Inquiry, 11*(1), 3–42.

————. (2005). *Radical possibilities: Public policy, urban education, and a new social movement*. New York: Routledge.

Bakhtin, M. M. (1981). *The dialogic imagination: Four essays by M. M. Bakhtin* (M. Holquist, Ed.; C. Emerson & M. Holquist, Trans.). Austin: University of Texas Press.

Butchart, R. E. (1994). Outthinking and outflanking the owners of the world: An historiography of the African-American struggle for education. In M. J. Shujaa (Ed.), *Too much schooling, too little education: A paradox of Black life in White societies* (pp. 85–122). Trenton, NJ: Africa World Press.

Costello, A. (2006). *New literacies in English: Integrating process drama and digital video in an urban, eighth-grade classroom* (Unpublished doctoral dissertation). University at Buffalo, State University of New York.

Creswell, J. W. (1998). *Qualitative inquiry and research design: Choosing among five traditions*. Thousand Oaks, CA: Sage.

Ely, M. (with Anzul, M., Friedman, T., Garner, D., & Stainmetz, A. M.). (1991). *Doing qualitative research: Circles within circles*. New York: RoutledgeFalmer.

Fecho, B. (2004). *"Is this English?" Race, language, and culture in the classroom*. New York: Teachers College Press.

Fine, M., & Weis, L. (2003). *Silenced voices and extraordinary conversations: Re-imagining schools*. New York: Teachers College Press.

Finn, P. J. (1999). *Literacy with an attitude: Educating working-class children in their own self-interest*. Albany: State University of New York Press.

Flinders, D. J. (1992). In search of ethical guidance: Constructing a basis for dialogue. *International Journal of Qualitative Studies in Education, 5*(2), 101–115.

Gee, J. P. (1996). *Social linguistics and literacies: Ideology in discourses*. Philadelphia: RoutledgeFalmer.

————. (2003). *What video games have to teach us about learning and literacy.* New York: Palgrave Macmillan.

Gordon, B. M. (1994). African-American cultural knowledge and liberatory education: Dilemmas, problems, and potentials in postmodern American society. In M. J. Shujaa (Ed.), *Too much schooling, too little education: A paradox of Black life in White societies* (pp. 57–78). Trenton, NJ: Africa World Press.

Heath, S. B. (1983). *Ways with words: Language, life, and work in communities and classrooms.* New York: Cambridge University Press.

Heathcote, D. (1984). Drama as a process for change. In L. Johnson & C. O'Neill (Eds.), *Collected writings on education and drama* (pp. 114–137). Evanston, IL: Northwestern University Press.

Hinton, S. E. (1967). *The outsiders.* New York: Puffin Books.

Kalantzis, M., & Cope, B. (2000). A multiliteracies pedagogy: a pedagogical supplement. In B. Cope and M. Kalantzis (Eds.), *Multiliteracies: Literacy learning and the design of social futures* (pp. 237–246). New York: Routledge.

Kress, G. (2000). Multimodality. In B. Cope & M. Kalantzis (Eds.), *Multiliteracies: Literacy learning and the design of social futures* (pp. 182–202). New York: Routledge.

Lankshear, C., & Knobel, M. (2003) *New literacies: Changing knowledge and classroom learning.* Philadelphia: Open University Press.

LeCompte, M. D., & Preissle, J. (1993). *Ethnography and qualitative design in educational research* (2nd ed.). San Diego: Academic Press.

Lincoln, Y. S., & Guba, E. G. (1985). *Naturalistic inquiry.* Beverly Hills: Sage.

Miller, S. M. (2007). English teacher learning for new times: Digital video composing as multimodal literacy practice. *English Education, 40*(1), 61–83.

Miller, S. M., & Borowicz, S. (2005). City voices, city visions: Digital video as literacy/learning supertool in urban classrooms. In L. Johnson, M. E. Finn, & R. Lewis (Eds.), *Urban education with an attitude: Linking theory, practice and community* (pp. 87–105). Albany: State University of New York Press.

National Council of Teachers of English (1982). *Guideline on informal classroom drama.* Retrieved from http://www.ncte.org/positions/statements/informalclassdrama

New London Group. (1996). A pedagogy of multiliteracies: Designing social futures. *Harvard Educational Review*, 66(1), 60–92.

Philbrick, R. (1993). *Freak the mighty*. New York: Scholastic.

Rosenblatt, L. M. (1978). *The reader, the text, the poem: The transactional theory of the literary work*. Carbondale: Southern Illinois University Press.

Vinz, R. (1996). *Composing a teaching life*. Portsmouth, NH: Boynton/ Cook.

Vygotsky, L. S. (1978). *Mind in society: The development of higher psychological processes*. Cambridge, MA: Harvard University Press.

Weiner, L. (2000). Research in the 90s: Implications for urban teacher preparation. *Review of Educational Research*, 70(3), 369–406.

Wilhelm, J. D., & Edmiston, B. (1998). *Imagining to learn: Inquiry, ethics, and integration through drama*. Portsmouth, NH: Heinemann.

Zigo, D. (2001). Collaboration in labor as a path toward equalizing power in classroom research. *International Journal of Qualitative Studies in Education*, 14(3), 351–365.

CHAPTER ELEVEN

Toward a Multimodal Literacy Pedagogy: Digital Video Composing as 21st Century Literacy

SUZANNE M. MILLER

University at Buffalo, State University of New York

Increasingly in digital practices outside of school, adolescent youth actively compose meaning through new kinds of texts in their social worlds (Lenhart, Madden, & Hitlin, 2005). In school, a declining percentage of graduating high school seniors (nationally only 28 percent) find what they do in classrooms meaningful and useful to their lives or futures (Bachman, Johnston, O'Malley, 2008). These two intersecting twenty-first-century trends provide a stark image of changes needed in education.

Although engaging in meaning making outside of school more than *in* school has influenced students for some time, current research narratives provide strong evidence for this trend. Analysis of student literacies outside of school—such as creating websites, fanfiction, and blogs—highlight these literacy lifeworlds that are often invisible to teachers in schools (Hull & Schultz, 2002; Selfe & Hawisher, 2004). The in- and out-of-school contrasts are so sharply drawn that some argue that most students lead double lives (Williams, 2005).

In these out-of-school literacy practices, print text is most often mixed with images, video, audio, and music; that is, the texts are multimodal, communicating by using different representational means. Facebook page creators, for example, use print text along with photos, videos, music, and links to webpages. But not just youth engage in these multimodal practices. Across generations, these practices flow into personal, civic, and workplace activities that are rapidly becoming pervasive cultural practices

(Kress & van Leeuwen, 2006). For evidence of the pervasiveness of multimodality, look at the design of webpages and the impact of webpage multimodality on media, such as newspapers, magazines, and TV news.

The swing in the landscape of communication from linear print to spatial images prompts the creation of many print-mixed texts (Kress, 1999). Professional literacy organizations promote these shifts in literacy as moving from the conventional sense of reading and writing *only* print text to an expanded sense of reading and writing multiple forms of nonprint "texts," as well (International Reading Association [IRA], 2001; National Council of Teachers of English [NCTE], 2005, 2008). In the technological and cultural contexts of the past two decades, that movement toward nonprint and print-mixed texts has accelerated due to the accessible digital affordances for creating and mixing print, images, sounds, video, and music. The underlying trend toward multimodality is not local and adolescent but global and multi-generational.

How do schools respond to the challenge of engaging students in the global, digital world of continual meaning making, expression, and social networking? Instead of drawing on these 21st century literacies for learning, the school "preference for print may preclude teachers from even noticing their students' competence with multi- and digital literacies" (King & O'Brien, 2002, p. 41). The literacy of school usually differs both from the blogs, fanfiction, and social networking sites around which millennial youth affiliate and from the multimodal literacies needed in twenty-first century personal, civic, and work spaces (Partnership for 21st Century Skills, 2008).

What's important to note are the underpinnings of these new multimodal literacies: they are *purposeful* literacy practices that are *meaningful* to users as *social communication*. These elements are often missing from technology use in school, where practicing software skills (e.g., PowerPoint, Excel) dominates (Lankshear & Knobel, 2003, 2006). In such school-based activities, the Web 2.0 information overload dramatized by New Literacies group scholars is ignored. They argue that what students need is *performance* knowledge: knowing *how* to find, gather, use, communicate, and imagine new ways of envisioning assemblages of knowledge

(Lankshear & Knobel, 2003). Yet, especially in the context of the high-stakes testing frenzy, students have fewer opportunities than ever to make meaning in school and little space to use their multimodal literacy strategies for school learning.

In short, we all live in new times of digitally accessible multi-modality for designing texts for social purposes. Those examining these trends in research have reached a clear consensus: facility with interpreting and designing multimodal texts will increasingly be required by human beings to communicate, work, and thrive in the digital, global world of the twenty-first century (Alvermann, 2002; Buckingham, 2008; Cope & Kalantzis, 2000; Gee, 2004; Jewitt & Kress, 2003; Kress, 2000, 2003; Lankshear & Knobel, 2003, 2006; New London Group, 1996, 2000; Street, 1995). Moreover, these scholars concur that significant changes will be needed in schooling, in teachers, and especially in educational beliefs about the status/design of nonprint modes of meaning as ways of knowing and communicating.

Some also argue that these social and cultural changes have special significance for English language arts classes in which making meaning from and composing texts are central issues (Albers & Harste, 2007; Ellis, Fox, & Street, 2008; Grabill & Hicks, 2005; Kadjer, 2006; Miller, 2007, 2008a; Miller & Borowicz, 2005, 2006, 2007). In what follows, I propose a framework and a method for drawing on these new social practices and developing performance knowledge for learning in schools.

Teaching and Learning in Classrooms Reframed by Digital Video Composing

Five years before YouTube brought easy access to videos around the world, the City Voices City Visions (CVCV) partnership was focusing on bringing multimodal composing into schools as a learning tool. Since 2000, the CVCV project has provided professional development institutes (twenty-eight hours over eight Saturdays) for more than two hundred urban teachers on using digital video (DV) as a high-interest means of composing and representing understanding of concepts in content-area classes such as English, social studies, science, English as a Second Language

(ESL), and foreign language. Teachers learned how to create DV projects as part of their curriculum, and the university team (five research assistants who were experienced teachers and I) provided ongoing in-classroom support for teachers as they introduced DV composing projects to their students.

What makes DV composing an effective instructional strategy? Creating videos is a high-status social practice and a quintessential multimodal literacy. Capturing, editing, and distributing video is widely and cheaply accessible, leading educational researchers and forecasters to now cite digital video as an emerging technology that will "significantly impact the choices of learning-focused organizations" in the next year (Horizon Report, 2008, p. 3). YouTube and other websites have made video content easy to share online to a worldwide audience. During one month, December 2007, Internet users in the United States watched more than 10 billion videos online (Lipsman, 2008).

The CVCV Institutes for professional development supported teachers in learning to create digital video using hand-sized DV cameras and engaging students in digital video composing on curricular concepts. In the early years of the project, all of us researchers and teachers were learning together how to integrate DV tools into the curriculum. In CVCV classroom sites, the university team learned from Keith Hughes and other Generation X teachers (born between 1965 and 1980) how to draw on the power of the visual genres that students already knew (e.g., movie trailers, ads, music videos) and how to create a digital video on a curriculum concept in one class period. The university team also documented the learning processes of teachers and student groups in their classroom video productions and often saw an almost total engagement in meaning making that I believe is the heart of literacy. A recurring image from these videos is a group of diverse students, heads together, intensely focused on the storyboard, the script, the camera LCD playback, or the computer screen.

The usefulness of DV composing as an important learning tool for the twenty-first century has been elaborated elsewhere in a series of case studies that involved following teacher and student learning through analysis of observations, interviews, and student products (Miller, 2007, 2008b; Miller & Borowicz, 2005, 2006, 2007; Miller, Hughes, & Knips, in press). The success of

DV composing as a student learning tool became evident over time through this research. DV composing also has been shown to be a powerful tool for transforming teaching and learning in English classrooms. The process begins with point-of-need support for English teachers in professional development and in their classrooms to help them critically reframe their pedagogical practices. In summary, DV composing in schools:

- helps teachers move away from print-only literacy;

- requires orchestration of representational modes—that is, requires multimodal design;

- engages students in a real-world literacy practice;

- makes intuitive sense to learners as a social practice that garners attention and viewers;

- connects to high-status youth media culture; and

- prompts deep attention to content and to communicating it for a familiar audience.

In all, DV composing provides students with multimodal learning in an authentic, high-status, social and media practice with powerful attention-getting qualities and expert models in the real world.

Elizabeth Rassler, a ninth-grade English teacher, introduced a DV project to her class in a process that is typical in CVCV classrooms. She asked each student to select an important passage from the memoir *Night*. They underlined the most powerful language in the passage that included imagery and turned that language into a found poem. In small groups, students read each other's found poems and selected one they liked the best to make into a short video representing *Night*. In one video, students in the class moved slowly by a pile of shoes and placed theirs on the pile, then moved on. In another, an image of flames, from a video retrieved online, flickered as a student in some sort of uniform stepped toward the camera and intoned sternly, "Men to the left, women to the right." These chilling videos captured students' aesthetic responses and the book itself through multimodal compositions that developed and demonstrated their understanding.

Learning to use and to teach digital video composing can

induce the changes in teachers' beliefs about literacy that promote changes in their pedagogies and students' learning (Miller 2008; Miller & Borowicz, 2006). A growing body of research situated in project classrooms provides evidence that DV composing can be a potent new literacy learning tool that leads to increased student engagement and achievement (Blondell, 2006; Borowicz, 2005; Costello, 2006; Lauricella, 2006; Miller, 2007, 2008; Miller & Borowicz, 2005, 2006, 2007). In the following, I illustrate how the essential components of digital video composing work in the CVCV context and in other classrooms.

A Multimodal Composing Framework for Pedagogical Change

Integrating multimodal composing in schools requires that teachers draw on the key components in literacies outside of school that entice students and others to engage so attentively—communicating and representing meanings with and for others to make sense of the world and oneself in the world. But how? In the New Literacies group at the University at Buffalo, my colleagues and I have developed a framework for pedagogical change based on theory and research from our cross-project analyses of studies in multimodal composing (Miller, Thompson, Boyd, & McVee, 2008). The resulting multimodal literacy pedagogy provides a model of changes needed in beliefs and practices and a reframing of how to support students as they engage in multimodal composing as a learning tool.

Four principles represent the key changes needed for teachers to transform the teaching and learning in their classrooms toward multimodal composing. The components that provide teachers direction toward this critical reframing include: (1) providing explicit multimodal design instruction and attention; (2) co-constructing authentic purposes for representing multimodal meaning for an audience; (3) designing multimodal composing activities that invite students to draw on their identity lifeworlds as resources; and (4) creating functional social spaces for mediating multimodal learning. (See Figure 11.1 for a representation of the framework for this multimodal literacy pedagogy.)

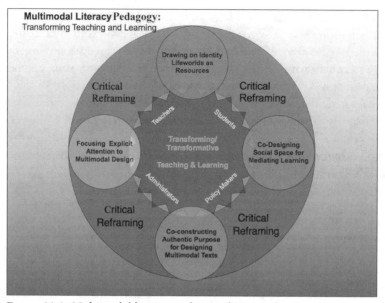

FIGURE **11.1.** *Multimodal literacy pedagogy framework.*

Creating a Classroom Social Space for Mediating Multimodal Learning

Successful CVCV teachers perceived digital video production as a social phenomenon that arises from collaborative participation in a group, what Leontiev (1978) calls an "activity system." Findings from CVCV studies are congruent with the sociocultural perspective that student participation within these activity systems, and the support they receive there, contribute not only to students' knowledge and thinking but to their values, beliefs, and identities (Lave & Wenger, 1991; Wells, 1999). Teachers initiated these social spaces by (a) changing their own and their students' classroom roles and (b) setting up tasks and processes to support collaborative work.

Successful youth programs outside of schools have a strong focus on collaborative activities (Hull & Nelson, 2005; Goodman, 2003; Buckingham, 2008). Researchers in those programs describe similar social practices, such as joint planning (Heath,

2004) and collaborative, authentic work experience (Goodman, 2003). The New London Group (2000) points to what they call "coengagement in designing" as essential to the new economy, to students' social and cognitive development, and to their democratic empowerment (p. 22). These social learning strategies are so important that, in the twenty-first century workplace, "socially skilled learners will be advantaged while 'monastic learners,' children who rely solely on independent learning strategies, may be disadvantaged" (Leu et al., 2004, p. 1598).

During DV production in CVCV classrooms, students are typically "networked with other people and with various tools and technologies . . . so that one can behave 'smarter' than one actually is" (Gee, 2003, p. 8). Successful CVCV teachers design the context for DV production first by shifting traditional teacher and student roles to create a shared DV social space in the classroom. In this shared workspace, the teacher shifts from role of expert to that of adult co-creator with the students. In most cases, the teacher literally moved from the desk at the front of the room to become a roving media guide, moving from student space to student space and occupying no significant physical space of her own. The teachers in these energy-charged classrooms described themselves as "guides," "facilitators," or "a third arm" in their students' learning events.

This change in teacher stance significantly alters the student space. Student participants tend to move between the roles of teacher and student in their joint endeavor of designing and producing the digital video within the group. When these teachers designed their classrooms as places of transformation, students' agency in their own learning emerged, with ongoing teacher support. This change allows students to bring to the digital composing task their media and community experiences. Leu et al. (2004) also noted this needed shift in teacher stance: "Teachers will increasingly need to orchestrate complex contexts for literacy and learning rather than simply dispense literacy skills, since they will no longer always be the most literate person in the classroom" (p. 1599).

Teachers created learning tasks and experiences that required students to take on new roles and identities as producers, designers, and resources for each other. Here is a typical description of teams collaborating in a DV workshop that was captured during a visit to Nate Russel's English class (Borowicz, 2005):

> The students attend to their tasks as soon as they come into the classroom. No one comes in late. Some students are at the computer looking for images on the Internet. Others are filming, and others are still planning, talking, sketching with their groups. John [a focal student] and his group have already filmed, and they are watching their raw footage on the camera screen. Two other boys join them to watch also. They laugh at footage of a staged fight scene, and Marty shouts out in his raspy voice, "Aw, that's dirty." The classroom is noisy, movement everywhere, electric. The kids are singing and dancing as they work. They're talking together, looking at each others' work, exchanging ideas, "Hey, man, look at this. Russel, you gotta' see this." Music is softly playing on DV sound tracks. Computers are replaying movies as they're being edited. Olivia and Portia are sitting on the windowsill viewing their footage in the camera; they're smiling, laughing, discussing how they will edit their footage.

Our research shows that such joint endeavors create the group; the common endeavor of digital video production and interest in DV composing organize the activity of this classroom. The concept of "affinity space," where a set of diverse people interact around a joint endeavor or activity (Gee, 2004, p. 83), operates in these social spaces. It may be that the only thing people have in common in an affinity space is the activity and experience of that particular space. In successful CVCV classrooms, teachers introduced and sustained activities so that such affinity spaces for digital video composing emerged through joint student work.

When a DV project is in process, students work in teams collaborating with each other and with cameras, computers, and props as mediating tools (Vygotsky, 1978) for the clear purpose of designing a digital video text. Whether students are creating a political commercial, interpreting a poem, or analyzing a scene from a novel through DV, the student space has an immediate focus, a common goal to play with and work toward. The content of the classroom DV space includes not just the textbook, the teacher, and other curricular texts (posters, worksheets), but also the multimodal signs students generate through the camera and design through the computer software. Students interact with each other around the content. They turn to and teach each other, drawing on knowledge distributed among the team and from outside sources on the Internet.

In successful CVCV classrooms, teachers construct an atmosphere of social ease in which what students bring to the composing task is as important as the curriculum represented in printed textbooks. The new ways that teachers organize these classrooms to set tasks and support joint endeavors invites students to talk for new purposes and to use what they know to create understanding of curricular concepts. For instance, in one eighth-grade English class about to read *Anne Frank*, students working in small groups were to create parts of a DV glossary on World War II terminology. The groups engaged in a lengthy conversation about what their terms really meant: Why was the swastika shaped the way it was? What were they trying to communicate? This attention to the meaning of symbolic representation—to semiotics—might be hoped for in a college seminar, but these 13-year-olds initiated such talk in order to understand the topic so that they could make a compelling DV entry into the class video. In many groups, the design of the film's message was shaped from students' collaborative language-in-use during planning, filming, editing, and assembling the video.

Even in a school where the atmosphere was sometimes interrupted by violent outbreaks, students noticed and appreciated the pocket of camaraderie in their classroom. "You get a lot out of it, working together with others and stuff," one student commented. DV composing creates an affinity space because it provides a prototype of joint production in a project-based activity that networks resources and people who share knowledge of all sorts.

An initial CVCV class activity in which a group-made video was completed in one class period demonstrates one way for teachers to create these social spaces. Social studies teacher Eric Mohammed asked each student to bring to school an artifact, an image, or a demonstration to answer the question, "What is culture?" The complexity of the question becomes apparent as the diverse verbal and visual answers are aggregated on a DV: a Muslim girl sets down a prayer rug, an African American boy has the camera circle his braids, and a girl shows a picture of her baby, all accompanied by explanations of his or her view of culture (Miller, 2007). The knowledge shared could not have been generated from one person; it required the distributed knowledge of all the students and their mediating visuals. Discussion of the DV prompted awareness of diverse perspectives on culture in the class.

After such initial collaborative movie-making experiences, the typical organization of DV classrooms is in production teams, which enables students to act with others "in such a way that their partial knowledge and skills become part of a bigger and smarter network of people, information, and mediating devices" (Gee, 2004, p. 86). In the wired world, the most effective way of learning and working is "by drawing from the expertise that lies outside ourselves" (Leu et al., 2004, p. 1598). Almost 20 years ago, the Department of Labor echoed the same social themes in its extensive study of the needs of the new workplace (The Secretary's Commission on Achieving Necessary Skills [SCANS], 1991), concluding that, along with fundamental thinking skills, high school graduates must be competent in collaborative capabilities such as participating as a team member, negotiating perspectives in diverse groups, and teaching others new skills. The U.S. Department of Education (1996) issued similar calls for getting American students ready for 21st century literacies and technology. DV composing in CVCV provides the kind of co-designing students need in "the collaborative work projects of the new economy" (Heath, 2004). Further, such collaborative practice empowers students as learners, engaged citizens, and community members.

Engaging Student Lifeworlds and Identities

Having students connect their lives to the curriculum was an explicit goal of the CVCV project. During the CVCV Institute, teachers learned how to engage students in DV curriculum projects linked to school and the community with the aim of both motivating student learning and developing teacher understanding of the urban community.

Drawing on student lifeworlds as resources in the curriculum so students could create new identities while learning was an essential component of multimodal literacy pedagogy that emerged in the multimodal composing research (Miller, 2007, 2008b; Miller, Thompson, Boyd, & McVee, 2008). Identity is involved in DV design because "the outcome of designing is new meaning, something through which meaning makers remake themselves" (Cope & Kalantzis, 2000, p. 23). As urban students have opportunities to reconstruct *who* they are in school through design activities that reconstruct *what* counts as learning, we have seen remarkable things happen. DV production provides an artful new literacy supertool that, with teacher support, can help students move out of passivity, alienation, and powerlessness (Miller & Borowicz, 2005).

When CVCV teachers created spaces that allowed students to redesign cultural forms (the genres and media familiar in youth culture), both curriculum *and* student identity were transformed. DV workspaces provided students opportunities to bring cultural and digital resources they had acquired outside of school *into* school learning. Music videos, movie trailers, and advertisements are all forms with which students are quite familiar through their everyday knowledge of television and movies. Working with teacher participants, the CVCV project has developed a series of media genres (different forms of video texts) from which teachers design lessons for student video composing. Working through an existing genre provides students with a resource, a familiar framework or structure for their thinking, allowing them to focus on redesigning the genre for their own interests and representational purposes. Literacy work in multigenre authoring suggests that mastering genres provides lenses on experience and instruments for making sense of the world (Romano, 2000). From this view, awareness of how media texts cluster into specific kinds of patterned forms, or genres, may in itself create a new lens for better understanding of the multimedia world. Frequently based on popular TV genres, well-liked genres in CVCV classrooms are poetry videos (based on music videos), movie trailers (for novels and new concepts), and uncommercials (selling an idea or concept, often based on TV ads).

Recruiting the designs and cultural forms of representation familiar to adolescents through youth culture provides opportunities for them to use their extensive media experiences as part of school learning. For example, in the ad genre, seventh graders enacted a short drama about buying groceries for various religious holidays that ended with the tagline, "The First Amendment: Priceless." Similar to music videos in which words to songs guide the video interpretation, an eleventh-grade class selected important speeches from *Oedipus Rex* and enacted them conceptually with a dramatic voice-over (access *The Queen Is Dead* at (http://www.gse. buffalo.edu/org/cityvoices/awards.html). A twelfth-grade class selected a poem they liked or wrote one and represented their interpretation as poetry videos (see the original poem and video *I Need to Run* at the Web address above). Ninth- and tenth-grade students created movie trailers to capture the essential conflicts and characters "coming soon" for the short story "Monkey's Paw" and The French Revolution (at the Web address above).

A recently developed DV genre is the confessional, based on reality TV shows, in which one of the participants enters a private place to share real thoughts and feelings about situations, relationships, and events. In Shakespearean plays, it would be called a soliloquy, but the confessional was a much more familiar form than the soliloquy for the group of eleventh graders who used it as a resource. For instance, to make sense of the play *Macbeth*, the students took on the roles of characters in a confessional to discuss their *real* feelings about who was to blame for what happened in the play. The three witches, played by young, African American women, took up a pose to show their connection and, in their home vernacular, blamed Lady Macbeth ("She be blamin' us, but she the one!"), who blamed Macbeth ("What's up with him?"), who blamed the witches and his wife ("I'm innocent—pretty much!). This video provoked discussion in the class about who really *was* responsible. Embodying these central conflicts through character performance provided an updated connection of the literature to students' lives, but the DV added the well-known media genre, linking the classic literary text to the familiar reality show confessionals with their complaining, blaming, and self-delusion. (View the video at http://www.gse. buffalo.edu/org/cityvoices/prod_v27.html.)

DV composing also recruits students' deep interests in music and spoken-word/rap poetry, thus further building on familiar youth culture. Music videos orchestrate signs, gestures, and images to create a strong youth message. TV shows like Def Jam Poetry portray the performance (gesture, voice, words) of spoken-word poetry. Hip hop is the most popular music form among youth (Morrell, 2004) and often was used by students as sound tracks for their movies. One Caucasian student, when asked to make a digital video on an important social issue, wrote his own rap song about his dating an African American girl, recorded it with his band, and produced a powerful video called *Zebrahead*, a reference to a movie about romance between people of different races.

When seniors were asked to write a poem and create a poetry video to represent it, one young woman wrote, "This is just a poem," drawing on hip-hop rhythm and a series of compelling images. She ended the video with a close-up of her praying to communicate the problem of dealing with life's stresses and concluded, as many authors do, that her writing will save her: "I'm gonna write my life away." (View the video at http://www.gse. buffalo.edu/org/cityvoices/prod_v19.html).

Inclusion of youth culture and social literacies in the classroom can create conditions for motivation, meaning making, and elevated student competence. Such changes in student positioning can lead to changes in their sense of identity and school achievement. Educational scholarship on identity has a central tenet: "identities are crucial to learning" (Sfard & Prusak, 2005, p. 19). Further, in their analysis of the influence of new media technologies on student identity, Weber and Mitchell (2008) argue that students construct their identities in action, adding bits through transaction with "whatever cultural and life material is at hand" as they improvise, experiment, construct meaning (p. 45). Evidence from CVCV classrooms suggests that these ideas emerged in student DV composing and tended to hold true across students and classrooms (Arora, 2009; Knips, 2009).

Finally, translating what seemed impersonal and distant into the local and personal was part of the affordance of DV composing. Subject matter such as the Jim Crow Laws became personal when the two girls who made a DV called "For Colored

Only" included images of lynching from the National Archives and put up a "Whites Only" sign at the water fountain outside the classroom door to enact scenes of discrimination. These girls were deeply changed by their video and broke up a fight in the cafeteria a week later saying, "You can't fight over stepping on sneakers—do you know what we've gone through to be here?" (Lauricella, 2006).

In her ethnographic case study in a CVCV English class, Borowicz (2005) found that when the teacher introduced DV composing, student engagement changed dramatically and students developed new school identities. One focal student, Darrius, who was perceived in school as nonresponsive and a troublemaker, composed a DV story in response to a novel to depict his vision of the importance of loyalty among friends. In an impressive change, he came to class early and often stayed late, sometimes giving up his lunch period to work on his movie. He orchestrated a tragic scene, demonstrating to the actor her language and movements before filming, then edited the footage using quick cuts and dramatic music to amplify the shock. He watched his movie over and over, sometimes talking to himself, sometimes singing along with the music he had imported, sometimes turning to a fellow student for assistance. On one occasion, he announced, "Man, I love this. I could stay here and work on this all day." For the first time in school, Darrius felt what it was like "being connected in a social space with resources for expressive productivity" (Borowicz, 2005). This connectedness to tools, peers, and the multimodal world is key to purposeful learning through all the senses and modes of communication—and to drawing on lifeworlds to remake identity.

Co-Constructing a Strong Sense of Purpose

Research in CVCV classrooms revealed another essential component of a multimodal literacy pedagogy: successful teachers worked with students to construct explicit purposes for multimodal composing. Seeing teachers "as designers of learning processes and environments" puts them in the position of initiating a felt need for multimodal composing, and when teachers communicated and students created strong integrative purposes, compelling composing processes and products resulted (New London Group, 1996, p. 73).

In her study of CVCV teacher Robert Williams, Lauricella (2006) described how Robert promoted an explicit purpose that supported his clear goals for teaching his urban students American history. Robert consistently communicated the need for ongoing inquiry into multimodal media texts in order to understand historical and current issues; they were "doing history" to become critical citizens of the twenty-first century. To that end, he showed TV news clips and other media texts to highlight that history springs from contested interpretations and should be constructed from multiple perspectives; students came to understand that both written and multimodal texts require analysis and contextualizing from a historical lens. They took up that purpose as their own in order to construct DV products of their voices and visions on history (e.g., *For Colored Only* was created by his students).

Student and school learning purposes often coalesced in DV composing activities, prompting student engagement in designing and embodied learning (that is, using all the senses to understand). In some classes, these patterns emerged *only* during DV composing. For example, the experience discussed earlier of Darrius in Nate Russel's urban English class (Borowicz, 2005) showed that students constructed personal purpose for their digital videos in composing their message. The teacher, however, constructed DV composing as a diversion from the "hard work" of "real learning." When Nate Russel suddenly returned the class to six weeks of written test-prep, Darrius and other students withdrew or stopped coming.

The importance of *purpose* was evident in Bailey's study (2006) of two ninth-grade English teachers, Carol and Terry, who used the same lesson plans and taught in adjoining rooms. Carol created a strong purpose for communicating to a real audience, and her students engaged in multimodal composing and learned content. However, the purpose Terry constructed orally for student tasks was monologic—merely "covering" authoritative content and not orchestrating modes in meaningful representation and communication. Student response generally was "mock participation and procedural display" (Bloome, 1986). In this inadvertent naturalistic experiment, the importance of initiating authentic purposes for digital composing with students becomes clear.

In the classrooms of teachers with strong, integrative purposes, patterns of change emerged for classrooms and students. Evidence reviewed here shows that, when engaged purposefully, students drew on social and cultural "funds of knowledge" that included youth media practices, home and peer language, vernacular history, and urban life experiences to connect to and make sense of curriculum from what they already knew (Moll, Amanti, Neff, & Gonzalez, 1992). This interweaving of modes and knowledge for meaning making mediated student understanding of the school curriculum and also served social and personal agendas of students—even those perceived to be struggling academically. The research in classrooms using DV composing suggests that the guiding purpose constructed by teachers for authentic multimodal composing in school cannot be low-level comprehension and memorization; it must be about designing multimodal texts to bring curriculum and youth culture, social literacies and experiences, together (reviewed in Miller, 2008b, 2008c).

Finally, in English classes aiming to communicate their interpretations of characters and themes through DV composing, students developed deep understanding of literary texts, which provided support for their thinking—even in timed essays of academic writing. Only the focal students who completed their literature digital video passed the schoolwide end-of-year essay test, with all students choosing to write about the book on which they had made a DV confessional (Costello, 2006); this finding argues against a dichotomy between multimodal literacies and print academic literacies. Costello concludes that the embodied experience of multimodal design "may be the basis for achievement on high-stakes essay assessments about literature." In this and other studies (Costello, 2006; Lauricella, 2006; McMaster, 2004), students' multimodal learning served them well as mediators and resources for more print-based reading and writing in passing high-stakes writing tests, though students' performance went well beyond learning standards and passing tests.

A vital implication of these studies is the need to explicitly support teachers' deep understanding of the possible influences of DV composing on students' interpretive strategies and reflective dispositions. Developing such understanding of how and what students learn, we may better introduce DV composing as a "pedagogical necessity" to support purposeful twenty-first century composing and achievement for all students.

Explicit Attention to Strategies for Multimodal Design

As mentioned earlier, students bring tacit knowledge and lived experiences to DV composing, but in a multimodal literacy pedagogy, it is the teacher's role to also focus students' attention on multimodal design to help them become aware of and effectively communicate what they know. That is, the teacher must teach explicit strategies for using and integrating modes. Teacher Keith Hughes, for example, used humor ("zooming in looks like a drunken wedding video") and directed attention to the importance of image, music, narrative, and kinesthetic modes during his introduction to DV, in screening samples of the genre, and throughout his visits to DV workgroups as they plan/video/edit. His questions and directions nudged students: "What's your concept?" "Don't shoot until it looks good." "How can you make that look better?" "Never shoot into the light unless you have a good reason!" "What kind of music would fit with that?" "What's your tagline for that ad?" With the camera hooked up to the TV, he showed two shots of a particular scene and asked which looked better.

When his eleventh-grade class made public service announcements (PSAs), he supported students finding topics of importance to them and then directed attention to how modes were orchestrated (designed) in both professional and student-made PSAs. As always, he emphasized using close-ups to focus attention, conceptual shooting instead of literal word to image representations, camera angles and perspectives to create meaning, the tone of music (from www.freeplaymusic.com), and the flow of spoken words—all aimed at communicating the message or concept. A brief look at how one group of Keith's students appropriated familiar multimodal resources and orchestrated modes to create their message illustrates the impact of this teacher's attention to design, particularly in how the design issues he addressed showed up on his students' design of their PSA video.

A dramatic opening shows a poignant close-up of a handsome, dark-haired young man bestowing a rose (it seems) to the viewer. The scene is backed with romantic Italian opera music. His slow motion wink with a magical "bling" sound from special effects is followed by a close-up of his hands delivering the red rose to the hands of a young woman. Then, the camera provides a close-up on him as he leans into her and says "I love you" in her ear. A dissolve to the next scene shows an overhead shot from the woman's point of view as she draws in a notebook a heart with two names, in the manner of schoolgirl romance. In the background, a chorus of young girls' voices chant, "Jimmy and Mary sitting in a tree, K-I-S-S-I-N-G." A cut to an extreme close-up of the youth's suddenly angry face, then to the heart as she continues drawing it, his raised hand, the heart, a slap in the face, the heart with an arrow through it, finally the young woman pushed, falling into the wall and crumpling (seen from high angle). The romantic aria continues ironically throughout.

In the last close shot, the young woman, a tear rolling down her face in slow motion, lowers her head in despair. Cut to black and the music changes to a woman singing about "keeping silent all these years . . . one more tragedy of love." The film ends with the message, white letters over black, each sentence flashing onto a different screen: "Love should not feel this way. Reach Out. Pick up the Phone. . . . Call Crisis Services. Local Number." (View video PSA on domestic violence at http://www.teachertube.com/view_video.php?viewkey=6426585b29f5335b619b.)

The orchestration of multimodal resources—the student design—includes the ironic contrast of romantic visual and musical symbols with the violent actions, the contrast of naïve notions of love and a harsh reality with visual cross-cutting, and the strong final message of speaking out. When local Crisis Services saw the video, they asked to use it as a public service announcement. This authentic topic was chosen by students who drew on what they knew about such occurrences. They created the PSA genre with careful multimodal design to communicate the problem and a solution. Drawing on and orchestrating all of the multimodal resources to communicate a meaningful message is at the heart of DV composing, and this teacher helped his students to focus attention on how the modes worked together.

In addition, students worked together to solve the problem of how to powerfully influence their peers through a conventional love story with a startling ending. They dramatized a perspective, a simulated situation, to imagine a social future in which choices lead to consequences, and new actions might lead to different ones—in their own lives and in the lives of their peers. Attention to multimodal design strategies assisted students in meeting their purpose of communicating powerfully what they know. And because the visual and auditory modes provide resources for understanding not available in the verbal mode, DV composing provided additional ways of coming to know through the process of creating a multimodal representation (Kress & van Leeuwen, 2006).

Conclusion

The quintessential multimodality of digital video composing provides an entry point for developing multimodal literacy practices for teachers and students, with the potential to develop the performance knowledge, design abilities, and social and cognitive strategies needed for 21st century literacies. Along the way, it has the potential to transform what goes on in schools.

Table 11.1 summarizes some of the strategies CVCV teachers have used in their Multimodal Literacy Pedagogy (MLP), many of them referenced in this chapter. The strategy lists are, of course, not comprehensive, but suggestive. Teachers who want to transform their classrooms and student learning through DV composing will likely develop many new ways to design their teaching with an eye to multimodal literacy pedagogy principles. The four key principles are ones teachers can work toward: initiating and sustaining social learning, co-constructing clear purpose for multimodal composing, providing explicit design instruction/mediation, and engaging student lifeworlds and identities. These principles clearly work in synergy, not separately. Providing design instruction serves little function if students don't feel the purpose for their multimodal composing. Social learning

TABLE **11.1.** Teaching Strategies for Multimodal Literacy Pedagogy with Digital Video

MLP Framework Principles	Teaching Strategies
INITIATING & SUSTAINING SOCIAL LEARNING	• Do movie-in-a-day that requires each student to create a brief scene (see directions at http://www.gse.buffalo.edu/org/cityvoices/teach_v2.html) • Explicitly identify the new roles that the teacher and students will play in multimodal composing workshops—orally and in writing. • Create two- to four-person production teams or allow students to form their own teams for DV composing. • Circulate among *groups* as a facilitator, providing possible strategies at the point of need—when groups need it (Could your group use titles there? Could all of you give the writer ideas?). • Direct students to each other as resources to solve problems (e.g., "Ask X to show you how—she figured it out."). • If you need to teach a skill (e.g., special effects), ask the students to go to another group and show them—X group needs to know. • In screenings, emphasize how the individuals worked together—T or S should say how the group came up with the idea, made decisions, negotiated shots, etc. • For younger students, list the activities of the group for check off as they are completed. • Re-direct student activity when it is not socially appropriate. • Provide an evaluation rubric to guide group work and give a group assessment/grade (separate grades for nonparticipants). • In some cases, allow an individual to work alone for one project if that seems to be a necessary step in learning to work socially.
CO-CONSTRUCTING CLEAR PURPOSE FOR MULTIMODAL COMPOSING	• Create consistent messages about using DV to *communicate* to an audience—on the assignment sheet, in production consults, etc. • On the rubric always have a category about clearly communicating meaning to the audience (the class and beyond). • Hold group-teacher approval sessions to review the storyboard or narrative "pitch" for the movie and focus on what idea students want to communicate. (See sample storyboards at http://docs.google.com/Doc?id=dcrwmnnh_40dvnghc). • Screen the completed digital videos to show audience response in a live, conversational way—and focus on these responses to create awareness of message and audience. • Post videos on a teacher website (or other venue) so students can show friends and relatives their DVs. • Suggest/assist with submitting to digital video contests—there are many contests posted online. OR create your own DV Festival.

continued on next page

Table 11.1 continued

PROVIDING EXPLICIT DESIGN INSTRUCTION AND MEDIATION	• Introduce the camera by connecting it to a display (TV, LCD) to demonstrate the effects of angle, close-up, lighting, etc. • Show professional examples of the genre (movie trailers, ads, music videos, news segments) and ask students to say what is working or not and why. (This is also a good time to point out media manipulation through multimodal design). • In group consults, ask design questions—How will you film that? Could you make that scarier? Can you fix the lighting? • Introduce editing by connecting the computer to a whole-class display (TV, LCD) to model designing while talking about the mood or tone of transitions, fonts and colors, special effects, juxtapositions, etc. • In camera handling and editing, focus attention on the *meaning*—how does that close-up or transition help show your meaning? • Focus attention on how elements in each mode contribute to the overall impact and meaning. (Are the parts working together?) • Ask students to explain why they used a mode in the way that they did—why did they use that music, that font, that visual, that text, that narrative, that transition, that effect?
ENGAGING STUDENT LIFEWORDS AND IDENTITIES	• Give students some choice of topics rather than assigning them. • Where possible, ask students to communicate their perspective on an issue or topic (For or against Iraq war? Hamlet—crazy or not?) • Use media genres that students know so they draw on that knowledge to organize the film and can focus more on what to say and how to say it. • When showing previous students' genre videos, point out what knowledge students drew on to show the remix of culture. • In group consults, ask questions and make comments to help students bring what they know to the video—e.g., can you think of a movie trailer that does that? Sounds like that Nike commercial—maybe you can find that clip online? • Encourage students to switch their group roles in order to extend their capacities—writer/storyboarder, camera person, editor, sound/music editor. • Encourage students to bring in props to aid in communicating their message—e.g., a hat, a robe, a kerchief to create context. • Always ask students to put credits at the end of the digital video to highlight specific roles of individuals. • Create a video quilt, in which each student brings something from his or her own writing to become part of the "quilt" that has a common theme (see In the World Today at http://nylearns.org/webpage/Default.aspx?UID=1236). • Allow students to use familiar music as sound tracks to films, preferably the music-only parts (or PG-rated lyrics).

spaces provide the best opportunity for engaging lifeworlds and identities as students work together to communicate something important. Explicit design instruction and mediation often draw on students' latent knowledge of media from lifeworlds, bringing it to conscious awareness in order to use and critique it.

Multimodal literacy pedagogy, as presented in this chapter, provides an explanatory framework for a critical reframing of teaching and learning. Multimodal literacy pedagogy as a theory helps highlight the dynamics of teachers in the process of transforming their teaching. It can lead to transformed classrooms and transformative literacy practices in schools. These are changes we need in teacher education in order to prepare teachers and their students for twenty-first century life in an increasingly digital democracy.

Acknowledgment

I am deeply grateful to all of those who over the years helped CVCV teachers in classrooms and traced teacher and student learning, most notably Monica Blondell, James Cercone, Stephen Goss, Merridy Knips, and Jonathan Federick. Many thanks to all the teachers who worked to innovate in their urban schools, especially Keith Hughes and Joel Malley.

Works Cited

Albers, P., & Harste, J. C. (2007). The arts, new literacies, and multimodality. *English Education, 40*(1), 6–20.

Alvermann, D. E. (Ed.). (2002). *Adolescents and literacies in a digital world.* New York: Peter Lang.

Arora, P. (2009, March*). Invisible students/multiple identities: "Low-level learners" design their first DV.* Paper presented at the 16th Annual Graduate School of Education Student Research Symposium. University at Buffalo, State University of New York.

Bachman, J. G., Johnston, L. D., & O'Malley, P. M. (2008). *Monitoring the future: Questionnaire responses from the nation's high school seniors, 2006.* Ann Arbor, MI: Institute for Social Research.

Bailey, N. (2006). *Designing social futures: Adolescent literacy in and for new times* (Unpublished doctoral dissertation). University at Buffalo, State University of New York.

Blondell, M. (2006). *Teachers' perceptions of DV composing in English classrooms: Blurring boundaries for understanding lives and curriculum* (Unpublished manuscript). University at Buffalo, State University of New York.

Bloome, D. (1986). Building literacy and the classroom community. *Theory into Practice, 25*(2), 71–76.

Borowicz, S. (2005). *Embracing lives through the video lens: An exploration of literacy teaching and learning with digital video technology in an urban secondary English classroom* (Unpublished doctoral dissertation). University at Buffalo, State University of New York.

Buckingham, D. (2008). Introducing identity. In D. Buckingham (Ed.), *Youth, identity, and digital media* (pp. 1–22). Cambridge, MA: MIT Press.

Cope, B., & Kalantzis, M. (2000). Introduction: Multiliteracies: The beginnings of an idea. In B. Cope & M. Kalantzis (Eds.), *Multiliteracies: Literacy learning and the design of social futures* (pp. 3–8). New York: Routledge.

Costello, A. (2006). *Digital video and drama production as literacy learning tools in English classrooms* (Unpublished doctoral dissertation). University at Buffalo, State University of New York.

Ellis, V., Fox, C., & Street, B. (Eds.). (2008). *Rethinking English in schools: A new and constructive stage.* London, UK: Continuum International.

Gee, J. P. (2003). *What video games have to teach us about learning and literacy.* New York: Palgrave Macmillan.

Goodman, S. (2003). *Teaching youth media: A critical guide to literacy, video production, and social change.* New York: Teachers College Press.

Grabill, J. T., & Hicks, T. (2005). Multiliteracies meet methods: The case for digital writing in English education. *English Education, 37*(4), 301–311.

Heath, S. B. (2004). Learning language and strategic thinking through the arts. *Reading Research Quarterly, 39*(3), 338–342.

The Horizon Report. (2008). Austin, TX: The New Media Consortium.

Hull, G. A., & Nelson, M. E. (2005). Locating the semiotic power of multimodality. *Written Communication, 22*(2), 224–261.

Hull, G. A., & Schultz, K. (2002). *School's out: Bridging out-of-school literacies with classroom practice.* New York: Teachers College Press.

International Reading Association. (2001). *Integrating literacy and technology in the curriculum: A position statement.* Retrieved from http://www.reading.org/resources/issues/positions_technology.html

Jewitt, C., & Kress, G. (Eds.). (2003). *Multimodal literacy.* New York: Peter Lang.

Kajder, S. B. (2006). *Bringing the outside in: Visual ways to engage reluctant readers.* Portland, ME: Stenhouse.

King, J. R., & O'Brien, D. G. (2002). Adolescents' multiliteracies and their teachers' needs to know: Toward a digital détente. In D. E. Alvermann (Ed.), *Adolescents and literacies in a digital world* (pp. 40–50). New York: Peter Lang.

Knips, M. (2009, March). *A student designer emerges: The story of Charles.* Paper presented at the 16th Annual Graduate School of Education Student Research Symposium. University at Buffalo, State University of New York.

Kress, G. (1999). "English" at the crossroads: Rethinking curricula of communication in the context of the turn to the visual. In G. E. Hawisher & C. L. Selfe (Eds.), *Passions, pedagogies, and 21st century technologies* (pp. 66–88). Logan: Utah State University Press; Urbana, IL: National Council of Teachers of English.

———. (2003). *Literacy in the new media age.* New York: Routledge.

Kress, G., & van Leeuwen, T. (2006). *Reading images: The grammar of visual design* (2nd ed.). New York: Routledge.

Lankshear, C., & Knobel, M. (2003). *New literacies: Changing knowledge and classroom learning.* Philadelphia: Open University Press.

———. (2006). *New literacies: Everyday practices and classroom learning* (2nd ed.). Philadelphia: Open University Press.

Lauricella, A. M. (2006). *Digital video production as a tool for learning: Exploring multiple text documents in an urban social studies classroom* (Unpublished doctoral dissertation). University at Buffalo, State University of New York.

Lave, J., & Wenger, E. (1991). *Situated learning: Legitimate peripheral participation*. New York: Cambridge University Press.

Lenhart, A., Madden, M., & Hitlin, P. (2005). *Teens and technology: Youth are leading the transition to a fully wired and mobile nation*. Washington, DC: Pew Internet & American Life Project. Retrieved from http://www.pewinternet.org/~/media/Files/Reports/2005/PIP_Teens_Tech_July2005web.pdf.pdf

Leontiev, A. N. (1978). *Activity, consciousness and personality*. Englewood Cliffs, NY: Prentice-Hall.

Leu, D. J., Jr., Kinzer, C. K., Coiro, J. L., & Cammack, D. W. (2004). Toward a theory of new literacies emerging from the internet and other information and communication technologies. In R. B. Ruddell & N. J. Unrau (Eds.), *Theoretical models and processes of reading* (5th ed., pp. 1570–1613). Newark, DE: International Reading Association.

Lipsman, A. (2008, February 8). U.S. internet users viewed 10 billion videos online in record-breaking month of December, according to comScore video metrix [Press Release]. Reston, VA: comScore. Retrieved from http://www.comscore.com/press/release.asp?press=2051

McMaster, R. (2004). *Collaborating for curricular change: Arts-based authentic assessments in the English classroom* (Unpublished doctoral dissertation). University at Buffalo, State University of New York.

Miller, S. M. (2007). English teacher learning for new times: Digital video composing as multimodal literacy practice. *English Education, 40*(1), 61–83.

———. (2008a). The multiple languages and literacies of English. In V. Ellis, C. Fox, & B. Street (Eds.), *Rethinking English in schools: A new and constructive stage* (pp. 174–182). London, UK: Continuum International Publishing.

———. (2008b). Teacher learning for new times: Repurposing new multimodal literacies and digital-video composing for schools. In J. Flood, S. B. Heath, & D. Lapp (Eds.), *Handbook of research on teaching literacy through the communicative and visual arts,* (Vol. 2, pp. 441–460). New York: Erlbaum.

———. (2008c). *Digital video composing for improving school achievement: Lessons from the CVCV-Buffalo Project*. Plenary presentation delivered at the CVCV Showcase Conference, Buffalo, NY.

Miller, S. M., & Borowicz, S. (2005). City voices, city visions: Digital video as literacy/learning supertool in urban classrooms. In L. Johnson, M. E. Finn, & R. Lewis (Eds.), *Urban education with an attitude: Linking theory, practice and community* (pp. 87–105). Albany: State University of New York Press.

————. (2006). *Why multimodal literacies? Designing digital bridges to 21st century teaching and learning*. Buffalo, NY: GSE Publications and SUNY Press.

————. (2007). New literacies with an attitude: Transformative teacher education through digital video learning tools. In P. J. Finn & M. E. Finn (Eds.), *Teacher education with an attitude: Preparing teachers to educate working-class students in their collective self-interest* (pp.111–126). Albany: State University of New York Press.

Miller, S. M., Hughes, K., & Knips, M. (in press). Teacher knowledge-in-action: Enacting multimodal literacy pedagogy for DV composing. In S. Kajder & C. Young (Eds.), *Research on technological pedagogical content knowledge in English classrooms*. Academic Information Press.

Miller, S., Thompson, M. K., Boyd, F., & McVee, M. (2008, March). *Why multimodal literacy practice? Lessons from students, teachers and teacher educators*. Symposium conducted at the Annual Conference of the American Educational Research Association. New York, NY.

Moll, L. C., Amanti, C., Neff, D., Gonzalez, N. (1992). Funds of knowledge for teaching: Using a qualitative approach to connect homes and classrooms. *Theory into Practice, 31*(2), 132–141.

Morrell, E. (2004). *Linking literacy and popular culture: Finding connections for lifelong learning*. Norwood, MA: Christopher-Gordon.

National Council of Teachers of English. (2005). *Position statement on multimodal literacies*. Retrieved from http://www.ncte.org/positions/statements/multimodalliteracies

————. (2008). *The NCTE definition of 21st century literacies* [Position statement]. Retrieved from http://www.ncte.org/positions/statements/21stcentdefinition

New London Group. (1996). A pedagogy of multiliteracies: Designing social futures. *Harvard Educational Review, 66*(1), 60–92.

————. (2000). A pedagogy of multiliteracies: Designing social futures. In B. Cope & M. Kalantzis (Eds.), *Multiliteracies: Literacy learning and the design of social futures* (pp. 9–36). New York: Routledge.

Partnership for 21st Century Skills. (2006). *Results that matter: 21st century skills and high school reform.* Retrieved from http://www.21stcenturyskills.org/documents/RTM2006.pdf

Romano, T. (2000). *Blending genre, altering style: Writing multigenre papers.* Portsmouth, NH: Boynton/Cook.

The Secretary's Commission on Achieving Necessary Skills. (1991). *What work requires of schools: A SCANS report for America 2000.* Washington, DC: United States Department of Labor. Retrieved from http://wdr.doleta.gov/SCANS/whatwork/whatwork.pdf

Selfe, C. L., & Hawisher, G. E. (2004). *Literate lives in the information age: Narratives of literacy from the United States.* Mahwah, NJ: Erlbaum.

Sfard, A., & Prusak, A. (2005). Telling identities: In search of an analytic tool for investigating learning as a culturally shaped activity. *Educational Researcher, 34*(4), 14–22.

Street, B. V. (1995). *Social literacies: Critical approaches to literacy in development, ethnography and education.* London, UK: Longman.

U.S. Department of Education. (1996). *Getting America's students ready for the 21st century: Meeting the technology literacy challenge.* Retrieved from http://www.ed.gov/about/offices/list/os/technology/plan/national/index.html

Vygotsky, L. S. (1978). *Mind in society: The development of higher psychological processes.* Cambridge, MA: Harvard University Press.

Weber, S., & Mitchell, C. (2008). Imaging, keyboarding, and posting identities: Young people and new media technologies. In D. Buckingham (Ed.), *Youth, identity, and digital media* (pp. 25–47). Cambridge, MA: MIT Press.

Wells, G. (1999). *Dialogic inquiry: Towards a sociocultural practice and theory of education.* New York: Cambridge University Press.

Williams, B. T. (2005). Leading double lives: Literacy and technology in and out of school. *Journal of Adolescent and Adult Literacy, 48*(8), 702–706.

Bringing Filmmaking into the English Language Arts Classroom

BRUCE ROBBINS
Boise State University

It doesn't take an expert to observe that the nature of literacy outside the English language arts classroom is quickly changing. As the NCTE position statement *Resolution on Composing with Nonprint Media* (2003) states:

> Today our students are living in a world that is increasingly non-printcentric. New media such as the Internet, MP3 files, and video are transforming the communication experiences of young people outside of school. Young people are composing in nonprint media that can include any combination of visual art, motion (video and film), graphics, text, and sound—all of which are frequently written and read in nonlinear fashion.

Like many English teachers, I recognized the need to adapt to the world of new media, not only to stay connected to the lives of students, but also because, as the NCTE statement goes on to point out, "with multiple opportunities for student expression in the English language arts classroom, these nonprint media offer new realms for teachers of composition" and, I would add, for language and literature. When I summoned the strength to peer over the barrier of learning new technologies (as I am quite comfortable with the old ones), I caught a glimmer of new possibilities for teaching English language arts. I asked myself: How might the new media, particularly digital video filmmaking, help educators teach in ways more connected to students today?

One of the new media with intriguing possibilities is video. Teachers have long shown movie versions of literature, and some (such as Dziedzic, 2002; Teasley & Wilder, 1996) have advocated teaching film viewing and analysis independent of written literary texts. In "Crafting an agentive self: Case studies of digital storytelling," Glynda Hull and Mira-Lisa Katz (2006) report personal and literacy efficacy for individual at-risk students who created media and filmmaking projects in an after-school community youth center. Kajder (2004) described her class' construction of digital personal narratives and attributed adolescents' increased literacy skills to digital filmmaking. Franek (1996) focused on teaching critical film viewing, engaged students in creating video productions of scenes from Shakespeare's *A Midsummer Night's Dream,* and concluded that his students' essays "often demonstrate that students have moved beyond passive, plot-centered watching to become active, critical viewers of film" (p. 54). Morrison (2002) reported that when her African American students produced video scenes from *Romeo and Juliet,* the students reached beyond white-only films to "see themselves" in Shakespeare's play. This work suggests that video and/or digital filmmaking can positively impact students by engaging them in literacies that develop personal and interpretive understandings.

In the schools in my region, however, what little filmmaking takes place is more likely to be found in a video production class focused on producing school news and public service announcements (i.e., broadcast journalism) than in an English language arts class, especially as a whole-class assignment in non-elective standard English. Video production equipment, which used to be a serious barrier, has now become widely available and simpler to use. Schools are better equipped with computers, too, and basic movie editing software now comes standard with computer software packages. Students even have greater exposure to filmmakers discussing or demonstrating their crafts, as these are now routinely provided as extras on movie DVDs. In such interviews or commentaries, the directors, actors, cinematographers, and designers talk about their craft in terms and concepts that are akin to the terms and concepts we teach in literature (plot, character motivation, mood, and so on). Filmmaking requires working in multiple modes of expression, yet written literacy continues to play important roles, especially in what filmmakers call "adaptations"—movie versions of written stories. The potential benefits of students making their own films include greater student engagement and more active learning about literature; if English teachers could overcome the unfamiliarity and technicalities of basic filmmaking, consider the connections between literature and storytelling in film, and orchestrate the components needed to make it work.

At the beginning, I did not know much about making films, but I knew that in order to explore the possible benefits of filmmaking in the English classroom, I had to roll up my sleeves and try it. Because I work at a university, I collaborated with a ninth-grade English teacher, Don Evans, who was also interested in the potentials of video but, like many teachers, was reluctant to get in over his head. Together we worked within Don's schedule of fifty-minute periods and his district's curriculum. We co-taught the nine-week unit in four ninth-grade English classes. All four classes read eight short stories, mostly anthologized classics, focusing on new critical elements of literature (Brooks & Warren, 1947) and skills in literary analysis. During the unit, we asked all students to visualize the stories in part by asking whom the students might cast for the characters, where they might choose to film the story, or how the stories reminded them of movies they had seen—common classroom prompts. We also viewed a film adaptation of Richard Wright's (1969) short story "The Man Who Was Almost a Man" and examined both its literary and cinematic features. Near the end of the unit, while two of the classes finished up with the usual essay of literary analysis, the other two classes were arranged in groups of four to six students and invited to create a film adaptation of a scene from one of the stories the class had read. This chapter reports on our experience of guiding students through the process of creating their video scenes.

Preparing the Movies

Like most kids, our students were eager to grab the cameras and start shooting, but they were not ready to make movies.

Filmmaking takes planning. To begin, we asked each student to select a scene that they thought was important and explain why. Then they sketched a simple storyboard for their scene. For a model, we looked at a few storyboard drawings from *Pirates of the Caribbean* (Verbinski, 2003), a movie that most students had seen. (The complete storyboard is available on the movie DVD.) We discussed how storyboards, like comics or graphic novels, narrate a story that relies on a sequence of images more than on words. Students noticed how storyboards indicate camera angles that suggest characters' relationships with each other and with the audience. At this point, we handed a camera to a student, had student volunteers stand in for actors or characters, and experimented with where we would put the camera to show various relationships and points of view. The demonstration led into ways a movie could be told in first person, third person limited, or omniscient point of view. At the end of one period, one student made a declaration about point of view: "This stuff finally makes sense now." Others agreed.

As the students created their storyboards, we saw what Wilhelm (1997) and others have pointed out—art activity supports better visualization of literature story worlds. For this activity we assumed that students would draw on their experiences of reading comics and graphic novels. Interestingly, however, many of the students drew pictures of isolated moments across the whole story that were more like traditional illustrations than sequential images of a single scene. We found that this might be a good place to broaden our definition of short story and read a graphic novel. We decided that in the future we should ask students to sketch the actions or pictures immediately before and after their central image. We might also teach a few basic art fundamentals such as framing, proximity, use of foreground and background, and balance or symmetry. Knowledge of art techniques could help deepen students' understanding of the story's characters, actions, conflict, point of view, mood, and theme, regardless of students' artistic ability. This moment of planning at the intersection between art and written text might be used to enhance students' understanding of both literacies.

At this point, we introduced the project requirements, including our decision that the film, as an "adaptation," must stay true to the intent of the original story and not be a spoof. We grouped students largely by the story they had chosen and had them discuss their individual ideas. Following lively discussion, groups came to a consensus about which scene they wished to film. After examining the opening pages of the screenplay for *Pirates of the Caribbean* as a model, each group wrote a script for their scene. We noticed that students did not have clear ideas about where the narrative scenes began and ended, so we returned to familiar terms associated with plot (e.g., inciting moment and climax) to help the groups frame their scenes and recognize the dramatic structure within the scene itself. As students wrote their scripts, they naturally began to make shifts that used their understanding of how printed stories and movies may work differently. Some groups cut lengthy dialogue, focusing their attention on essential dialogue and deciding what could be told with pictures instead. Others invented dialogue to dramatize moments that the stories had narratively glossed over.

While some groups struggled with writing, others created wonderfully descriptive and evocative scripts—scripts that would require multimillion dollar budgets. To make the projects more realistic, we next asked the groups to develop a shooting plan in which they wrote their initial decisions about filming locations, camera angles, and actors' movements and indicated who would play what roles in front of or behind the camera. Groups specified whether they would use a school camera or provide their own (about half of our groups brought in family cameras). Students also listed props or costume pieces needed for the shoot and who was responsible for bringing them, any special lighting needed, and their plans for transportation if they intended to shoot in locations away from school. We asked for a shooting schedule and found that we needed to give ninth graders lots of guidance, so Don and I created a master schedule for each class. The practicalities of the shooting plan helped some groups more fully develop their ideas, and it brought others down to earth. One group pondered, for example, where they could find a jungle island in Idaho, and another realized that they had no access to a boat that they had planned to use for their opening shots.

Producing the Movies

When filming began, the classroom resembled a journalism or play production class in that not all students were involved in the same activities or even in the same locations. For instance, groups might be involved in rearranging desks to suggest a dining room, filming outside on the school lawn, borrowing a cart from the library, filming in a conference room or empty classroom, rehearsing in a hallway, or retrieving props from a locker. Teaching in this setting meant roaming from one group to another, supervising behavior, encouraging, helping students anticipate problems, asking thought-provoking questions, and monitoring students' experiential learning. For example, as one group filmed their General Zaroff character, in "The Most Dangerous Game" (Connell, 1924/1999), approaching his quarry Rainsford, who was hiding in a tree, Don asked them if they had considered whose point of view they wanted the audience to see. The group realized that their camera operator had to climb the tree in order to produce the viewpoint they wanted. I helped another group use their interpretation of Rainsford's character to determine how he should come through a doorway. We were teaching students some basics about acting, costume, lighting, and camera angles, but our questions and comments were also intended to deepen how the students understood and interpreted their characters and stories. Frequently students came to insights that they had not expressed earlier when their story had been discussed in class.

Although some kids are very comfortable with technology, we found that many of our students were not necessarily skilled with video and required some initial instruction. Some were confused about when the camera was recording or not, and some accidentally taped over their previously recorded footage. Others did not attend to battery life, which was especially problematic when shooting outdoors. Students also learned that without external microphones, the longer the shot, the harder it was to hear the dialogue. Even though we guided students to plan a variety of camera angles, they tended to shoot their scenes in one continuous take from only one camera location. It was also challenging for students to attend to what moviemakers call "continuity," so that story moments shot today would fit with those shot tomorrow. In final cuts, for example, some of our characters appeared to mysteriously change clothing in the blink of an eye. Very soon Don and I discovered that rather than becoming technicians ourselves, we could address many of these problems by simply asking the groups to regularly review their footage, similar to what Hollywood calls "dailies." The routine daily review motivated student self-discovery, interpretation, and revision in this new form of composing.

For film editing we used Windows Movie Maker. (Apple's iMovie is a similar introductory program.) The program is simple but nevertheless effectively enables students to edit their films and to add a sound track, transition effects, titles, and credits. As with the cameras, our students were quick to start using the editing program but reluctant to read instructions. So learning the basic operations of the program was important for us as teachers, but it was not as daunting as we imagined it might be. I found that I could teach myself the basic program in two or three hours by experimenting with some practice video footage. Working with someone who already knows the program is even faster, and we discovered that some of our students already knew the program from home use.

In addition to learning how to make basic editing moves, Don and I looked for potential problems that students might fall into so that we could warn them away. In Movie Maker, for example, we learned that if we save a "project," we have saved only our editing commands but not the actual film footage itself, which requires selecting "Finish Movie" even if we are not really finished editing. One way to avoid this problem was to have student groups always use the same computer. We also regularly saved backup copies of students' video footage and movies.

We found that it was not practical to expect a whole group of four to eight students, using one computer, to edit together. Similarly, not everyone in a group could be actively involved in every part of planning, performing, or filming, which is why we asked the groups to identify each student's major responsibilities in their shooting plan, including designating one or two film editors. Students often took on multiple responsibilities, of course, but when the student editors were not directly involved in writing, rehearsing, or preparing for filming, they could get acquainted with the software by playing with some practice footage. After the first day of shooting, editors could begin to trim and edit the first batch of footage even while the rest of the group was out shooting more.

In any filmmaking, problems often arise (and, in fact, we found the project to be a great opportunity to teach some problem-solving skills). The constraints of a fifty-minute period added to the common problem of not having enough time to set up and to shoot multiple takes. Students also discovered that their selected locations had surprising traffic noise. On a couple of days when exterior shots were planned, it rained. We had days when certain groups could not do their work in class because they were going to film after school at someone's house, or because someone forgot a key prop or camera, or because shooting was finished but editing was not. So during the filmmaking project we also assigned an additional story for independent silent reading whenever students had unproductive filmmaking time.

Presenting and Discussing the Movies

When presentation day arrived, the groups played their movies for the class, finished or not. As teachers, we were interested in using the presentations to promote further learning, not just as show-and-tell. As we projected the "final" movies, the students were most intent on seeing themselves and their peers on the screen. Some groups included "bloopers" after the credits for fun. After each showing we had the groups discuss their ideas and interpretive choices, which led to further discussion of the stories themselves. We asked all of the groups to reflect on changes they would make to their scene if they could direct a Hollywood production of their story. This reflection allowed them to ex-plain away any production limitations and make their intentions clearer. But the question also moved us from the immediacy of the films to the mental images and interpretations that the stories had evoked in the students.

Here is an example from a group who chose a scene from James Hurst's (1960/1999) story "The Scarlet Ibis." The house in the movie, says Jeremy (all students' names are pseudonyms), should be a big old country house with a fireplace and old trees by it.

> BRUCE: Okay, and what about outside where he buries this thing, the ibis? What would that be like?
>
> JEREMY: I'd have it more dreary, like darker, behind the house.
>
> BRUCE: Like shady, or bad weather, or . . . ?
>
> JEREMY: Shady, yeah.
>
> DEVON: Have like one of those trees that was described at first.
>
> BRUCE: Which tree are you thinking of, Devon?
>
> DEVON: That bleeding tree or whatever.
>
> BRUCE: Yeah. So just have it right there where he's burying the bird? So you'd have the red tree and the red bird and Doodle all in the same picture?
>
> DEVON: Yeah.

Discussion of students' visualizations not only nudged students to elaborate on the "movies in the mind" that they had of the story but, as in the previous example, the discussion also set the stage for further literary ideas, such as symbolism in this case.

Another group also chose "The Scarlet Ibis," in which the narrator, only referred to as Brother, remembers his relationship with his invalid little brother nicknamed Doodle. This group elected to film the story's major turning point, though they didn't quite realize that until their presentation discussion.

> CRYSTAL: Well, we just thought this was the most exciting part.
>
> BRUCE: Yeah, that moment when the Brother runs away from Doodle is really important, isn't it? . . . So if you could make a professional movie out of this, and you had lots more money and time and everything, how would you try to dramatize that moment—or showing that Brother made a decision to run away so it looks like a choice and not an accident?
>
> LORNA: Maybe it could be longer and more drawn out?
>
> CRYSTAL: I think the way I would want to do it would be like you'd hear us talking about the storm coming and stuff, and then I was kind of falling on my knees and saying I can't go any farther, and Brother saying yes, you can. And getting up

like expecting me to follow, and I try to get up and follow him, and then—not.

BRUCE: So you'd see one down, and the other one up—

CRYSTAL: And then going "come on" and start walking, and then running.

BRUCE: Interesting. Any other ways to see that, maybe?

CYNTHIA: I think that, well, that's why I was so disappointed that the music wasn't working because you really portray emotions with music . . . dramatic music, and also the camera might follow the Brother a little instead of just staying from Doodle's perspective.

BRUCE: What emotions would you want to get across with the music?

CYNTHIA: Anger, mostly. Because Brother is just trying to drop it all. Like that's the point where he's just done, and he wants it out of his life, and he's just running away. So I think rage.

Crystal, who played the role of Doodle in her group's film, appeared to have been imagining another version with more developed and heightened drama than she and her group had been able to create. In this sense, the students' films often functioned in much the same way that classroom drama activities do, where acting out an aspect of a story not only clarifies an action or situation, but it also prompts further imagination and analysis that expands what Judith Langer (1995) calls "the horizon of possibilities" (p. 26) of students' "envisionments" (p. 9) of literature. In this case, Crystal appears not just to be imagining a more dramatic version of the story, but also to be empathizing with the character and feeling the pathos of the situation. Cynthia's concern about the music for the scene also reflects the emotions that the scene evokes for her and that she wished to re-create for the audience. This dimension of emotional response to the stories, as well as statements suggesting empathy for the characters, frequently surfaced during the presentation discussions but was rare during the more traditional class discussions following each story.

From all of the students' films, productive discussions came from our noting an interpretive decision that they had made (consciously or not) and inviting discussion about the choice and the interpretive implications behind it. Often these decisions focused on portrayals of character and the traits and motivation suggested by these depictions. For example, we asked about choices for close-ups. A group filming part of "The Necklace" (de Maupassant, 1907/1999) decided they would closely show the protagonist Madame Loisel's face as she looks at her friend's jewels, portraying there the greed, envy, and pride that the group felt drove the character and plot. Don followed up with this question:

> DON: If you had to make the whole movie, how would you show Madame Loisel's dynamic character change from the start to the finish?
>
> SONJA: At the beginning she's like really, really greedy and she wants—well, not at the very beginning, but she'd be like I want more instead of less. But then at the very end she would be repaying her debt. Like because she went and bought a fancy necklace for a fake one and traded it. And so you'd see she's different because she didn't want to keep the necklace for herself. She gave it to her friend. And she took fifteen years to repay it.
>
> BETH: And she actually did repay it.
>
> BRUCE: So are you seeing her as a morally good character at the end because she worked off her debt?
>
> BETH: More than she was at the beginning. Not greedy much anymore.

Another group's choice to film the end of "The Most Dangerous Game" by staging the final fight between Rainsford, the protagonist, and General Zaroff, the antagonist, raised this question: "If this fight were the climax of the story, the major turning point in the conflict, then what resolution would the group film as the end of the complete movie?" Two of the group members suggested showing dogs tearing Zaroff apart. As we talked, we worked beyond these boys' initial reactions—to show as much blood and gore as possible—to the thematic implication that bad guys who do not value human life deserve severe punishment. Other members preferred ending with a shot of Rainsford, the victorious protagonist, seated at the same table where we previously had seen his adversary dining, which raised the question of whether we should now see the protagonist as different from the antagonist or whether we should see that the protagonist is beginning to become like his nemesis. One student suggested Rainsford should be eating a salad because the experience would turn him into a vegetarian. Clearly our discussion of choices in depicting the film ending was also a demonstration for students about how interpretive choices emerge and how skilled readers recognize and choose among interpretive possibilities.

Multimodal Intersections

Filmmaking involves an intriguing mix of work with print and nonprint texts across several sign systems. As an integration of the arts, creating a film adaptation of a story from literature builds on the blend of arts in drama that traditionally include elements such as literature, acting, dance, mime, costume design, props, scenery (architecture and painting), lighting, music, and sound effects. The languages of drama are visual, auditory, and kinesthetic. The texts of this work include scripts and prompt books, lighting plots, costume designs, scenery designs consisting of elevations, floor plans, and three-dimensional models, musical scores, dance or movement notation, as well as actors' movements, gestures, facial expressions, and their words and intonations. The successful play is an invisible synthesis of such disparate elements unified to create a desired effect for both the director and the audience. Filmmaking then adds more elements from the visual arts, including the arts of storyboarding, photographic camera work, musical scoring, and editing. The shift from stage to screen necessitates shifts in the conventions and uses of the dramatic elements and their potentials within the genres of the stage play or the movie. In the classroom, film blends familiar uses of reading print texts and enacting classroom drama with the newer technology of digital videography in which students can now compose as well as view film texts.

Our ninth-grade students naturally came to school with a good deal of film viewing experience, but making a movie is quite different from watching one. They had some adapting to do. The tasks involved in creating even their short scenes forced many students to think in and across unfamiliar modes. Furthermore, some of the technical decisions required of students directly fostered learning in the elements of literature, such as point of view (illustrated by the next discussion with Megan). In our discussion, for example, of the scene from "The Scarlet Ibis" in which Doodle buries a rare scarlet ibis that has died in a storm, Megan came to a new idea about how her movie might look:

MEGAN: It would be good if it was like the family watched him out of the window of the living room. Show a shot of them all sitting back down at the table and looking out the window at him burying the bird outside. (She gestures both hands moving away from her eyes forward.)

BRUCE: So seeing him through their eyes, their point of view?

MEGAN: Yeah. And then when Brother was running back to Doodle. . . . I think it would be kind of cool, in the rain, to shoot it from his point of view, from his eyes (she gestures again), like moving around when he's looking around for his brother. And then finding him and it kind of . . . (She gestures raising the camera, aiming it slowly up).

CRYSTAL: Like the camera was inside of his eyes.

BRUCE: So you shot this in kind of an omniscient point of view, which was "I can see this, and then I can see that, and I can look all around wherever I want." But you're talking about actually limiting it, too, aren't you, to what the people are seeing?

MEGAN: To what HE is seeing, like inside his head. Like if Doodle is over there, and it's his eyes looking, running, and trying to find him.

BRUCE: So we would see Doodle just when Brother finds him, then?

CRYSTAL: Yeah, like the audience would see Doodle the same time Brother does.

BRUCE: So that would change it to a first-person point of view, or a limited point of view. That would be an interesting change or choice.

The classroom discussions are, of course, interpretable, but in the previous discussion, Megan's discovery appears to be based largely on her entering into film-based thinking, imagining what a camera operator would do and how it would look to an audience. She entered into a photographic concept of point of view that is more visually based than print-based. Yet clearly this kind of discovery will better support her understanding of point of view in print stories as well, because she is also learning to traverse between the two sign systems to find meaning and understand technique.

The discussions after each presentation became opportunities to explore changes that students made because they sensed that while the printed stories might present a story in a certain way, movies sometimes operate by different conventions. One group that filmed a part of "The Most Dangerous Game" decided to film not only the first effort of escape out in the jungle by the protagonist Rainsford but also to show the antagonist General Zaroff back at his chateau calmly preparing to hunt his human prey—a scene not included in the original story. As we discussed this decision, we talked about why movies might shift a printed story's limited point of view to an omniscient viewpoint in the film mode. For the same story, another group decided to film a final fight between Rainsford and Zaroff. In the short story, the narrative leads up to the confrontation, establishes that the winner will sleep in Zaroff's fine bed, and the loser will be thrown to the dogs, and then cuts off abruptly with "On guard, Rainsford . . . ." When next we read, "He had never slept in a better bed, Rainsford decided," we infer that he has won; the fun comes partly from the inferential work that we as readers contribute. But the students knew very clearly that movies, unlike short stories, are obliged to show the fight; it's just how the movie mode works.

One of our groups simply could not stick to our dictates to play their scenes straight. They, too, had chosen "The Most Dangerous Game," focusing on a long conversation between the characters over a gourmet meal. We asked why they decided to create a parody of the scene.

> KENNETH: We thought it was kind of boring, so we figured we'd spice it up a little bit.
>
> BRUCE: You think the story "The Most Dangerous Game" is boring?
>
> KENNETH: Just the scene we did.
>
> ISAAC: (At the same time) Just the way we were filming it, the scene was kind of—
>
> KENNETH: It was boring because it was all talking.

BRUCE: Did you realize that after you started filming it, or when you picked the scene?

KENNETH: After, because it was just kind of back and forth talking, so we were like oh, we should add stuff in.

BRUCE: So you were afraid WE would be bored if you did it straight, is that right?

BRYAN: Yeah.

It is, of course, a common maxim that movies have to move, and that boring an audience is an egregious offense. This group had spent considerable time cutting the story's original dialogue, but in the end, they still did not trust the material enough because of their fear that, in movie form, the restriction of camera shots (only two people sitting and talking) would not allow their movie to move enough to satisfy their audience—their classmates.

One of "The Scarlet Ibis" groups ended their final tableaux by panning from Brother crying over his dead brother to their red ibis bird propped in a tree above the boys in order to visually suggest the symbolic connection between the two—even though it does not happen that way in the printed story. After the class viewing, a student asked:

HUMPHREY: I have a question. Did the bird come back alive?

MEGAN: No, no, it's symbolism.

CRYSTAL: It's a symbol. You know, the bird fell out of the tree and died, and so we decided to just show the bird in the tree as a symbol of Doodle dying.

LORNA: It symbolizes Doodle and the bird are, like, similar.

CYNTHIA: They both struggled, like—well, they were both weak. Like the bird had been thrown around in a storm and it was just weak and it couldn't go on anymore. And Doodle was weak; he was born that way, and he struggled with things that normally people wouldn't struggle with.

When seen as a multimodal activity, the students' simple filmmaking set up the kind of flexible, reflective thinking and discovery that is inherent in having students work across sign systems, thinking that Suhor (1991) called "transmediation." Converting their short stories to the film mode appeared to prompt new thinking.

Student Engagement

I doubt I need to convince many classroom teachers that our film-making project enlivened the English classroom and fostered high student interest and engagement. They will not be surprised that many of the students in the essay group begged to make movies instead. Filmmaking is "cool," and it creates variety. Filmmaking is social, too, and while that creates challenges posed by the need for greater cooperation, diplomacy, and personal responsibility to the group than the traditional classroom requires, it also appeals to the social nature of adolescents. In his *English Journal* column's review of research on engaged learning, VanDeWeghe (2006) summarizes three categories of student engagement: behavioral, emotional, and cognitive. Whereas the traditional classroom normally invites only cognitive student engagement, we observed our filmmaking project stimulating all three. As one of our students put it, "I think English is way more enjoyable when you do more than just read and write."

Finis

Because this was the first time that Don or I had tried using film-making for teaching, and because neither of us had much technical skill, at times this unit felt pretty messy. Even though we knew that projects can promote active learning and construction of knowledge, and even though this first experience helped us see where we could manage this kind of project more efficiently next time, we still wondered whether the filmmaking was worth the extra time it took (a week longer than the essay group). Often too, with group projects, teachers wonder whether students are learning or just playing. In the final reflections about the film-making project, students told us that filmmaking turned out to be harder than they thought. We took that to mean that there was more thinking involved than the students had anticipated, and as teachers we considered that a good sign.

The point of the project had never been to produce high-quality films. We considered filmmaking to be a vehicle, a means to an end in which learning was the real goal. To further track student learning, we gave all four classes a pretest and a post-test. In understanding of literary terms on the tests, as well as in classroom assignments, the project classes performed virtually the same as the essay classes. But the quality of their presentation discussions suggests that some students were getting deeper learning experiences than the assessments measured. In addition, the filmmaking students were clearly more positively engaged in the work of the class, and we believe that when students put more effort into their work, they get more learning value out of it.

We believe that our filmmaking project demonstrates a small-step way that many regular English language arts teachers could begin to incorporate filmmaking into their teaching without necessitating a curriculum overhaul. The project was also an opportunity to consider what English classroom filmmaking might offer both students and teachers. In *Literacy in the New Media Age*, Gunther Kress (2003) asserts that mode and choice of mode are significant issues, and that for any mode we should ask, "What are its limitations and potentials? What are the *affordances* of a mode?" (p. 45). We left our first classroom filmmaking experience with new understandings about the valuable affordances of filmmaking as a classroom activity. The project had engaged students in deep interpretation and reflection about literary concepts, such as characterization, point of view, tone, mood, and conflict, and the multimodality of the project made more visible to students the genre conventions of both fiction and film. We were hungry to do more with filmmaking in the classroom in order to discover yet more affordances of this complex media.

Works Cited

Brooks, C. Jr., & Warren, R. P. (1947). *Understanding fiction*. New York: F. S. Crofts.

Connell, R. (1999). The most dangerous game. In *Prentice Hall literature: Timeless voices, timeless themes: Gold Level* (pp. 16–45). Upper Saddle River, NJ: Prentice Hall. (Original work published 1924).

de Maupassant, G. (1999). The necklace. In *Prentice Hall literature: Timeless voices, timeless themes: Gold Level* (pp. 536–541). Upper Saddle River, NJ: Prentice Hall. (Original work published 1907).

Dziedzic, B. B. (2002). When multigenre meets multimedia: Reading films to understand books. *English Journal, 92*(2), 69–75.

Franek, M. (1996). Producing student films: Shakespeare on screen. *English Journal, 85*(3), 50–54.

Hull, G. A., & Katz, M.-L. (2006). Crafting an agentive self: Case studies of digital storytelling. *Research in the Teaching of English, 41*(1), 43–81.

Hurst, J. (1999). The scarlet ibis. In *Prentice Hall literature: Timeless voices, timeless themes: Gold level* (pp. 484–521). Upper Saddle River, NJ: Prentice Hall. (Original work published 1960).

Kajder, S. B. (2004). Enter here: Personal narrative and digital storytelling. *English Journal, 93*(3), 64–68.

Kress, G. (2003). *Literacy in the new media age.* New York: Routledge.

Langer, J. A. (1995). *Envisioning literature: Literary understanding and literature instruction.* New York: Teachers College Press.

Morrison, J. D. (2002). Using student-generated film to create a culturally relevant community. *English Journal, 92*(1), 47–52.

National Council of Teachers of English. (2003). *Resolution on composing with nonprint media* [Position statement]. Retrieved from http://www.ncte.org/positions/statements/composewithnonprint

Suhor, C. (1991). *Semiotics and the English language arts. ERIC Digest.* Bloomington, IN: ERIC Clearinghouse on Reading and Communication Skills. Retrieved from ERIC Database. (ED329960)

Teasley, A. B., & Wilder, A. (1996). *Reel conversations: Reading films with young adults.* Portsmouth, NH: Boynton/Cook.

VanDeWeghe, R. (2006). Research matters: What is engaged learning? *English Journal, 95*(3), 88–91.

Verbinski, G. (Director). (2003). *Pirates of the Caribbean: The curse of the black pearl* [Motion picture]. United States: Walt Disney Pictures.

Wilhelm, J. D. (1997). *"You gotta BE the book": Teaching engaged and reflective reading with adolescents.* New York: Teachers College Press; Urbana, IL: National Council of Teachers of English.

Wright, R. (1969). The man who was almost a man. In R. Wright, *Eight men.* New York: Pyramid Books.

CHAPTER THIRTEEN

Digital Literacies, Aesthetics, and Pedagogies Involved in Digital Video Production

RICHARD BEACH AND THOM SWISS

University of Minnesota

Any attempt to incorporate an aesthetic orientation into the English curriculum needs to recognize the high level of students' use of digital technologies, such as blogs, wikis, podcasts, digital video, and social networking—online participation which involves both reading *and* composing of digital texts (Beach, Anson, Breuch, & Swiss, 2009; Morris & Swiss, 2006).

In this chapter, we focus on one type of digital production, digital video production, describing ways in which students respond to and produce videos from an aesthetic perspective. With the development of easy-to-use digital video cameras and editing software, coupled with outlets such as YouTube and Google Video, the production of digital videos has exploded, creating audience interest in online video viewing as a regular entertainment pastime. One study found that while the number of television viewers will grow by about 5.3 percent over the next five years, online video viewers will grow by about 60 percent (Hallerman, 2008). Gold (2008) notes that young people prefer to watch the online version of the teen soap opera program *Gossip Girl*, the most downloaded show on iTunes in early 2008, to watching the television version because they could watch it according to their own schedule and then chat with their peers about the show. Another survey found that for adolescents, short videos were the most popular form of media viewed on any device, followed by comedy skits/stand-up routines and music videos (Eggerton, 2008).

In addition, students can now readily produce their own digital videos. In one survey, 64 percent of online adolescents were engaged in some form of content creation, with 28 percent operating as "super-communicators," for example, creating videos to share on YouTube (Lenhart, Madden, Macgill, & Smith, 2007). The increased popularity of digital videos is also evident in the growing popularity of video blogging, or vlogging, in which students voice their opinions using video (Verdi & Hodson, 2006). (For a set of tutorials on creating vlogs created by Richard, see http://digitalwriting.pbwiki.com/Vlog+production+tutorials.)

This viewing and production experience provides students with tacit knowledge of effective use of video production techniques (Albers, 2007) as well as knowledge of digital literacies employed in creating digital videos: multimodality, interactivity, modularity, automation, and collection/appropriation (Lankshear & Knobel, 2003; Manovich, 2001; Kress, 2003). These literacies are "digital" in that they are facilitated through uses of digital video production and editing tools, such as iMovie or Windows Movie Maker, to readily move video clips around as "modules" (the use of modularity), as well as to automatically add certain editing transitions or music—the use of automation (Manovich, 2001).

Aesthetics and Digital Videos

This increased digital video production raises the question as to what kinds of aesthetic concerns students apply in creating their digital videos. Traditional notions of aesthetic design relevant to analyzing a painting or song may not be relevant to judging the aesthetic aspects of digital video. Evaluating the aesthetic design and perspective employed in a Picasso painting doesn't necessarily apply to analyzing the appeal of a YouTube digital video.

Applying aesthetic concerns to digital video production involves going beyond simply analyzing beauty and form. Like Mark Johnson (2007), we believe that aesthetics involves "how human beings experience and make meaning. Aesthetics concerns all of the things that go into meaning—form, expression, communication, qualities, emotions, feeling, value, purpose. . . ."

(p. 212). Responding to and creating a digital video involves aesthetic considerations related to not only camera shots and angles, music, sound effects, and editing transitions, but also how the power of moving images, sound, and music serves to rhetorically engage their audiences' emotions and create involvement in narrative development.

This rhetorical focus requires that students make aesthetic judgments about potential audience response to their digital videos. They can begin to consider potential audience response by studying ratings assigned to YouTube videos that often have more to do with the content or physical performances than the quality of the cinematography, as evident in the YouTube 2008 award-winning videos (http://hubpages.com/hub/youtube-awards-2008). They may then understand that videos' aesthetic appeal derives from portraying content as a social practice that engages audiences interested in a video producer's particular perspective or identity. As Kelly Wissman (2008) notes:

> Envisioning photography as a social practice recognizes that the images produced are not simply a transparent recording of reality; rather, the images encapsulate a particular framing of that reality that is highly intentional and unique to the individual photographer. Envisioning photography as a social practice also entails considering the social context in which images are produced and received and considering the shaping influence of those contexts on the images and interpretations of those images. To envision photography as a social practice also means to envision photographers as social beings with historical legacies, emergent identities, and social commitments, all of which can inform the production of the images. (p. 14)

By perceiving video production as a social practice, students focus on how their use of images, sounds, and music derives from shared social and cultural understandings operating within a particular social context, for example, their high school world. The aesthetic appeal of their videos, therefore, depends on how effectively students portray places, events, or people from the high school that have particular emotional appeals or meanings for their peer audiences. In this study, students often enhanced that appeal by making intertextual references in their videos to their peers' shared knowledge of larger popular cultural images, sounds, and music. For example, they employed or parodied storylines based on familiar Hollywood movie genres (mystery, horror, science fiction, romance, detective, etc.), references that positioned their audiences as being "in the know."

High School Students' Digital Video Production

To illustrate students' aesthetic considerations in their digital video productions, we turn to examples from Elizabeth Boeser's digital video production class (open to ninth through twelfth graders) at Jefferson High School in Bloomington, Minnesota. In Elizabeth's class, students began by creating iMovie slideshows with only images, followed by videos without editing, leading to videos with interviews and news broadcasts, and then moved on to producing ads before ending with a narrative video. (For descriptions of specific activities and topics covered in this class, see http://sites.google.com/site/missboeser/Home/tv-production.) In planning, filming, and editing their videos in teams, students were collaboratively making aesthetic judgments based on their sense of peers' potential engagement with their videos.

To study the videos produced in Elizabeth's class from 2005 to 2008, we analyzed the ways in which they employed the use of interactivity, multimodality, modularity, automation, and collection/appropriation in producing and editing their videos. We also cross-checked our perceptions with Elizabeth's and her students' aesthetic assessments as to which videos were particularly popular. We also identified certain consistent themes in these videos that reflected students' interest in parodying or critiquing aspects of popular culture, including an example we will further discuss of how the body is portrayed in popular culture, particularly in terms of gender differences.

Interactivity

In creating their videos, students continually shared their videos, during and after production, with each other in their production groups and then with the entire class, resulting in ongoing peer and teacher feedback and further editing. To help students adopt an audience's perspective, Elizabeth had them create video ads employing what J. Anthony Blair (2004) calls a "visual argument"—a reliance on visual images to persuade audiences and carry the weight of their arguments, images whose meanings were based on shared, intertextual references to popular culture texts. In their ads, students parodied the ad narrative formula—if you use product X, you will be instantly transformed into Y. For example, in parody of iPod commercials, one student was shown walking down the school hallway followed by another student. When the student in front turned on his iPod, the student behind began dancing, referencing actual iPod advertisements showing people dancing as they listen to their iPods, a visual argument that using an iPod conveys one's coolness. The use of the iPod image of the dancing person with an iPod built on intertextual references to Apple's massive advertising campaign to equate use of the iPod with the emotional pleasure of enjoying and dancing to music. The aesthetic appeal of the students' video depended on audiences' shared knowledge of the iPod advertising campaign.

Multimodality

Another digital literacy involved in digital video productions is multimodality—the ability to employ and combine different modes, such as images, language (dialogue/voice-over), music, and sound effects. Combining different modes in multimedia productions appeals to audiences' sensory memory, particularly important for visual-spatial learners (Metiri Group, 2008).

The use of multimodality in digital video productions is evident in the increased popularity of digital storytelling that combines writing, photographic images, and a musical sound track to create representations of students' personal experiences (Miller, 2008; Ohler, 2007). In an after-school digital storytelling program for middle and high school students located in Oakland, California, the D.U.S.T.Y. project (oaklanddusty.org/index.php), students used digital storytelling to portray their lives in urban Oakland. To do so, they combined images, video clips, audio, and text based on the aesthetics of digital rhetoric. One student, Randy, created "Lyfe-N-Rhyme" (oaklanddusty.org/videos.php), described by Hull and Katz (2007):

Randy narrates the movie, performing his original poem/rap to the beat of a Miles Davis tune playing softly in the background. He illustrates, complements, or otherwise accompanies the words and the message of his poem/rap, along with the Miles Davis melody, with approximately eighty images. Most of these images are photographs taken by Randy of Oakland neighborhoods and residents, while others he found on the Internet, and a few screens consist solely of typed words.

Hall and Katz note how this video functions effectively on an aesthetic level by connecting Randy and his social world with "works of art and African American icons, past and present" and "recontextualizing them in his own creative universe of this digital story" (p. 58).

In producing their videos, Elizabeth's students worked collaboratively in groups of three and four to plan, shoot, and edit their videos. In doing so, they were making decisions about which material to retain or cut, as well as the use of certain transitions between shots, music, and sound effects. Therefore, they had to consider how to effectively combine images with music, sound effects, and voice-over audio in multimodal ways. For example, in one video, three werewolves attacked students in the high school. The student producers employed grainy, black-and-white color to mimic older werewolf movies as well as parody some of the werewolf genre techniques, using sound effects and classical music typically associated with these movies. In creating this video, these students were aware of potential audience appeal based on shared knowledge of the werewolf movie genre as well as how they transformed their sterile high school setting into a scary werewolf world.

Modularity

A third digital literacy involves the idea of modularity which acknowledges that media samples or data bits (e.g., stills, video clips, and sounds) can function as separate objects or "modules" that also can be combined without losing their autonomy (Lankshear & Knobel, 2003; Manovich, 2001). A website consists of different objects that can be stored independently on the site or a network to create a page, and then combined. Objects can be added, deleted, or revised without having to completely redo the overall website. Students can also remix digital videos using sites such as Remix America (http://remixamerica.org) to create their own documentaries.

Given the modular nature of digital texts, students can readily mix and match digital material. Once Elizabeth's students learned the editing options in iMovie, they could then readily import and move clips, music, and sound effects to construct their videos. Students worked collaboratively around the same computer to make mutual editing decisions based on aesthetic judgments as to how to best edit material in ways that would appeal to their peer audiences. For example, in one video, a student driving a car in the school parking lot "hits" some students. After the car drives away and a dispatcher reports on the incident, there is a shot of some police squad cars turning around and beginning their pursuit of the car, a shot taken from some stock footage of police squad cars imported into the video. In editing this sequence, the students wanted to appeal to their audiences by drawing on the genre conventions of the action/car-chase movie genre with fast-paced cutting.

In another video, students created a set of questions to ask their teachers such as "What do you think about corporal punishment or overt public displays of emotions?" The students then edited the answers that represented positions that were quite different from what the teachers might normally espouse, for example, that corporal punishment is a good idea—noting in the final credits that these answers were not the teachers' actual answers. The aesthetic appeal of this video derived from their peers' knowledge of individual teachers within their school and how their answers conflicted with their actual beliefs.

Automation

A fourth digital literacy involves what Manovich (2001) describes as automation, the use of highly automated systems in the production and combination of modular parts. Digital photo and video editing tools, such as Photoshop, Windows Movie Maker, and iMovie, automatically adjust images, transitions, and sound effects. These automation features are based on certain aesthetic assumptions regarding audience perceptions of desirable visual experiences. For example, the iMovie 2009 uses "image stabilization" to automatically correct unstable shots to create a stable viewing experience. Hollywood filmmakers can also employ computer graphic or 3-D systems to create animation images, such as the images of thousands of soldiers in the *Lord of the Rings* film series.

Elizabeth's students learned to exploit iMovie automation features for adding transitions, titles, special effects, and music to their videos. In the video about werewolves attacking the school, students used an iMovie editing option that automatically blurred all of the shots to create a dream-like atmosphere associated with the horror genre. In another video, a student was transported into a music-video world in which his peers mimicked different music-video groups dancing to music in the school hallways. The student had difficulty understanding how and why he was being transported into this world, so at the end of the video, he attempted to explain these events by reading a graphic novel. Through use of an iMovie special effects tool, the student was transported into the graphic novel itself as a character in black-and-white line drawings moving around within a comic-book frame with the other characters (see Richard's VideoAnt—http://ant.umn. edu—annotation comments numbers 26 and 27 about the use of this comic-book image effect at http://tinyurl.com/lrrl7k).

Collection/Appropriation

In creating digital texts, students collect and appropriate digital material, a time-honored practice by artists such as Roy Lichtenstein, Claes Oldenburg, and Andy Warhol who all appropriated pop culture and commercial art images. Much of new media digital art or poetry productions involve collecting digital popular culture images, texts, and videos (Hocks & Kendrick, 2003; Morris & Swiss, 2006). In these productions, artists collect and re-appropriate material to adopt critical perspectives on these images, texts, or videos. For example, in what he describes as the commercial rhetoric art project, Steven McCarthy (2007) collected images of junk mail, commercials, packages, branded material, and websites, and then combined them to create online

collages (faculty.che.umn.edu/dha/smccarthy/CommercialRhe-
toricArtProject/index.html).

His purpose in creating these collages was to critique the
pervasive advertising driving consumerism in American culture.
He notes that, "Through the lenses of design and art, one can appreciate the aesthetic pleasure and formal qualities of re-arranging
the commercial rhetoric of other designers" (p. 3).

Students can create remix or parody videos, which are popular items on YouTube. For example, the "David after Dentist"
YouTube video (http://www.youtube.com/watch?v=txqiwrb
YGrs), which had some eight million hits, was shot by a father
of his son sitting in the back seat of a car after having an extra
tooth removed, still somewhat disoriented by the anesthetic drugs.
This video resulted in numerous remixes of the original material
with some videos accentuating the disorientation through editing
and others substituting adults with the boy's language. Another
popular YouTube video parody is the Nice White Lady (http://
youtube.com/watch?v=ZVF-nirSq5s) that pokes fun at the Hollywood movie genre of the white teacher "savior" figure portrayed
in *Dangerous Minds* or *Freedom Writers Diaries*, who suddenly
transforms her students from resistant to engaged learners.

Elizabeth's students also used appropriation and remixing in
creating video parodies. For example, students created a parody
of fast-food hamburger television commercials in which a student orders a burger with "extra lard." As he eats the burger, his
stomach grows larger and he appears to be ill, recontextualizing
images of happy, healthy consumers in fast-food restaurants.
Elizabeth's students also appropriated film and television genre
techniques by creating parodies of trailers. In one video parody
of the movie theater's warning trailer to turn off cell phones,
a student believes that he will fail a test, so he sneaks into the
teacher's office to steal a copy of the test. In going through the
teacher's file, his cell phone goes off and he is caught. The video
ends with the admonishment, "please turn off your cell phones."

The aesthetic appeal of these parodies derived not only from
their creative use of images, such as the student's stomach bulg-
ing out as he eats the hamburger, but also from their rhetorical
appeal to the audience's prior knowledge of what is being ridi-

culed. Audiences know that they are bombarded with fast-food hamburger ads glorifying high-fat food and reminders to turn off their cell phones, and being positioned as "in the know" as to what's being ridiculed is typically aesthetically appealing.

Another video parodied the popular teen film *Mean Girls* (Waters, 2004), depicting a new student who had been home-schooled and then started attending public high school. This student is socialized by three "mean girls" who inform her about the cliques in the school, telling her that by hanging out with their group, she is learning the practices associated with being in the "girl world." The aesthetic appeal of this video lies in its intertextual references to peers' insider knowledge of the original *Mean Girls* film as well as gendered social practices in their school.

The Theme of Embodiment

Students collected and appropriated familiar visual images to engage in critical inquiry about the challenges of being an adolescent. One common theme in many of their videos dealt with issues of embodiment in which students' underwent a physical transformation from weak to strong or unattractive to attractive. Through making these videos, students challenged the consumerist myth of the instant physical transformation through the use of a "miracle" product. In one video, a girl perceived to be unattractive and unpopular receives a makeover and is suddenly attractive and popular; this video critically examined society's focus on physical appearance as primary in female popularity.

This focus on embodiment reflects adolescents' concern with how to physically perform certain identities according to norms derived from popular cultural representations of the body. In their discussion of the aesthetic aspects of embodiment, Misson and Morgan (2006) note that portrayals of film or television stars serve to socialize adolescents in ways of talking, dressing, gesturing, walking, or standing that serve to define their identities so that, for example, a Latina girl might adopt "the look" of a Jennifer Lopez:

The influence of the movie star or the rock star does not stop at our taking on their clothing style, their hairstyle, their "look," but we can take on their whole way of moving the body, their way of being in space. More subtly, if reading a literary text allows us to rehearse different ways of seeing the world and different emotional reactions, these are felt on the body, and they shape our repertoire of bodily reactions just as they do our mental ones. And to repeat Eagleton's words, "Aesthetics is born as a discourse of the body." (p. 136)

Elizabeth's students created videos that allowed them to embody and challenge stereotypical notions of masculinities and femininities. One paraplegic student used specific camera shots and angles to film his video from the perspective of someone in a motorized wheelchair moving throughout his school day in different school spaces and greeting different people, thereby positioning his audience to experience the perspective of someone in a wheelchair. In addition, many of the students' commercials featured products designed to bolster one's status as a young man or young woman. One video promoted a drink designed to enhance mens' muscular strength and become popular with women, whereby interrogating the use of a product for defining one's masculinity based primarily on physical appearance. Another video portrayed students calling up a service that provided men to liven up lethargic parties. In the ad, after a large, muscular, hired man shows up at a party and begins dancing, the party suddenly comes to life. This storyline examined the larger assumption that muscular men are valued for their social presence and power.

The students' concern with an emphasis on male physical prowess was also reflected in several video ads portraying the problematic status of being perceived as a "nerd" in school. In one video, a "nerd" is initially harassed in the hallways by bullies. The ad then shows the product being advertised, a tree in a pot that a student can carry around the school and hide behind, preventing him from being detected by bullies. In another video, a group of elves continually bullies one nerd-like elf, who then seeks out combat training in order to get revenge on the bullying elves. These portrayals of being a "nerd" reflected an interest in what it means to be perceived as having bodies that do not conform to media representations of the muscular, masculine body.

Students also used their videos to demonstrate how spaces control the body, for example, how school spaces control student bodies by stressing punctuality, grooming, dress, self-control, and being "on-task." To resist these controls, students looked for less restrictive spaces to perform alternative identities—what Konrad Glogowski (2006) describes as "third spaces." Third spaces are informal public spaces, such as restaurants, bars, parks, malls, or social networking sites such as Facebook or MySpace, where people interact; these spaces are distinct from the "first space" of home and the "second space" of work or school. In their use of video production, students examined the control of official school space on their bodies by transforming school spaces into "third space" alternatives that allowed for unconventional, resistant displays of the body. For example, one student-produced video showed students transforming a classroom into a dance club with flashing strobe lights. In the previously cited video (http://tinyurl.com/lrrl7k) in which the school was transformed into a music-video world, the students mimicked various music-video groups performing songs and engaged in choreographed dancing in the hallways and parking lot in ways that appealed to their peers' prior knowledge of music videos.

Students used their video productions to transform institutional, utilitarian school "second spaces" constituted by rules of physical control and regimentation into alternative "third spaces" in which students can sing and dance in the hallways. The students' videos themselves mediated constructed, alternative "third spaces" in which students displayed physical engagement with embodied literacies as well as critical inquiry of the stereotypical conceptions of embodiment. They discovered how images, sound, and music could be employed to parody and interrogate these stereotypes, challenging the social and cultural images of masculinity, femininity, physical ability, and the institutional norms of schooling.

In summary, students' use of digital video production involved use of the digital literacies of interactivity, multimodality, modularity, automation, and collection/appropriation. Students employed these literacies based on an aesthetic sensibility of what appealed to their audiences given their audience's prior knowledge of references to popular culture and advertising texts. They also portrayed issues of embodiment by critiquing stereotypical gendered representations of the body as well as using the physical display of the body to transform the controlling school space into an alternative "third space," celebrating appealing enactments of the body. In all of this, they used their video productions to create aesthetically appealing, imaginative "third spaces" as alternatives to controlling school spaces.

Fostering Reflection through Peer and Teacher Feedback

Acquiring an aesthetic sensibility in producing digital videos requires that students reflect on how and why they are using certain digital literacies. To foster this meta-awareness, Elizabeth provided students with feedback during the process of scripting, storyboarding, collecting images, videotaping, and editing. To assess the students' videos, Elizabeth used a rubric (summarized next) based on ratings from 1 to 4 for the following features:

- *Script/storyboard*: The degree of planning and development of detailed descriptions of shots, movement, narration, and dialogue.

- *Video*: The degree to which the camera was always in focus and steady, the variety of planned shots and angles, and effective use of composition based on the rule of thirds.

- *Audio*: The clarity of sound and use of silence.

- *Lighting*: The use of sufficient lighting to eliminate shadows and glare.

- *Editing cuts*: The degree to which cuts are used to eliminate unnecessary slack time.

- *Transitions:* The appropriate use of transitions to create a smooth flow between scenes.

- *Titles:* The inclusion of clearly displayed titles that enhance the story or content.

- *Pacing/continuity*: Use of steadily paced clips to maintain audience interest.

◆ *Music/sound*: Use of well-balanced music or sound that enhances the mood and pacing.

◆ *Graphics/animation*: Clear graphics or animation that enhance the topic and mood.

◆ *Content:* The extent to which the video tells a compelling story with a connected structure.

◆ *Creativity:* The use of imaginative creativity suitable to the content.

The following descriptive feedback was Elizabeth's response to a student's video that portrayed a conflict between the main character, a Dungeons and Dragons Wizard, and his archrival who both are seeking to win a Dungeons and Dragons tournament:

> Your video was exceptional, as you had to do it twice. Some shots were a little unbalanced, but considering the time restraints, you did quite well. I'm not taking points off for audio, although I feel like you could have used more music, especially in the beginning and during scenes that showed a progression of time. You only used ambient light, but none of the shots were too dark. The cutting was very good, but a little off in a couple of spots. You could have done without repeat scenes and perhaps Charles (all student names are pseudonyms) announcing to save time. Your opening was only so-so, but your end credits were better. Always check your spelling and grammar. Pacing was great. The end scene was so funny, with the screaming, awesome comic timing. Your voice-overs were good, but I think you could have had more action and less of Martha standing around and talking in front of the blue screen. That made the movie a little dull. You did not include extra graphics, but you showed that you could use the title sheets. You could have used subtitles to add more to the movie. You did not use many extra effects. The content was fantastic and the project, although based on actual TV, was funny. Overall, I think this group worked the best as a team. If you had more time, I think this would have been one of the best projects I've seen all year.

Elizabeth's descriptive feedback provided students with both positive comments and constructive criticism. While Elizabeth notes limitations in use of techniques, she is still impressed with the use of content from the Dungeons and Dragons popular culture material. Her response to the content reflects our larger point that the aesthetic experience of digital videos derives from how these videos appropriate popular culture material. Teachers also may use the previously mentioned video annotation tool, VideoAnt (http://ant.umn.edu), to provide descriptive annotations at specific points on a video (for an example of Richard's annotations to the students' video about the student entering into a music-video world in the school, visit http://tinyurl.com/lrrl7k).

Students also wrote reflections on their sense of purpose and audience (Albers, 2007) that Elizabeth described as an "artist statement for public display with the video." She directed the students to "create the statement to reflect your definition of video and how it relates to your point of view on the subject of your work. Include anything else that you would like to communicate to the audience about yourself, your artwork, the subject, or the video form." Students then had to evaluate their own work by answering the following questions:

- To what extent does the completed work fulfill your artistic intent?

- What are its strengths and weaknesses?

- How did feedback affect the development of the work?

- Give at least two examples of technical problems you encountered.

- Explain how these problems were resolved in the creation of the piece.

One student, Andrea, reflected on her group's video, "Hallway," a horror movie trailer in which three girls ridicule another girl about her doll. This girl then hangs herself in the school bathroom but returns as a ghost to avenge her death by hunting down the three girls and killing one of them in the bathroom. The producers employed lighting techniques throughout the video to enhance the horror aspects, for example, turning on and off the lights in the bathroom. Andrea noted how they derived the idea of using lighting in the bathroom:

> We went to the girls' bathroom down the hall. Someone turned the lights off and we all said, "Oh, that's creepy!" We went to the mirror and shut the lights off again, looked in the mirror, and each one had an idea of how to make a scene about that . . . we left and forgot to turn on the lights. As we left, Martha got scared when she heard someone inside flushing the toilet. For a second we all thought it was haunted, *but just for a second.*

In her reflection, Andrea drew on knowledge of technical uses of lighting in horror films consistent with her group's "artistic intent" for the trailer to "scare and persuade the audience to watch the movie."

Andrea also noted that the group carefully planned how to shoot a scene in which the three girls were chasing Martha as she ran from side to side down a long hallway, a scene that would be shot:

> in a "stop-and-go" way: play, pause, move, repeat. We also thought there could be a shot where the camera follows the lockers like a path. So the camera tilts a little to show there's many lockers and she runs by all of them. But there is a moment where, there is a door in between the lockers, and we put Martha there to make it scary.

Andrea's reflection shows that she and her group members drew on their knowledge of conventional horror-movie camera techniques to heighten the "scary" aspects of the video and indicates her awareness that these techniques would appeal to her peers.

In another artist statement, Linda reflected on her group's production, "Stunning 16," a parody of the MTV television show *Super Sweet 16*, in which wealthy families throw lavish birthday parties for their adolescent daughters featuring celebrity performers, large venues, expensive cars, and designer dresses. In the video, the fictional character, Alecia Whitmore, is shown handing out guest invitations, selecting the gym as a site for the 300 guests, choosing an expensive dress, and selecting an escort from a lineup of young men, ending with Alecia and her escort coming out from behind stage curtains to loud applause. In her reflection, Linda described the intent of the video as ridiculing the excessiveness of *Super Sweet 16* birthdays:

Just as *South Park* brings unnecessary drama and conflict to a part of society they find ridiculous, we have created a film with an overly dramatic diva, Alecia Whitmore. We replicated the same idea that films such as *Austin Powers* express, bringing excessive importance and cheesy actions to the life of a spy . . . . We endorsed ideas of modesty, humility, and thankfulness. Making the attitude of Alecia look distasteful, we made the above virtues appear desirable.

Linda also noted how camera techniques were used to parody the typical *Super Sweet 16* show's portrayals of selecting a dress, venue, and escort:

The main direction for the film was to imitate the show, yet we desired to draw special attention to the outrageous demands of the spoiled 16-year-old. We wrote the script to give our character, Alecia, an extremely pompous and arrogant attitude. Technically, we attempted to over exaggerate shots to draw importance to trivial things. For example, we put the escort scene in slow motion and did several pedestal shots to make the escort seem excessively gorgeous and important. In addition, we glorified materialism by adding ridiculous music. The "Hallelujah Chorus" was attached to the spinning pedestal of the dress.

Linda's reflections represented her group's aesthetic awareness of the rhetorical use of visual argument to parody the MTV show and critique what they perceived to be the shallow values of a celebrity media culture.

Elizabeth's feedback and these students' self-reflections were based on their aesthetic assumptions regarding their videos' effectiveness in engaging their peer audiences. These aesthetic assumptions were based on popular cultural codes that constituted the meaning of social practices, artifacts, and various media representations. In their artist statements, Andrea and Linda both recognized how their appropriation and parodying of popular culture material resonated with their peer audiences. They were also aware of how their production techniques, such as use of editing, appealed to audiences who appreciated inventive techniques.

Summary

In this chapter, we argue that the concept of aesthetics is important when thinking about digital literacy and its relationship to the production and consumption of digital videos. Understanding the aesthetic aspects of digital productions requires that we see these expressions, as both readers and writers, in a social context. It requires that we notice and value students who are engaged in a shared "participatory culture" (Jenkins, 2006), just as Elizabeth's students were in their work with digital video. As members of this "participatory culture," students bring knowledge of various digital literacies and popular cultural codes to their aesthetic responses to digital videos. They then use that knowledge to make aesthetic judgments about the effectiveness of videos in building social relationships with audiences and critiquing popular culture. They also appreciate the inventive uses of digital literacies, for example, how students combine video, text, and music from different sources to create engaging multimodal productions or how they appropriate and remix popular culture material to parody that material. And they recognize the need to continually consider the knowledge their potential audiences bring to viewing their videos so that their intertextual references to that knowledge will draw in those audiences.

All of this suggests the value of media literacy instruction in English or literacy classrooms. Knowledge of the digital literacies applied in video production enables students to build on and critique the operating popular cultural codes as well as analyze the multimodal combinations (modularity, automation, appropriation, remixing, etc.) employed in the video's production. In doing so, students can identify intertextual references to specific cultural codes and recognize how digital literacies are used to foster audiences' interactive, social connections to those intertextual references. Through digital literacies instruction and digital video production, students learn how to make aesthetic judgments. They also draw on their insider membership in "participatory cultures" (Jenkins, 2006) in responding to videos as commentary on those cultures. All of this suggests that English language arts teachers can use digital video production to help students learn to appreciate the aesthetic power of digital videos to engage audiences and foster critical inquiry.

Works Cited

Albers, P. (2007). Supporting literacy with student-made documentaries. *Classroom Notes Plus, 25*(2), 1–15.

Beach, R., Anson, C., Breuch, L.-A., & Swiss, T. (2009). *Teaching writing using blogs, wikis, and other digital tools.* Norwood, MA: Christopher-Gordon.

Blair, J. A. (2004). The rhetoric of visual arguments. In C. A. Hill & M. Helmers (Eds.), *Defining visual rhetorics* (pp. 41–61). Mahwah, NJ: Erlbaum.

Eggerton, J. (2008, April 7). CTAM study: Teens watching mostly short-form videos: Cable and Telecommunications Association for Marketing examines teens' media consumption. *Broadcasting and Cable.* Retrieved from http://www.broadcastingcable.com/article/ CA6548585.html?industryid=47174

Glogowski, K. (2006). *Classrooms as third places?* [slidecast]. Retrieved from http://www.slideshare.net/teachandlearn/classrooms-as-third-places

Gold, M. (2008, January 27). The buzz on "Gossip Girl." *Los Angeles Times.* Retrieved from http://articles.latimes.com/2008/jan/27/ entertainment/ca-gossip27

Hallerman, D. (2008, February). *Online video content: The new TV audience.* Retrieved from http://www.emarketer.com/Reports/All/ Emarketer_2000454.aspx

Hocks, M. E., & Kendrick, M. R. (Eds.). (2003). *Eloquent images: Word and image in the age of new media.* Cambridge, MA: MIT Press.

Hull, G. A., & Katz, M.-L. (2006). Crafting an agentive self: Case studies of digital storytelling. *Research in the Teaching of English, 41*(1), 43–81.

Jenkins, H. (with Clinton, K., Purushotma, R., Robison, A. J., & Weigel, M. (2006). *Confronting the challenges of participatory culture: Media education for the 21st century.* Chicago, IL: MacArthur Foundation. Retrieved from http://digitallearning.macfound.org/

atf/cf/%7B7E45C7E0-A3E0-4B89-AC9C-E807E1B0AE4E%7D/
JENKINS_WHITE_PAPER.PDF

Johnson, M. (2007). *The meaning of the body: Aesthetics of human understanding*. Chicago: University of Chicago Press.

Kress, G. (2003). *Literacy in the new media age*. New York: Routledge.

Lankshear, C., & Knobel, M. (2003). *New literacies: Changing knowledge and classroom learning*. Buckingham, UK: Open University Press.

Lenhart, A., Madden, M., Macgill, A. R., & Smith, A. (2007). *Teens and social media: The use of social media gains a greater foothold in teen life as they embrace the conversational nature of interactive online media*. Washington, DC: Pew Internet and American Life Project. Retrieved from http://www.pewinternet.org/~/media//Files/Reports/2007/PIP_Teens_Social_Media_Final.pdf.pdf

Manovich, L. (2001). *The language of new media*. Cambridge, MA: MIT Press.

McCarthy, S. (2007). *The commercial rhetoric art project*. University of Minnesota. Retrieved from http://faculty.che.umn.edu/dha/smccarthy/CommercialRhetoricArtProject/index.html

Metiri Group. (2008). *Multimodal learning through media: What the research says*. Retrieved from http://www.cisco.com/web/strategy/docs/education/Multimodal-Learning-Through-Media.pdf

Miller, C. H. (2008). *Digital storytelling: A creator's guide to interactive entertainment* (2nd ed.). Burlington, MA: Elsevier/Focal Press.

Misson, R., & Morgan, W. (2006). *Critical literacy and the aesthetic: Transforming the English classroom*. Urbana, IL: National Council of Teachers of English.

Morris, A., & Swiss, T. (Eds.). (2006). *New media poetics: Contexts, technotexts, and theories*. Cambridge, MA: MIT Press.

Ohler, J. B. (2007). *Digital storytelling in the classroom: New media pathways to literacy, learning, and creativity*. Thousand Oaks, CA: Sage.

Verdi, M., & Hodson, R. (with Weynand, D., & Craig, S.). (2006). *Secrets of videoblogging: Videoblogging for the masses*. Berkeley, CA: Peachpit Press.

Waters, M. (Director). (2004). *Mean girls*. [Motion picture] United States: Paramount Pictures.

Wissman, K. K. (2008). "This is what I see": (Re)visioning photography as a social practice. In M. A. Hill & L. Lasudevan (Eds.), *Media, learning, and sites of possibility* (pp. 13–46). New York: Peter Lang.

INDEX

Abbott, L., 90
Across the Wide Dark Sea: The Mayflower Journey (Van Leeuwen), representation of danger and fear in, 196–98
Action,
  in advertisements, 35
  in counter-narrative texts, 36
Advertisements
  action in, 35
  as curricular resources, 33–35
  language in, 33
  vision in, 34–35
Aesthetics, 5
  digital videos and, 301–3
Aesthetic texts, 165–67
Afflerbach, P., 189
Akers, N., 223
Albers, P., 2, 3, 5, 9, 10, 11, 15–16, 28, 32, 33, 35, 36, 113, 118, 158, 160, 163, 164, 173, 178, 180, 188, 191, 206, 235, 256, 301, 314
Alvermann, D. E., 10, 235, 256
Amanti, C., 270
Androes, K., 6
Anson, C., 300
Anstey, M., 68, 228
Arizpe, E., 189, 190, 205
Arnheim, R., 136, 152
Arora, P., 267
Arter, J., 136
Art(s), 5–8
  aesthetics and, 5
  backpack lesson, 138–54

as catalyst for literacy skills, 158–59
effect on literacy, 6–7
integration with writing, 115–31, 138–54
representation of danger and fear in, 194–202
research in, 6–8
visual, 190
ArtsConnectEd website, 19
Arts-integrated curriculum, 192–93
  classroom application of, 143–45
  planning unit of study for, 216–19
  semiotics and, 188–89
  teaching of, 219–25
  in urban setting, 157–80
Arts Together Institute (IUPUI), integration into classroom, 213–16
Au, K., 30
Automation, of digital media, 306–7

Bachman, J. G., 265
Backpack lesson, 138–54
  classroom application of, 143–45
  format of, 139
  history of, 138–43
  implications of, 152–54
  moving from tangible to intangible in, 145, 151–52

EDITORS

Peggy Albers is a professor of language and literacy education at Georgia State University in Atlanta, Georgia. She is the author of two books, *Finding the Artist Within: Creating and Reading Visual Texts in English Language Arts Classes*, and *Telling Pieces: Art as Literacy in Middle School Classes*. Her research interests include visual discourse analysis, arts-integrated literacy instruction, critical literacy, and children's literature. Albers is the author of numerous professional articles and chapters on arts and literacy, visual analysis, and multimodality. She also serves as an NCTE consultant in adolescent literacy, English education, and arts-based literacy instruction. She is an active potter who shows and sells her work nationally.

Jennifer Sanders is an assistant professor of literacy education in the School of Teaching and Curriculum Leadership at Oklahoma State University. She teaches a variety of literacy undergraduate and graduate courses, including language arts and children's literature. Her research interests revolve around writing instruction, writing and art integration, and children's literature from multicultural and critical perspectives. Recent reserch includes a content analysis of religious pluralism in children's literature and a longitudinal study with her colleague, Sue Christian Parsons, on teachers' nonfiction genre knowledge and nonfiction literacy instruction. Jennifer is on the board of directors for the children's literature and reading special interest group of the International Reading Association and served as co-chair of NCTE's Commission on Arts and Literacies (COAL) from 2007–2009.

CONTRIBUTORS

Richard Beach is professor of English education at the University of Minnesota. He is author of *Teachingmedialiteracy.com: A Web-Linked Guide to Resources and Activities* and coauthor of *Teaching Writing Using Blogs, Wikis, and Other Digital Tools*. He received the Computers in Reading Research award in 2009 from the International Reading Association.

Beth Berghoff is an associate professor of literacy, culture, and language education at Indiana University–Purdue University in Indianapolis (IUPUI), where she serves as chair of graduate programs in the School of Education and teaches reading and literacy classes for K–12 teachers. Her research interests include school change, professional development, writing assessment, and arts-infused curriculum. Beth has served as the language arts consultant for Indiana Department of Education, on the editorial boards of *Language Arts* and the *National Reading Conference Yearbook*, and on NCTE's Commission on Arts and Literacy. Her publications include numerous chapters and articles as well as the coauthored books *Arts Together: Steps toward Transformative Teacher Education* and *Beyond Reading and Writing: Inquiry, Curriculum, and Multiple Ways of Knowing*.

Sharon Blecher graduated from Cornell University in 1971 and received an MA in teaching from Northwestern University in 1972. After teaching in Chicago and at the university level in Hong Kong, she joined the Oberlin, Ohio, schools in 1976, and Eastwood School's Open Room in 1983. In 1990, the Open Room was named a Center of Excellence for Teaching Children at Risk by the National Council of Teachers of English. In 1994, she was awarded an NCTE teacher-researcher grant to study the ways students are empowered in their literacy learning when the fine arts are woven into the curriculum. This became the catalyst for her book *Weaving in the Arts: Widening the Learning Circle* (Heinemann, 1998; coauthored with Kathy Jaffee), as well as several articles in education journals. In 2001 she became a National Board Certified Teacher. She has been a resident consultant for the Cleveland Opera education program and the Mississippi Arts Council. Sharon and her teaching partner, Gail

Burton, continue to study the literacy implications of arts integration with their first and second graders, in particular as they work with their students to compose the music and write the libretto for an original opera.

Cindy Bixler Borgmann is associate professor of art education at the Herron School of Art and Design, Indiana University–Purdue University Indianapolis (IUPUI), where she teaches graduate and undergraduate courses for teachers in art and education and is supervisor of youth programs. Cindy has served as project consultant for the Indiana Department of Education in K–12 visual art standards and assessment, and serves on the board of the Art Education Association of Indiana and the National Art Education Association. Her research interests and publications are in aesthetics, critical inquiry, the cognitive characteristics of visual art, and professional development, and include the coauthored book *Arts Together: Steps toward Transformative Teacher Education.*

Gail Furline Burton has been a teacher since the day she walked into an elementary classroom and said hello to her first-grade teacher. She can name every teacher she ever had and tell you stories about her days with them. But it wasn't until she began to team teach with Sharon Blecher thirty years into her professional career that music found its way into her classroom, projects, and lessons. Gail has now completed the production of four operas and would not have a class be cheated of that experience. Opera! Who knew? Gail now teaches second grade in the Eastwood Open Room in Oberlin, Ohio, in a continuing partnership with Sharon Blecher. "Nothing without joy . . ." is a philosophy gleaned from Reggio Emilia studies and the desire to bring more of that program to her own students. She has been part of several presentations to the National Council of Teachers of English and enjoys a special affiliation with the Commission on Arts and Literacies.

Adrienne M. Costello is an assistant professor of English at Buffalo State College, where she teaches a range of courses on teaching, literature, and educational research. Her teaching and research interests are influenced by her background in musical theater and include multimodality, twenty-first century approaches to teaching Shakespeare, and integrating the arts and literacy. She has served as co-chair of NCTE's Conference on English Education Commission on Arts and Literacies (COAL) since 2008.

Keri-Anne Croce is an assistant professor in the elementary education department at Towson University. She teaches both undergraduate and graduate course work in language and literacy, facilitating the development of the nonnative English speaker, and assessment. Her research includes investigating students' meaning making of pictorial and written texts, and assessment of nonnative English speakers.

Esther Cappon Gray is an associate professor of literacy studies in the Department of Special Education and Literacy Studies at Western Michigan University. Her research examines ways that meaning-making and learning are affected by motivation, confidence, prior knowledge, social interactions, ownership, and semiotic literacies. She is fascinated by the ways that learners find voice when they approach content by stepping into role as adults in fictional workplaces. In addition to the Holocaust literature unit described in this book, she and Susan Thetard co-taught a Russian literature unit during which the class established identities in role as the serfs on a large estate shortly before the end of serfdom. Gray and colleague Will Rabidoux collaboratively taught two social studies units with urban fifth graders who learned about the branches of the U.S. government in role as discount store executives and learned about the American Colonial Era in role as researchers and writers of a publishing company. She is writing a historical book about the origins of Carl Orff's Schulwerk, an educational approach popular in the United States and around the world, in which students learn to express themselves through improvising, composing and arranging original or folk music, rhythms, movement, and poetry.

Jerome C. Harste is a past president of the National Council of Teachers of English as well as a coauthor of numerous professional publications (*Beyond Reading and Writing: Inquiry, Curriculum, and Multiple Ways of Knowing; Language Stories and Literacy Lessons; Creating Classrooms for Authors and Inquirers; Whole Language: Inquiring Voices Want to Know; New Policy Guidelines for Reading;* and the list goes on). Harste sees curriculum as a metaphor for the lives we wish to live and the people we wish to be. Harste's areas of expertise are early literacy, reading, teacher education, social semiotics, and critical literacy. Instructionally he advocates critical literacy, multiple ways of knowing, and inquiry-based education. Harste holds the rank of emeritus professor at Indiana University in the Department of Literacy, Culture, and Language Education. In addition he is currently teaching courses on how to use the arts to make our classrooms critical for Mount Saint Vincent University in Canada. In 2008, the elementary section of NCTE recognized Harste as an outstanding educator in the language arts.

Melissa Helmerick is a visual arts teacher at Deer Run Elementary School in Indianapolis, where she has taught for more than twelve years. She has her MA in fine arts from Herron School of Art and Design at IUPUI. She is interested in visual thinking strategies and arts-integrated curriculum.

Catherine Maderazo is an assistant professor of elementary education at Towson University, teaching literacy methods to undergraduate and graduate students. Her research interests include how children become literate in the twenty-first century, why some children's literacy is less valued than others, and how to best prepare elementary teachers to teach children responsively. She is married and has two sons.

Prisca Martens is a professor in the Department of Elementary Education at Towson University, where she teaches courses in reading, children's literature, and language arts. Her research focuses on reading, miscue analysis, retrospective miscue analysis, and early literacy and, most recently, on how to support children in reading both the written and pictorial texts in picture books. She is the author of *I Already Know How to Read* and numerous articles and is an active member of several professional organizations, including the National Council of Teachers of English (NCTE) and the Center for the Expansion of Language and Thinking (CELT).

Ray Martens is an assistant professor in the Department of Art, Art History, and Art Education at Towson University, where he is also the graduate director of art education. He teaches graduate art education courses and also two undergraduate/graduate courses for art education majors that fulfill state reading and writing requirements for certification. His research deals with the pictorial and written text in picture books. He is an active member of several professional organizations, including the National Art Education Association (NAEA) and the National Council of Teachers of English (NCTE). He is also a practicing studio artist and has work in many collections around the world.

Suzanne M. Miller is associate professor of English education at the University at Buffalo—State University of New York, and director of the City Voices, City Visions (CVCV) digital video composing project, a partnership with the Buffalo Public School District. She is a national leader in English education, who has served as chair of the executive committee of the Conference on English Education (CEE)—the arm of NCTE whose members are engaged in the preparation, support, and continuing education of ELA teachers. She has published widely on her ethnographic research that traces the impacts of sociocultural contexts in classrooms and schools on teaching and learning. In 2007 she won the Janet Emig award for her research report on preparing English teachers to use digital video composing as a twenty-first-century learning tool. In 2008 she received the Rewey Belle Inglis award for outstanding woman in the teaching of English. In 2009, Miller received NCTE's Janet Emig award for excellence in English education research.

Sherelle Jones Patisaul is an English language arts and drama teacher at Winder-Barrow High School in Barrow County, Georgia. Now in her fifth year of teaching, she is a graduate of the English education program at the University of Georgia. Her goals include teaching to students' emerging strengths, positioning herself as a learner alongside her students, and embracing the arts in her English classroom. Sherelle has presented her work in breaking the restraints of the five-paragraph essay as well as work in creating spaces for the visual arts within language arts at state and national conferences. She is an active member in two theater companies and worked closely with drama productions at a local middle school.

Joanna Robertson recently finished her graduate work at Syracuse University in reading education. She received a bachelor's of music in music performance from the Crane School of Music and a master's of music in music education from the University of Maine. She has had publications appear in the *Journal of Children's Literature* and the *Music Educators Journal*. She is currently working as a literacy educator, music educator, and professional musician. Robertson assisted a local military hospital in starting a Reach Out and Read program, which provides books to families and educates parents on early literacy practices. In addition to this work, other teaching and research interests include children's literature, literacy across the curriculum, connections between literacy and the arts and literacy and music, and multimodality and multiliteracies.

Bruce Robbins is an associate professor of English education at Boise State University. He taught high school English in Oregon for thirteen years and now teaches undergraduate and graduate courses in English teaching. His research interests include classroom drama and filmmaking, English teacher induction and mentoring, curriculum development, technical communication, and teachers as writers.

Richard Siegesmund is associate professor and co-chair of art education at the Lamar Dodd School of Art, University of Georgia. He coedited with Melissa Cahnmann-Taylor, *Arts-Based Research in Education: Foundations for Practice*. His scholarly interests focus on the theory, curriculum, and assessment of arts-based inquiry. Before focusing on arts education, his career in museum administration included serving as director of The Fabric Workshop, Philadelphia, and deputy director for curatorial affairs at the San Francisco Museum of Modern Art. Siegesmund earned his PhD and MA from the Stanford University School of Education and a BA from Trinity College, Hartford. In addition, he studied graduate painting and printmaking at the University of Hawaii. He has received fellowships from the Getty Education Institute for the Arts and the National

Endowment for the Arts. In 2009, he was artist-in-residence at the University of Georgia campus in San Luis, Costa Rica.

Thomas Swiss is professor of culture and teaching at the University of Minnesota. His books include two collections of poems, *Rough Cut* and *Measure*; edited collections on popular music, including a recent book on Bob Dylan, *Highway 61 Revisited* (University of Minnesota Press); and volumes on new media, including *New Media Poetics* (MIT Press); and was also a coauthor of *Teaching Writing Using Blogs, Wikis, and Other Digital Tools*.

Susan A. Thetard teaches English and theater at University High School, a laboratory school within the Department of Curriculum and Instruction at Illinois State University in Normal, Illinois. Susan holds a BFA in theater and English from Illinois Wesleyan University and an MFA in theater from Illinois State University. In addition, Susan has taken courses in the doctoral program in curriculum and instruction at Illinois State University. Her teaching career spans more than fifteen years at the high school level in English. She has held National Board Certification in English language arts/young adolescents for ten years and was just recertified. The classes she teaches are observed by hundreds of future teachers, and she works with six or more preservice teachers each semester helping them develop lesson plans to teach a three-day unit in her classes. Many years she also has a teaching intern, a program much like the PDS model. Thus, modeling new approaches to teaching is something for which she strives. Learning about process drama and working with Gray on this Holocaust-focused unit introduced a new approach using drama that she uses today.

Carol Thorne is a music teacher at Deer Run Elementary School in Indianapolis, where she has taught for more than eleven years. She has a bachelor's degree in music education from the University of Indianapolis. She is interested in learner engagement and arts-integrated curriculum.

Michelle Zoss is assistant professor of English education at Georgia State University. She began her career in education as both an art and English teacher. Her scholarly interests focus on theory and curriculum of integrating the arts in English language arts classrooms. Zoss earned her PhD in language education from the University of Georgia and an MA in curriculum and teacher education from Stanford University. She earned an honors BA in art and English, and a K–12 art and secondary English teaching certification at the University of Iowa. Seeking to learn more about integrated subjects in multiple contexts, she presented research on arts integration at international conferences in Spain and England, as well as several national conferences in the United States. In 2009, she was awarded the Terry Furlong prize for the best research presentation at the 2008 annual national conference of the National Association for the Teaching of English in England.

This book was typeset in Sabon by Barbara Frazier.
Typefaces used on the cover include Formata Bold, Helvetica Neue Bold
Condensed, and Univers 47 Condensed Light.
The book was printed on 50-lb. Williamsburg Offset paper
by Versa Press, Inc.